"Ralph Block delivers succinct, accessible advice that even novice investors will appreciate. *INVESTING IN REITS* **IS A VALUABLE DISCOVERY FOR INVESTORS OF EVERY STRIPE.**"

JON FOSHEIM
Principal and cofounder
Green Street Advisors

"**A MUST-READ FOR ANYONE INVESTING IN REITS**—and that should be everyone!"

R. BRUCE ANDREWS
President and Chief Executive Officer
Nationwide Health Properties

"**RALPH BLOCK IS A STOREHOUSE OF KNOWLEDGE ON REAL ESTATE INVESTMENT TRUSTS.** He is insightful on the important issues, intuitive to future trends, and instructive in a clear, folksy way. His book is **A MARVELOUS GUIDE TO THE REIT INDUSTRY.**"

MILTON COOPER
Chief Executive Officer
Kimco Realty Corporation

"Given the continued transformation of private real estate to the public markets, **THIS BOOK IS AN ESSENTIAL RESOURCE** for students, individual and institutional investors, and anyone else interested in understanding the REIT market."

DAVID J. HARTZELL
Distinguished Professor of Finance and Real Estate
Director of the Real Estate Program
The Kenan-Flager Business School
The University of North Carolina at Chapel Hill

INVESTING IN

REITs

Also available from
BLOOMBERG PERSONAL BOOKSHELF

Smart Questions to Ask Your Financial Advisers
by Lynn Brenner

Staying Wealthy—Strategies for Protecting Your Assets
by Brian H. Breuel

Investing in Small-Cap Stocks
by Christopher Graja and Elizabeth Ungar, Ph.D.

A Commonsense Guide to Your 401(k)
by Mary Rowland

The New Commonsense Guide to Mutual Funds
by Mary Rowland
(October 1998)

BLOOMBERG PERSONAL BOOKSHELF

INVESTING IN

REITs

Real Estate Investment Trusts

RALPH L. BLOCK

EDITED BY

VERONICA J. McDAVID

BLOOMBERG PRESS

PRINCETON

First edition published 1998
3 5 7 9 10 8 6 4 2

Block, Ralph L.
    Investing in REITs: Real Estate Investment Trusts / Ralph L. Block; edited by Veronica J. McDavid.
        p.   cm. — (Bloomberg personal bookshelf)
    Includes index.
    ISBN 1-57660-055-6
    1. Real estate investment trusts. I. McDavid, Veronica J. II. Title. III. Series.
    HG5095.B553   1998
    332. 63'247--dc21   98-24139
                                                               CIP

Chart illustrations by Myra Klockenbrink

Edited by Veronica J. McDavid

Book design by Don Morris Design

To my father, Jack,
who has always been the original "REIT man"
and without whom this book,
in more ways than one,
would never have been possible.
My only regret is that he was not
able to see its completion.

ACKNOWLEDGMENTS

"No man but a blockhead ever wrote except for money."

—SAMUEL JOHNSON

FIRST AND FOREMOST, I'd like to express my sincere appreciation and gratitude to Gary, Bill, Steve, Craig, Libby, Sylvia, Sally, Claudia, and all my friends at Bay Isle, without whose support, encouragement, and steadfast assistance this book would, truly, never have been written. It's almost unbelievable that such highly competent professionals can also be such nice people. Thanks, too, to my highly capable and enthusiastic editor, Veronica J. McDavid, for her many hours of tireless contributions, and to my new friends at Bloomberg, Alan Fass, Jared Kieling, Jacqueline Murphy, and Christina Palumbo, for their extremely valuable input and guidance.

I'd also like to express my appreciation to Jon Fosheim, Mike Kirby, John Lutzius, and all of their associates at that quintessential research firm, Green Street Advisors, for their outstanding research and analysis on REITs over the years. Thanks, also, to the many REIT and real estate enthusiasts I've had the pleasure of meeting and corresponding with, including Michael Dowd, Barry Vinocur, Dan Guenther, Ralph (of the East) Manton, and Dean Altshuler, who have helped me to sharpen my understanding of the world of real estate and REITs.

I owe much to Milton Cooper, a giant of the REIT world and a gentleman in every respect, who provided me with the necessary moral support to undertake this project, and to the folks at NAREIT, including Chris Lucas and Chuck DiRocco, who were always available with the requested REIT statistics and information. Limited space prevents me from noting specifically the many other individuals whose support and assistance I gratefully acknowledge and to whom I'm very much indebted.

Finally, allow me to express my gratitude to my lovely wife, Paula, who has put up with a great deal of "benign neglect" during the time it's taken me to complete this project.

INTRODUCTION

ALL OF US THINK we know real estate, and we have all interacted with it in one way or another since our arrival in the hospital delivery room. That building, our earliest impression of the world, is real estate; the residence we were taken home to, whether a single-family house or an apartment, is real estate; the malls and neighborhood centers where we shop, the factories and office buildings where we work, the hotels and resorts where we vacation, even the acres of undeveloped land—all are real estate. Real estate surrounds us. But do we really understand it?

For many years we have had a "love-hate relationship" with real estate. We love our homes and fully expect that they will appreciate in value. We admire real estate tycoons such as Joseph Kennedy, Conrad Hilton, and the Rockefellers; we even find Donald Trump and Leona Helmsley fascinating. Yet we believe real estate to be a risky investment and marvel at how major Japanese companies have spent hundreds of millions of dollars on U.S. hotels, golf courses, major office buildings, and other "trophy" properties during the 1980s, only to see their values plummet in the real estate recession of the late 1980s and early 1990s. As we approach the new millennium, real estate has clearly recovered, but we worry whether the good times will continue.

Is real estate a good investment? Real estate investment trusts, or "REITs," own real estate, but to what extent are they dependent upon the fortunes of real estate in general? Can we make money in REITs regardless of how real estate fares?

This book answers those questions and more. It not only makes a convincing case for investing in REITs, but also provides all the details, background, and guidance investors should have before delving into these highly rewarding investments. Here's what's in store:

Part I: Meet the REIT serves as an introduction to REITs. The first order of business is to explain why REITs are terrific investments that belong in every well-diversified portfolio. From there, we'll explore the "nature of the beast," and obtain a good working familiarity with REITs and their characteristics. Furthermore, we will follow with a description of the types of properties REITs own and the investment characteristics of each. And, finally, this section compares REITs with other traditional investments and also describes the structure and evolution of REITs.

Upon reaching **Part II: History and Mythology**, readers should find REITs such an intriguing investment that they'll wonder why these mystery moneymakers have been unpopular for much of their history. This section answers this question and dispels some old myths about REITs.

We'll take a look back to study the thirty-six–year history of the REIT world since its inception in 1962, and trace their progress up to today, when REITs have finally come of age.

Part III: Choosing REITs and Watching Them Grow provides the basic tools investors need to understand the dynamics of REITs' revenue and earnings growth, distinguish the blue-chip REITs from their more ordinary relatives, and find investment bargains among REIT shares. It will also get into the nitty-gritty of building REIT portfolios with adequate diversification.

Finally, **Part IV: Risks and Future Prospects** presents a necessary discussion of the risks investors face as they wind their way through the REIT world. And, at last, we'll do some speculating as to the future growth of the REIT industry and how we might profit from future trends.

By the time you finish this book, you will have a firm understanding and appreciation of one of the most highly rewarding investments on Wall

Street. Even more important, you will be able to build your own portfolio of outstanding real estate companies that should provide you with attractive current dividend yields and the prospects of significant capital appreciation in the years ahead. By investing in investment-quality REITs, investors large and small have been able to earn total returns averaging at least 12–14 percent annually, with steady income, low market-price volatility, and investment safety.

REIT investors today have a much wider choice of investment properties than ever before and can choose from some of the most experienced and capable managements that have ever invested in and operated real estate in the United States. As you'll see as you read on, REITs should be an essential part of every investor's portfolio; REIT investors have done quite well over the past 30 years, but the best is yet to come!

MEET THE
REIT

PART I

CHAPTER

1

What They Are
AND HOW THEY
WORK

W HAT'S YOUR idea of the perfect investment? How about one that promises not to double overnight or make you an instant millionaire, but instead will pay you a *consistent* 6 or 7 percent in quarterly dividends that go up another 6 or 7 percent annually as surely and steadily as if they were, say, rent? How about real estate?

Sure, you say, but only if there were a way to buy and own real estate in a hassle-free way, so an experienced professional dealt with the business of owning and managing it and just gave you the profits. And only if you could sell your real estate— if you wanted to—easily, as easily as you can sell a common stock. Well, read on. This is all possible with real estate investment trusts, or REITs, as they are commonly called.

REITs have provided individual investors all over

the country with a way to buy skyscrapers and shopping malls and health care facilities and apartment buildings—in fact, just about any kind of real property you can think of. REITs give you the perk of the cash flow that real estate leases provide, but with the benefit of a common stock's liquidity. Equally as important, REITs have access to capital and can therefore acquire and build additional properties as part of their ongoing real estate business.

Besides that, REITs can add stability to your investment portfolio, because real estate as an asset class has long been perceived as an inflation hedge and therefore adds diversification.

REITs have been around for 35 years, but it's been only recently that most people have really started buying into these high-yield investments. During 1997 alone, over $32 billion was raised in

REITS ARE A LIQUID ASSET

A LIQUID ASSET or investment is one that has a generally accepted value and a market where it can be sold easily and quickly at little or no discount to that value. Direct investment in real estate, whether it be a golf course in California or a skyscraper in Manhattan, is not liquid. The right buyer must be found, and even then, the value is not clearly established. Most publicly traded stocks *are* liquid. REITs are real estate–related investments that enjoy the benefit of a common stock's liquidity.

REIT offerings, but, according to many experts, the REIT industry, having so far captured only about 4 percent of the $3.5 trillion commercial real estate market, still has plenty of room left for growth.

Stan Ross, managing partner of E&Y/Kenneth Levanthal Real Estate Group, defines REITs by saying, "They are real operating companies that lease, renovate, manage, tear down, rebuild, and develop from scratch." That helps define a REIT, but you need to know not only what a REIT is, but also what it can be to you and what you can expect from it in terms of investment behavior.

REITs provide substantial dividend yields, which generally range between 4 and 8 percent, making them an ideal investment for an IRA or other tax-deferred portfolio. But unlike most high-yielding investments, REIT shares have a strong likelihood of increasing in value as the REIT's properties generate higher cash flows and additional properties are added to the portfolio.

REITs own real estate, but, when you buy a REIT, you're not just buying real estate, you're also buying a business.

When you buy stock in Gillette, for example, you're buying more than razor blades. REITs are corporate real estate entities overseen by financially sophisticated, skilled management teams who have the ability to grow the REITs' cash flows by 6 to 10 percent annually—and sometimes much more. Adding a 6 percent dividend yield to capital appreciation of 6 to 10 percent, resulting from 6 to 10 percent annual increases in operating cash flow provides for total returns of 12 to 16 percent.

A successful REIT's management will accept risk only where the odds of success are very strong. This is because, generally, they are investing their money right alongside yours and don't want to risk loss of capital any more than you do. REITs run the properties in such a way that they throw off good income; but they also have an eye to the future and are interested in growth of the property portfolio and in taking advantage of new opportunities.

TYPES OF REITS

THERE ARE TWO basic categories of REITs: equity REITs and mortgage REITs.

An equity REIT is a publicly traded company that, as its principal business, buys, manages, renovates, maintains, and occasionally sells real properties. It also acquires properties and frequently develops new properties when the economics are favorable. It is tax advantaged in that it is not taxed on the corporate level, and, by law, must pay out at least 95 percent of its net income as dividends to its investors.

A mortgage REIT is a REIT that makes and holds loans and other obligations that are secured by real estate collateral.

The focus of this book is equity REITs rather than mortgage or hybrid REITs (REITs that own both properties and mortgages), because, for the individual investor, equity REITs are less vulnerable to changes

EQUITY REIT PROPERTIES AND LOCATIONS

AN EQUITY REIT MIGHT OWN SUCH PROPERTIES AS:	AN EQUITY REIT MIGHT BE REGION SPECIFIC TO:
Apartment Houses	The East Coast
Neighborhood Shopping Centers	Washington, D.C.
Regional Malls	The Mid-Atlantic Region
Factory Outlet Malls	Texas
Health Care Facilities	California
Office Buildings	The Southeast
Industrial Parks	The Southwest
Self-Storage Facilities	New York
Hotels	The West Coast
Manufactured-Home Communities	Florida
Golf Courses	Nationwide U.S.A.

in interest rates and have historically provided better total returns, more stable market-price performance, lower risk, and greater liquidity. In addition to that, equity REITs allow the investor to diversify not only in the type of property he or she invests in, but also in the geographic location of the properties.

GENERAL INVESTMENT CHARACTERISTICS

PERFORMANCE AND RETURNS

DURING THE FIVE-YEAR PERIOD ending February 28, 1998, equity REITs have delivered an average annual total return to their investors of 15.08 percent. Compared to the remarkable performance of the stock market in recent years, those returns aren't bad, are they? Look at the chart shown at right. According to the REIT trade association, The National Association of Real Estate Investment Trusts, or NAREIT, equity REITs have generally provided their investors with compounded annual total returns right in line with the S&P 500.

SOURCE: NAREIT

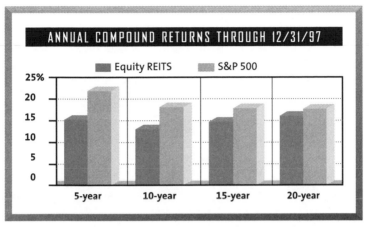

ANNUAL COMPOUND RETURNS THROUGH 12/31/97

■ Equity REITS   ▨ S&P 500

However, if REITs had only matched the S&P Index, you wouldn't be reading a book about them. The performance of lots of high-risk stocks have substantially exceeded the returns provided by the broad market. Here's the difference: REITs have matched the S&P's total return in spite of having benefits not usually enjoyed by stocks that keep pace with the market, namely low "betas," low market-price volatility, limited investment risk, and high current returns.

LOW BETAS

YOU'VE PROBABLY ENCOUNTERED the term "beta" in assessing different categories of stocks. A stock's beta is simply an evaluation of its volatility and return relative to an index of stocks, such as the S&P 500. With the base being 1, a stock with a beta greater than 1 is more volatile than the index; a stock with a beta less than 1 is less volatile than the index. Compare technology stocks, which, as a group, have a high beta, with utility stocks, which as a group have a low beta. A stock with a beta of 2 will move up twice as much as the overall index percentage in periods of rising prices—and down twice as much in periods of falling prices.

Many high-beta technology stocks have big price swings. Utility stocks, on the other hand, usually move up or down incrementally, or trade in a very limited range. Although technology stocks as a group have had a good overall return, you personally might have bought a tech stock at $22, seen it drop to $12, and, even though it eventually went up to $35, have had to wait six months or perhaps much longer for that to happen. That's okay when you can afford to hold out—but what if you can't wait? What if you need to sell in hurry? You know what happens: you lose.

Modern portfolio theory (MPT) equates "risk" in a stock with its tendency to rise or fall more than a broad stock market index, such as the S&P 500. The theory is that higher-risk stocks provide investors with higher returns in order to compensate them for the extra risk.

According to Lehman Brothers' *1996 Annual Review and Outlook for REITs,* the REIT industry beta, in relation to the S&P 500 beta, using monthly data for the prior ten years, is 0.59.

What this means, according to "beta theory," is that price movements in REIT stocks will have only a 59 percent correlation with the broad market, as measured by the S&P 500 Index. Theoretically, in a "hot market," when the S&P 500 Index is rising sharply, REITs' relatively low beta will act as a drag on their performance relative to the broad stock market indices. This happened in 1995, when REIT stocks lagged behind the popular indices but still provided investors

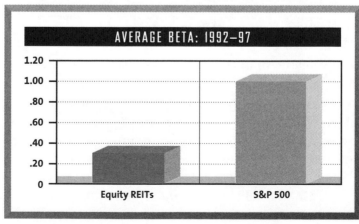

AVERAGE BETA: 1992–97

SOURCE: NAREIT

with total returns of 15.3 percent. Conversely, in a bear market, low-beta stocks such as REITs should provide stability to cushion the drop in the value of a fully diversified portfolio.

REITs offer diversification to your portfolio because they don't necessarily move in correlation with the rest of the market.

It is interesting to note that in 1996 there was an interesting anomaly, when REIT stocks' performance flew in the face of beta theory and turned in a performance substantially *higher* than the broader market. In 1997, however, they reverted to what might normally be expected; REITs' total return in 1997 was 20.3 percent vs. 33.4 percent for the broader market as measured by the S&P 500 Index. Trading in high-beta stocks can be compared with high-stakes gambling: you can win big—or you can lose big. For the last 20 years, REITs as a group seem to have defied that theory, having been simultaneously less volatile than the major indices and yet having matched their total return. What's the reason for this apparent contradiction?

One possibility is that, because of the myths and

VALUE INVESTMENTS

A VALUE INVESTMENT is an investment that is priced cheaply relative to its true value. Money managers scouting for value investments look for stocks that have been unfairly beaten down in price, perhaps, for example, because there has been some bad news about one of their competitors, and all the stocks in the sector get "tarred with the same brush." Value investors believe that, in time, such investments will rise, as soon as the market realizes their intrinsic worth.

misperceptions concerning REITs that we'll explore later, REIT stocks are not efficiently priced and are, in fact, priced *below* what one would expect in a perfectly efficient market. In other words, in addition to all their other advantages, REITs may be considered *value* investments.

LOW VOLATILITY

A STOCK'S "VOLATILITY" refers to the extent to which its price tends to bounce around from day to day, or even hour to hour. Volatility is different from beta, as a stock may yo-yo wildly intraday or from day to day, yet its closing price may move pretty much with a market index over slightly longer periods.

REITs' high current yields act as a shock absorber against daily market fluctuations.

Equally important, there is a predictability and steadiness to most REITs' operating and financial performance from quarter to quarter and from year to year, and there is simply less concern about major negative surprises.

There's no getting around it: our biggest investment mistakes are emotional ones. When our stocks are going up, we tend to throw caution to the winds in our pursuit of ever greater profits. Likewise, when our stocks are dropping, we tend to panic and dump otherwise sound investments, because we're afraid of ever greater losses. When is the "right" time to sell or buy? Prudent investors have learned through experience to temper their emotional reactions, but low volatility in a stock can make patient and disciplined investors of us all.

Sometimes our financial decisions are not based on prudent market strategy but on what's going on in our personal life. Let's say the market is having a bad week. You know this is not the time to sell, but your daughter's tuition is due. Not to worry. If your shares are in a REIT instead of a tech stock, chances are you can sell them at very close to the price at which they were trading last month or even last year—and they've been paying all those fat dividends in the meantime.

LOW RISK

THERE'S JUST NO WAY to avoid risk completely. Simple preservation of capital carries its own risk— inflation. Since inflation came along, there's no such thing as "no risk." Real estate ownership and management, like any other business or commercial endeavor, is subject to all sorts of risks. Mall REITs are subject to the changing tastes and lifestyles of consumers; apartment REITs are subject to overbuilding and declining job growth in their properties' geographical areas; and health care REITs are subject to the politics of government cuts in health care reimbursement, to cite just a few examples.

Yet, despite this, property owners are somewhat insulated from the failures of their tenants—if they are diversified in sector and geographic location. If one tenant is doing badly, for instance, there are usually other tenants who are doing fine. This kind of thing happened repeatedly in 1989–90 in the retail industry, and the retail REITs came out of it virtually unscathed; they merely found new tenants to replace the losers. Beware, however, of real property designed for a single use, in which case the departure of the one and only tenant could present a real problem for the property owner.

Holders of most common stocks must contend with yet another type of risk, related not to the fundamentals of a company's business but to the fickleness of the financial markets. Let's say you own shares in a company whose business is doing well. The earnings report comes out and the news is that earnings are double what they were last year—right in line with analysts' expectations. Just because there was no *positive* surprise, the price of the stock drops. This is fairly common in the stock market, but REIT investors to date have rarely suffered from this syndrome.

Analysts who follow REITs are normally able to forecast quarterly results, within one or two cents, quarter after quarter, year after year.

This is because of the stability and predictability of REITs' operating cash flows, rents, built-in increases, and real estate operating costs. True, compared to tech stocks, REITs are not very exciting, but think of what you'll save on aspirin and Maalox.

When you look at the riskiness of equity REITs, you see that very few have gotten into serious financial trouble over the years. Those that have had difficulties have done so through excessive debt leverage, wild promises on the part of management, or questionable transactions with directors or major shareholders. Such shenanigans can occur in any company. Remember, there is no such thing as no risk. If you're investing primarily in the higher-quality REITs (and we'll tell you how to be the judge of that), the long-term risk of REIT investments is far lower than that of most other common stocks.

HIGH CURRENT RETURNS— PLEASURES AND IMPLICATIONS

THERE ARE CERTAIN distinct advantages to owning high-yield stocks such as REITs. One is that it is at the shareholder's, rather than the management's, discretion to decide what to do with one's portion of the company's operating income. As REITs pay substantial dividends, you can choose to plow the money back into the REIT (albeit on an after-tax basis in taxable accounts), invest the funds somewhere else altogether, or blow it on a trip to Hawaii. Shareholders in companies like Netscape, which pay little or nothing in dividends, have no such choice. Essentially, all of "their" share of net income is reinvested for them by management.

Of the 11 percent–plus average annual total return on stocks since the mid-1920s, approximately 40 percent of that return has come from dividends.

And consider the psychological benefit of seeing significant dividends roll in each month or each quarter. If, like most of us, you have to work to earn a salary, seeing a check come in for several hundred dollars— without your having to show up at the office—gives you a very warm feeling regardless of whether you intend to spend it or reinvest it.

A third advantage is based on the wisdom of balancing your portfolio. One of the first rules of investing is to be diversified. From an overall portfolio perspective, REITs can provide that diversification.

ARE HIGH CURRENT RETURNS SLOWING GROWTH?

IT DOESN'T TAKE a Ph.D. to figure out why a lot of investors like REITs' high returns. But what effect does the high payout ratio have on the REIT? With investors receiving at least 95 percent of the taxable income

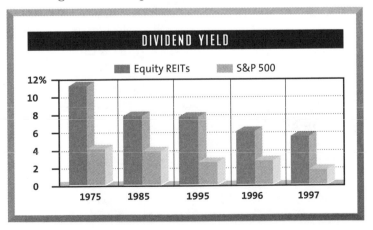

SOURCE: NAREIT

(excluding capital gains), the REIT has very little retained capital with which to expand the business and, therefore, its future operating income. To the extent that stock price appreciation results from rapidly rising earnings, a REIT's share price should normally rise at a slower pace than that of a non-REIT stock. However, the REIT investor doesn't mind that; he or she expects to make up the difference through higher dividend payments, and thus maintain a high *total* return. The chart that follows gives a picture of the impact of high dividends on total return.

EVERGREEN REITS			
EVERGREEN REIT	BEGINNING	END	RETURN
FFO	1.00	1.06	
P/FFO Multiple	10.0	10.0	
Price	$10.00	$10.60	6.0%
Dividends		$0.70	7.0%
TOTAL RETURN			13.0%

Nevertheless, for the REIT, there are other alternatives by which it can propel growth. If management wants to expand, it can do so through additional stock or debt offerings, through private equity placements, by exchanging new shares or partnership units for properties, or through loans from banks or insurance companies. There are some times when such capital flows freely, some times when it dries up altogether, and still other times when it is available but at a price that is prohibitive. Generally, however, high-quality REITs can expect to have good access to capital during most market environments.

When selecting REITs for investment, remember, it is the strong ones that can attract additional capital — and this provides the most growth potential.

Since being able to attract reasonably priced capital is a crucial asset for a REIT, it is those companies with excellent reputations in the investment community that have the clear advantage.

The need to raise additional capital for growth should normally mean that REITs will be slow-growing investment vehicles. Lately, however, some REITs have been acting in a very un-REITly way, growing by 10 to 20 percent annually. It's as if grandma suddenly got off her rocking chair and started doing handsprings. What's going on here? The phenomenon can probably be explained by the fact that some REIT management companies have combined their capital-raising capabilities with many institutions' need to liquefy their real estate investments, and thus created rapidly growing real estate businesses. Of course, the national real estate recovery has greatly facilitated this process.

REITs are the easiest way for individual investors to participate in the real estate recovery.

As small investors became aware that there was a way they could participate in this trend, the big money managers and institutional investors also started getting involved. For better or for worse, heavyweights leave big footprints. They're not just *in* the market; sometimes they *make* the market. Now we're seeing the effects of momentum, a factor not always related to value. REITs were attractive even before they became such an investment trend. This trend has enabled growth-oriented investors to find REITs meeting their criteria, but value-oriented investors can still find plenty to like in the REIT world. We'll tell you how to find REITs that meet your specific objectives, "momentum" notwithstanding.

SUMMARY

◆ REITs own real estate, but when you buy a REIT, you're not just buying real estate, you're also buying a business.

◆ REITs' total returns, over reasonably long time periods, have been very competitive with those provided by the broader market.

◆ REITs offer the liquidity of being publicly traded.

◆ REITs offer diversification to your portfolio because they don't necessarily move in correlation with the rest of the market.

◆ REITs' high current yields act as a shock absorber against daily market fluctuations.

◆ Analysts who follow REITs are normally able to forecast quarterly results within one or two cents, quarter after quarter, year after year, thus minimizing the chances for "negative surprises."

◆ REITs' high yields raise the overall yield of the portfolio, thus minimizing volatility and providing stability even in major bear markets.

◆ REITs are the easiest way for individuals to participate in the real estate recovery.

CHAPTER

2

REITs
vs. COMPETITIVE
INVESTMENTS

BEFORE DECIDING if REITs are the right investment for you, it's important to measure their merits, point by point, against those of other investments. That comparison is only meaningful, however, if the comparison is made with investments that are truly similar. This point brings us to a concept known as "relevant market."

In antitrust law, relevant market is very significant. Suppose, for example, that Nestlé wanted to acquire Hershey Foods. In order to determine whether this might create an antitrust problem arising from a company's acquisition of a competitor, you have to figure out what the "relevant market" is. Is the market simply chocolate bars, is it a wider market such as "candy," or is it a still wider market such as "snack foods"? There might or might not be an antitrust problem, depending upon which market is perceived as being the "relevant market."

A similar issue arises when we compare the merits of REITs to those of other investments. Is it appropriate to compare REITs with *all* common stocks, or does it make more sense to compare them with the more narrow "market" of high-yield investments? Up to this point we've been comparing them to the broad spectrum of common stocks, which, technically, they are. Many investors, however, see them as somehow different from stocks in such companies as Merck, Ford, Disney, or Intel, because of their higher dividend yields and lower capital appreciation prospects.

REITs might be more accurately compared to securities investments with similar characteristics: utility stocks, preferred stocks, bonds, and convertibles. These are the investments of choice for those investors who normally invest in higher-yielding securities.

The easiest comparison is to electric utility stocks, since, with their comparable yields, prospects of dividend growth, and capital appreciation, they are closer to REITs than most other investments. And, although they are not as close, we'll also make the comparison to nonconvertible bonds and preferred stocks, and with convertibles and other real estate investments.

REITS *vs.* ELECTRIC UTILITIES

BACK IN 1994 I did an informal study of REITs' popularity in relation to utility stocks. According to a *Barron's* mutual fund section in April 1994, 71 mutual funds had been specifically designed to invest in utilities, compared with only 11 designed for real estate securities. The aggregate asset value of these utility funds was $25.3 billion *vs.* only $1.27 billion for the REIT funds. Five utility funds each had assets greater than all 11 of the REIT funds combined. So, historically, utilities have been much more popular investments than REITs—but this situation is reversing rapidly.

Most analysts expect nothing more from utilities than that their earnings will keep pace with inflation at best. An April 1996 article in the *Los Angeles Times,* "Safe Widow and Orphan Utility Stocks May Be History," made the point that utility stocks, for many years regarded as some of the safest investments around, may no longer be so. The reporter, Tom Petruno, observed that, for the "utes," whether because of deregulation, increased competition, or poorly executed diversification, ". . . times have changed, and generally not for the better. . . ."

True, in the past year, there has been more interest in electric utilities than there has been in a long time, but Robert McConnaughey, of Prudential Real Estate Securities, believes that "while utilities have seen a bounce based on some M&A activity and the perception that the stocks are cheap, there are tremendous unanswered questions facing that industry in the face of deregulation. What are the electric companies really worth," he asks, "if the market evolves in the Enron model and power is openly traded at the lowest cost of generation?" People know utilities; they trust them. But are they a better investment than REITs? The answer is no.

There is a strong case to be made that REITs are clearly superior investments to utilities and that smart investors who have a large segment of their portfolios in electric utilities should be reallocating those funds to REITs.

Milton Cooper, CEO of Kimco Realty Corporation and former chairman of The National Association of Real Estate Investment Trusts (NAREIT), observed in January 1997, that "income-oriented investors, who dropped their utility stocks last year when lower inflation depressed stock yields and the threat of deregulation increased the risk of holding a utility, found a safe harbor in REITs."

GROWTH PROSPECTS
REITS' TOTAL ANNUAL RETURNS to shareholders for the five-year period ending December 31, 1997, was 18.3 percent. Utilities' average total return for the same period, as measured by the Dow Jones Utility Average, was only 10.6 percent per year (*see chart on the following page*).

In the current environment, growth is difficult for electric utilities. Most can charge customers only what state regulators will allow. In addition, in the past, they have been locked into one geographical area, and, although this is changing, the verdict isn't in yet on their expansion.

REITs are not threatened by the twin specters of deregulation and new competition; utilities are.

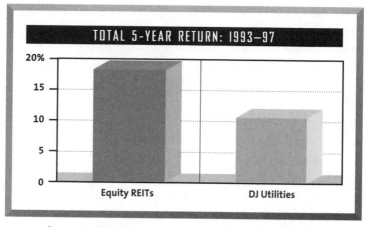

TOTAL 5-YEAR RETURN: 1993–97

Some utility company managements, in an attempt at more aggressive growth, expanded into other businesses, only to realize—after big expenditures—that the diversification was not an improvement. Will the current efforts by some utilities to expand internationally turn out any better? Don't count on it. With obstacles like these, it's unlikely that even the most ardent supporters of utility stocks will enjoy future growth rates in excess of 3 percent.

MANAGEMENT

WHILE THERE ARE certainly some REITs being run by "caretaker" managements that do not seek to use imagination and their available resources to grow the business, the good ones are run by extremely capable companies or individuals who have had many years of experience in the successful ownership and management of real properties. They are energetic, entrepreneurial, and quick to seize new opportunities.

It is very important to note that many REITs are managed by people who have most of their own net worth invested in the shares.

Although the managements of some of the utilities may be very capable, most are not entrepreneurial types known for their vision and innovation. Further, they are not as heavily invested in their own companies as are most REIT managements.

REGULATION

FOR ELECTRIC UTILITIES, regulation is the ultimate obstacle to growth. For the regulatory commissions of most states, rate regulation is a "heads-we-win, tails-you-lose" proposition. Look at the utilities who decided to build nuclear power plants. In many areas, the common perception seems to be that it was not a sound idea, because of the risks to the surrounding population and the problem of disposing of nuclear waste. Management goofed in assessing the situation, and many nuclear plants now stand empty as a result.

Who pays for the mistake? It's not hard to figure out. When it comes to counting votes, there are more people using utilities than running and owning them. Regulators, having been appointed by elected officials, will simply pass on the costs to shareholders. REITs, on the other hand, are not subject to significant regulatory supervision.

COMPETITION

ELECTRIC UTILITIES TODAY are facing something they have never had to deal with: competition. Until recently, the power companies had a Faustian bargain with regulators: "You tell us what we can charge our customers and how much we can keep, and we get a monopoly on supplying all the power in our area." But that bargain is beginning to crumble as former monopolies are being opened up to new competition.

These new competitors, whether upstart cogeneration companies or major power companies, are siphoning off large commercial electricity users, causing the local companies to seek significant rate increases from the consumer to make up for lost revenue. Power company managements are not used to the streetfighting of competition.

REIT managements, on the other hand, have been competing with real estate companies, merchant builders, and knowledgeable private investors since they first got into the business. They know their way around the block.

INFLATION

AT THE TIME of this writing, whether thanks to the gods, the Feds, or the Force, inflation is still not a problem, but it's a situation no one seems to trust. Even now, threats of wage inflation can throw the markets into a tailspin. It seems inevitable that interest rates will eventually rise. Utilities are prodigious borrowers and thus particularly vulnerable to rising interest rates. While regulators may allow utilities to pass on some of their costs to users, it's always a game of catch-up, with the increases in user rates seriously lagging behind rising interest rates. Investors who anticipate the market have made utilities even more sensitive to interest rates, to the point that utility share prices on any given day have an inverse relationship to the day's interest-rate charts, even though the actual effects of rising rates may not be felt for some time to come. Utilities have therefore traded like fixed-income securities, declining in the face of rising inflationary expectations.

At first glance it may seem as if REITs are in the same position as utilities. After all, they do carry a substantial amount of debt, and borrow frequently. They, too, are often highly leveraged. The difference, however, is that *investor perception* of REITs is that they are primarily real estate companies and that the values of their underlying assets will tend to increase with inflation. Consequently their prices will frequently move up with the price of gold, oil, and actual real property, which are often seen as hedges against inflation, in situations where supply and demand for commercial space is in equilibrium. In addition, the highest-quality REITs today have relatively small amounts of variable debt, and, therefore, are unlikely to be seriously affected by rising interest rates in the short term.

INVESTMENT TRENDS

THE INVESTMENT MERITS of utility stocks are already widely known. It's unlikely that there will be a major surge of new investors who suddenly discover their virtues. REITs, on the other hand, have been largely ignored by investors since their arrival on the scene approximately 35 years ago. Although their popularity has increased substantially in recent years, they are not yet heavily represented in investment portfolios. The point here is that there are hundreds of thousands of potential REIT investors out there, both individual and institutional, looking for excellent yields with reasonably good growth prospects, who are not yet invested in REITs. Will they all necessarily become REIT enthusiasts? No one knows for sure, but REITs began a new surge of popularity in 1996. The prospect of a substantial increase in the amount of new investment funds flowing into REITs instead of into utility stocks is very enticing.

A sea change is already under way. At the end of 1997, real estate mutual fund cash flow from 1994 had increased by $10.63 billion, compared with a *decrease* of $4.8 billion for utility mutual funds. So, it's not only fundamentals that move markets. It's also investment styles.

YIELDS

RIGHT NOW, THE most widely regarded electric utility companies are paying dividends of approximately 5 percent and are expected to grow at 2 to 3 percent annually. Top-quality REITs in the United States, on the other hand, while paying a similar current yield, have growth prospects of at least 6 to 10 percent

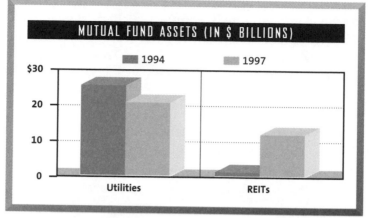

SOURCE: AMG DATA SERVICES

annually over at least the next several years. Which would you rather own?

REITS *vs.* BONDS

WHILE REITS DO COMPETE directly with utilities for the funds of yield-oriented investors, they are not *quite* so analogous with bonds. Although bonds generally provide higher yields than the best-quality REITs, the investor gets only the interest coupon, but no growth potential. Bonds do offer something that REITs cannot provide: repayment of principal at maturity so that, in the absence of bankruptcy or other default, the investor will always get back his or her investment. It is this feature that makes the comparison between REITs and bonds (or REITs and preferred stocks) flawed. For that reason, if absolute safety of capital is paramount regardless of what it costs you, REITs may not be the ideal investment for you. But let's look at the returns each can yield.

With bonds, what you see is what you get: pure yield and very little else. Let's assume that you invest $10,000 in a bond that yields 7 percent and matures in ten years. At the end of ten years, you will have your $10,000 in cash, plus the cumulative amount of the interest you received (10 x $700), or a total of $17,000, less taxes on the interest.

$10,000 invested in Bonds:

(with 7 Percent Coupon and 10-Year Maturity)

$10,000 (value at maturity) +

(10 yrs. x $700/yr. interest) = $17,000

$10,000 invested in REITs:

(with 6 Percent Dividend over 10-Year Period)

$16,895 (value at maturity) +

$7,908 (10 yrs.' cumulative dividends) = $24,803

If, however, you invest the same amount of money in a REIT, the total return would probably calculate something like this: Assume the purchase of 1,000 shares of a REIT trading at $10 per share, providing a 6 percent yield (or $.60 per share). Let's also assume that the REIT increases its "funds from operations" (funds from operations, or "FFO," is essentially cash flow) by 6 percent annually and increases the dividend by 6 percent annually. Finally, let's assume that the shares will rise proportionately with increased FFO and dividend payments. Ten years later, the REIT will be paying $1.01 in dividends, and your total investment will be worth $24,803 ($7,908 in cumulative dividends received plus $16,895 in share value at that time). That's $24,803 from the REIT, *vs.* only $17,000 from the ten-year bond, or a difference of $7,803. Taxes, of course, will have to be paid on both the bond interest and the dividend payments *(see chart on the following page)*.

Of course, conventional wisdom says that REITs *should* provide a higher total return, because they are much riskier than bonds. However, that's not always true if you look at the facts. It *is* true that, unlike bonds, REIT shares offer no specific maturity date, and there is no guarantee of the price you'll get when you sell them. However, with bonds you get no inflation protection, and so you are at a substantial risk of the declining purchasing power of the dollar.

REITS' HIGHER TOTAL RETURN

REIT's 6 PERCENT Annual Dividend Compounded at 6 Percent Annual Growth Rate

YEAR	PRICE	DIVIDENDS
1	$10.00	$0.60
2	$10.60	$0.64
3	$11.24	$0.67
4	$11.91	$0.71
5	$12.62	$0.76
6	$13.38	$0.80
7	$14.19	$0.85
8	$15.04	$0.90
9	$15.94	$0.96
10	$16.89	$1.01
		$7.91
x 1, 000 shares	$16,894.79	$7,908.48
TOTAL INVESTMENT		$24,803.27

If history is any guide, REITs, unlike bonds, will appreciate in value as the value of their underlying real estate appreciates and the rents from their tenants increase over time.

With respect to price and earnings volatility, the chart at right shows the path of the FFO (funds from operations) and the stock price of United Dominion Realty, a long-established and very well-run apartment REIT, over the last ten years. As you can see, there are no rollercoaster rides here; there are only the normal price fluctuations you might see with bonds as well.

In fact, the risks are stacked against the bond investor, since, if inflation rises, so generally will interest rates, which reduces the market value of the bond while it's being held and results in an actual loss of capital if the bond is sold prior to maturity. On the other

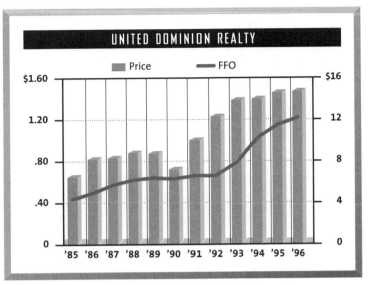

hand, if inflation slows, resulting in lower interest rates, many bonds are "called" before their maturity dates, depriving the investor of what, with hindsight, was a very attractive yield and forcing him or her to find some other investment vehicle, one that will pay a much lower rate of interest.

U.S. Treasury bonds are not callable prior to maturity and entail no repayment risk, but their yields are lower than those of corporate bonds and also fluctuate with interest rates.

REITS vs. PREFERRED STOCKS

NOW LET'S TAKE a look at how well REITs stack up against preferred stocks. Unlike bonds, preferred stocks do not represent the promise of the issuer to repay a specific amount at a specific date in the future, and in the legal pecking order their claims against the corporation are below those of every other creditor. Unless the terms of the preferred stock provide for the right of the holder to demand redemption, preferred shares enjoy the worst of all possible worlds: neither do they have a fixed maturity date, nor are their holders considered creditors. They do, however, provide relatively high yields in today's market, many offering in excess of 8 percent. The problem here is, as with bonds, what you see is what you get: pure yield and very little else.

REITs are not as interest-rate sensitive as bonds, preferred stocks, or utilities.

While the high dividends are enticing, preferred stocks, unlike REITs and common stocks, offer little in the way of price-appreciation potential or hedge against inflation. Their prices, like bonds', are very interest-rate sensitive.

REITS vs. CONVERTIBLES

WHEN WE COMPARE REITs to *convertible* bonds and *convertible* preferred stocks, we finally come to an investment that does, in fact, provide direct competition for REITs. These securities offer yields comparable to REITs' *and* appreciation potential—if the common stock into which the convertible bonds or preferred stock may be converted rises substantially. In the case of convertible bonds, there is the security of a fixed maturity date in case the underlying common stock fails to appreciate in value. Convertibles can be a relatively attractive investment concept.

The problem with good convertibles is that most companies don't issue them. The yield-hungry investor just has to keep an eye out for these "hybrids," and, from time to time, there is a small window of opportunity to purchase them. Then, if the underlying common stock appears to be a good investment, the convertible may also be a good investment.

REITS vs. OTHER REAL ESTATE INVESTMENT VEHICLES

AS AN ASSET CLASS, real estate can be a very good investment. A well-situated, well-maintained investment property may grow in value over the years, and its rents may grow with it. While buildings may depreciate over time and neighborhoods change, only a finite amount of land exists upon which an apartment, store, or building can be built. If you own such a facility in the right area, it can be, if not a gold mine, a cash cow whose value is likely to increase over the years. New, competitive buildings will not be built unless rents are high enough to justify the development costs. Then these higher rental rates on the new buildings might well establish a new prevailing level of market rents that enable the owners, even of older buildings, to increase rents.

However, contrary to popular wisdom, there is no necessary correlation between inflation and the value of real estate. One real estate observer (Pablo Galarza, in *Financial World,* January 2, 1996) has concluded that, based upon a study of real estate performance data between 1978 and 1993, the net operating income of the properties studied did not even come close to keeping up with inflation in that period. Nevertheless, that was a period of high inflation and substantial overbuilding, and history has shown that well-maintained properties in economically healthy areas, if they are protected against competing properties because of land scarcity or zoning restrictions, are likely to rise in value over time.

REIT ownership addresses all the problems raised by every other real estate investment vehicle: diversification, liquidity, management, and, in most cases, conflicts of interest between management and investors.

Accepting that commercial property is generally a good long-term investment and accepting our view that REITs are the best way to invest in commercial property, how does real estate as an asset class affect the rest of your portfolio? Since it behaves differently from all your other assets—stocks (both foreign and domestic), bonds, cash, or possibly gold or art—it adds another dimension and therefore helps to diversify your holdings. There are a number of ways, however, in which you can choose to hold real estate.

PRIVATE OWNERSHIP

PRIVATE OWNERSHIP MEANS that you're in the real estate business. Do you have the time to manage property, or do you already have a full-time career? Do you know when it's a good time to buy, sell, or hold? Sometimes buying real estate at cheap prices, then selling it, is more profitable than holding and managing it, depending on the market climate. Would you recognize when it's smarter to sell the property than to run it? For most individual investors, having a real estate professional make this decision is far wiser than being in real estate directly. Effective and efficient property management is also crucial; the importance of competent, experienced management cannot be overstated, and individuals often lack the resources to accomplish this.

Private ownership may sometimes offer higher profits than investing in a REIT, but you probably don't have the time or experience to be in the real estate business.

Although it is sometimes more profitable not to have to share returns with anyone else, it is also clearly riskier. The investment value of real estate is quite often determined by the local economy; at any given time, apartment buildings may be doing well, say, in Los Angeles, but poorly in Atlanta. Most individuals simply do not have the financial resources to buy enough properties to be safely diversified, either by property type or by geography.

Then there is the problem of liquidity: selling a single piece of real property may be very difficult and costly. Furthermore, it may not happen when you want it to, although selling may be your only way to cash out.

Finally, even if you are willing to accept all the inconveniences and disadvantages of inexperience, risk, and illiquidity, would you want to be the one that gets the call that there's been a break-in, or the air conditioning is on the fritz, or the elevator's stuck? And if you utilize an outside management company, your profits will be substantially reduced.

C-CORPORATIONS

AS WE HAVE SAID, the REIT is the most tax-efficient way for individuals to own real estate in public form, since the REIT pays no taxes on its net income if the REIT distributes at least 95 percent of that income to shareholders in the form of dividends. However, there is another publicly traded security that can own real estate, to which we referred earlier. It is the "C-corporation." A C-corporation is not a REIT and thus it pays taxes on its net income, whether or not distributing any income to its shareholders. One example of a C-corporation that owned real estate would have been The Rouse Company, a shopping-center owner that was a C-corporation for many years. Recently Rouse decided to convert to a REIT.

Since a C-corp. is not required to distribute any income to shareholders, it may thus have more capital available for growth and expansion. For the shareholder, however, this is not necessarily an advantage, depending on his or her investment goals. The dividend yields of C-corporations are puny compared to REIT yields, and most investors who choose to own real estate prefer high dividends. The bottom line is that aggressive real estate investors who are more interested in capital appreciation than income might want to take a look at the C-corps. that own and manage real estate. That's a different type of investment altogether—another story for another day.

PRIVATE PARTNERSHIP

OWNERSHIP THROUGH A private partnership—whether with 2, 10, or 20 partners—really isn't much better. Here, the investor gets to delegate, either to a general partner or to an outside company, the tasks of property leasing and management—at a price, of course. Usually, however, most private partnerships of this type own only one or very few properties, and those properties are rarely diversified in terms of property type or location.

In a private partnership, liquidity often depends on the financial solvency of the investor's partners. Although it might be theoretically possible for one partner to sell his or her interest to another partner without the underlying property's being sold, it often just doesn't happen that way. Also, in private partnerships, conflicts of interest abound between the general partner and the limited partners, often with regard either to compensation or to the decision to sell or refinance the partnership property. Finally, there is the question of the personal liability of the individual partners if the partnership gets into financial trouble, a situation not uncommon in recent years.

PUBLICLY TRADED LIMITED PARTNERSHIP

THERE IS A WORLD of difference between REITs and real estate limited partnerships. The limited-partnership sponsors of the 1980s plucked billions of dollars from investors who were seeking the benefits of real estate ownership combined with liquidity. Unsuspecting investors during that time did *so* poorly that they were lucky to recover 10 or 20 cents on the dollar.

There were several reasons for their failure: Sometimes it was that fees were so high that there were no profits for the ultimate owner, the investor. Sometimes it was that the partnerships bought too late in the real estate cycle. After they grossly overpaid for the properties, they hired mediocre managers—failing to recognize that, particularly in the 1990s, real estate was—and still is—a very management-intensive business. Other times, these limited partnerships had conflicts of interest with the general partners, to the detriment of the investors. There are big differences between real estate limited partnerships and REITs, as we shall discuss in detail later.

SUMMARY

◆ There is a strong case to be made that REITs are clearly superior investments to utilities and that smart investors who have a large segment of their portfolios in electric utilities should be reallocating all or a portion of those funds to REITs.

◆ REITs are not threatened by the twin specters of deregulation and competition—utilities are.

◆ Many REITs are managed by people who have most of their own net worth invested in the shares.

◆ If history is any guide, REITs, unlike bonds, will appreciate in value as the value of their underlying real estate appreciates and the rents from their tenants increase over time.

◆ REITs are not as interest-rate sensitive as bonds, preferred stocks, or utilities.

◆ Bonds and preferred stocks have no potential for dividend income growth, and utilities have low growth potential—but REITs have substantial dividend yields and growth prospects of 6 to 10 percent annually.

◆ REIT ownership addresses all the problems raised by every other real estate investment vehicle: diversification, liquidity, management, and, in most cases, conflicts of interest between management and investors.

◆ Private ownership may sometimes offer higher profits than investing in a REIT, but most individuals don't have the time or experience to be in the real estate business full time.

CHAPTER

Today's
REITs

N OW THAT YOU have a general sense of what REITs are and how they compare to other investments, let's take a closer look at the structure of REITs and how they've adapted over the years.

THE FIRST REIT

THE REIT WAS defined and authorized by the U.S. Congress, in the Real Estate Investment Trust Act of 1960, and the first REIT was actually formed in 1963. The legislation was meant to provide individual investors with the opportunity to participate in the benefits, already available to large institutional investors, of owning and/or financing significant commercial real estate on a tax-advantaged basis.

The avoidance of "double taxation" is one of the key advantages to the REIT structure.

The tax advantage is that a REIT is not subject to corporate tax. It must, however, by law, pay out 95 percent of its net income to its shareholders. The shareholders, of course, must pay income taxes on the dividends, unless the REIT shares are held in an IRA, 401(k), or other pension plan, although often not all of a REIT's dividend is immediately taxable.

THE TAX REFORM ACT OF 1986

THE TAX REFORM ACT of 1986 relaxed some of the restrictions historically binding REITs. Originally, management was legally obliged to hire outside companies to provide property leasing and maintenance for its tenants, but a REIT is now

UNIQUE LEGAL CHARACTERISTICS OF A REIT

1 The REIT must distribute at least 95 percent of its annual taxable income, excluding capital gains, as dividends to its shareholders.

2 The REIT must have at least 75 percent of its assets invested in real estate, mortgage loans, shares in other REITs, cash, or government securities.

3 The REIT must derive at least 75 percent of its gross income from rents, mortgage interest, or gains from the sale of real property. And at least 95 percent must come from these sources, together with dividends, interest, and gains from securities sales.

4 The REIT must have at least 100 shareholders and must have less than 50 percent of the outstanding shares concentrated in the hands of five or fewer shareholders.

allowed to do such work within its own organization. This change was highly significant because imaginative and efficient property management is a key element in being a successful and profitable property owner.

Today's REITs are fully integrated operating companies that can handle all aspects of real estate operations internally:

◆ Acquisitions and sales of properties
◆ Management and leasing
◆ Maintenance
◆ Property rehabilitation and repositioning
◆ Property development.

In studying different REITs, you might come across the terms "UPREIT" and "DownREIT." These are terms used to describe differences in the corporate structure of REITs. The UPREIT concept was first implemented in 1992 by creative investment bankers. Its purpose was to enable long-established real estate operating companies to bring properties they already own under the umbrella of a REIT structure, without actually having to sell the properties to the REIT, since by such a sale the existing owners would incur significant capital gains taxes.

UPREIT

UPREIT JUST MEANS "Umbrella Partnership REIT." Generally, the way it works is this: The REIT itself might not own any properties; what it does own is a controlling interest in a limited partnership that, in turn, owns the real estate. The other limited partners often include management and private investors who had indirectly owned the organization's properties prior to its having become a REIT. The owners of the limited-partnership units have the right to convert them into shares of the REIT, to vote as if they were REIT shareholders, and to receive the same dividends as if they held publicly traded REIT shares. In short, they enjoy virtually the same attributes of ownership as the REIT shareholders.

DOWNREITS

DOWNREITS ARE STRUCTURED similarly but are usually formed after the REIT becomes a public company, and generally do not include members of management among the limited partners in the controlled partnership.

REITs structured as UPREITs or DownREITs can exchange operating partnership (OP) units for interests in other real estate partnerships that own properties the REIT wants to acquire. Such an acquisition does not threaten the sellers with adverse tax implications. By receiving OP units in a "like-kind" exchange, the sellers can then not only defer the payment of taxes but also gain the advantage of having a more diversified form of investment. This gives the UPREIT or Down-REIT a competitive edge over a regular REIT when it comes to making a deal with tax-sensitive sellers.

Originally conceived as a tax-deferral device, the UPREIT structure has also become an attractive acquisition tool for the REIT.

There is one caveat with the UPREIT structure, however, in that it creates an opportunity for conflicts of interest. Management often owns units in the UPREIT's partnership rather than, or in addition to, shares in the REIT, and their OP units will have a low cost basis. Since the sale of a property could trigger taxable income to the holders of the UPREIT's units but not to the shareholders of the REIT, management might be reluctant to sell a property or even the REIT itself—even if, for instance, the property is a disappointment or the third-party offer is a generous one. What remains to be seen is how management handles the conflict issues and to what extent OP units will be used to finance acquisitions of attractive properties.

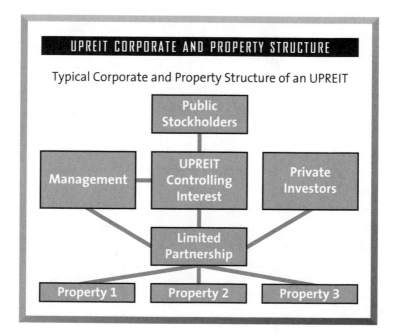

UPREIT CORPORATE AND PROPERTY STRUCTURE

Typical Corporate and Property Structure of an UPREIT

Public Stockholders

Management

UPREIT Controlling Interest

Private Investors

Limited Partnership

Property 1   Property 2   Property 3

UPREITs and DownREITs are simply variations on REITs that enable existing property owners to "REITize" their existing property without incurring current capital gains taxes.

THE INFAMOUS LIMITED PARTNERSHIPS OF YESTERYEAR

THE LIMITED PARTNERSHIPS of the 1980s were designed for the purpose of owning and managing properties and generating a positive cash flow, but, in many cases, the properties did not live up to expectations. What investors really bought was the tax shelter these properties offered, along with the hope of capital appreciation. In a rapidly rising real estate market, simply holding the property for six months or a year, even if it was running at a loss, would mean that investors could enjoy a nice capital gain. When, however, in 1986 the tax laws were changed, the arrangement no longer worked. Investors were unwilling to continue suffering losses for any length of time when the loss was no longer a tax shelter.

Today's REITs are an entirely different animal from the notorious real estate limited partnerships of the late 1980s.

Initially, investors still hoped for the capital gain, but, the properties' having lost their tax-shelter status meant they had also lost value. Furthermore, real estate was then entering a protracted period of stagnation and overbuilding. The anticipated capital gains became losses. Eventually, investors walked away from their properties, and there was an epidemic of bankruptcies.

Let's compare the two different investment vehicles point by point:

Limited partnerships were marketed mostly as tax shelters, rather than investments that were profitable in themselves. When investors were buying a tax shelter, many of the partnerships, even though operationally unprofitable, made sense. Once the properties were rendered useless as a tax shelter, the bottom line suddenly became significant. As a tax shelter, the partnership investment could afford high management fees, high interest payments, and multiple mortgages. It was still a good investment as a tax shelter; it was just a bad investment as real estate.

Today's REITs are not tax shelters. What they emphasize is excellent total returns, consisting of both current income and capital appreciation. The REIT's success is measured by its ability to increase its FFO (funds from operations) and its dividend payments to its shareholders.

The limited partnership had a built-in recipe for trouble: the management's fee system. Usually, outside advisers were hired whose fees were based on the value of the properties. This gave them a strong incentive to add properties that would generate increased fees, but these properties did not necessarily attract good tenants or offer rent growth potential; often only caretaker managers were hired who had no incentives to manage the properties efficiently.

Today's REITs are allowed to be managed internally, and the management of well-regarded REITs is comprised of experienced executives who generally have a significant stake in the company, which often comprises most of their net worth.

With the limited-partnership structure, the only chance for growth was through increasing the rent roll and thereby directly affecting capital appreciation, since property prices were generally quoted in multiples of annual rent rolls. Here again, for tax-shelter investors, operating, cash-flow growth was not the primary goal.

Today's well-run REIT is a dynamic business. It

achieves growth through increasing the operating profit on the properties it owns and by raising capital for acquisitions and new property development. Good REIT managements have a successful track record of being able to raise such capital and find attractive opportunities.

Limited partnerships were not liquid investments. Since most of the limited partnerships were creatures of syndicators, the partnerships could not be traded in public markets. If you wanted out of the investment, you were in trouble. Eventually narrow trading markets were created, but the "bid-ask" spreads were large enough to make a pawnbroker blush.

Today's REITs, on the other hand, can be bought or sold quickly, several thousand shares at a time, in organized markets such as the New York Stock Exchange.

Limited partnerships were promoted by brokers as having high yields, and many did pay 9–10 percent with, they claimed, "appreciation potential." A rate of 9–10 percent sounds good now, but remember, in 1989, the prime rate was as high as 11.5 percent. A 9–10 percent yield wasn't extraordinary in that interest-rate climate, and, as far as the potential for yield growth went, it was quite often only that—potential.

Today's good-quality REITs offer very good yields in today's lower-interest-rate climate, and, what is more, they deliver on dividend growth rates, many of them growing in the vicinity of 7 percent or more a year.

Limited partnerships, when it came to capital appreciation, presented two very different pictures. Those who came early to the party, when real estate inflation was still spiraling upward, enjoyed reasonably good capital appreciation, but the late arrivals were lucky to get out with their shirts on their backs.

Today's good-quality REITs have been able to generate steadily increasing FFO, which, coupled with their high dividends, provides total returns comparable with the S&P 500, yet in a low-risk investment.

REITs and the traditional real estate limited partnerships have almost nothing in common except the nature of their underlying assets, but, until recently, REITs have suffered from an undeserved guilt by association.

LENDING REITS *vs.* OWNERSHIP REITS

WE DISCUSSED EARLIER what the statutory requirements were for a REIT. According to those requirements, there is nothing in the legislation requiring a REIT to own real properties. It is within the boundaries of the legal definition for the REIT merely to lend funds on the strength of the collateral value of real estate by originating, acquiring, and holding real estate mortgage loans. These mortgages might be secured by residential, business, health care, or other properties. Hybrid REITs both own and hold mortgages on properties. They were popular some years ago, but, except for certain health care REITs, have long since faded into obscurity.

In the late '60s and early '70s, lending REITs were the most popular type of REIT, as many large regional and "money-center" banks and mortgage brokers formed their own REITs. Almost 60 new REITs were formed back then, all lending funds to property developers at high interest rates. In 1973, interest rates rose substantially, new developments couldn't be sold or leased, nonperforming loans spiraled way out of control, and most of these REITs crashed and burned, leaving investors holding the bag. A decade later, a number of REITs sprang up to invest in collateralized mortgage obligations (CMOs), and they didn't fare much better. Today, while some lending REITs have been successful, they generally occupy specialized niches of the REIT world.

The vast majority of today's REITs own real property rather than make real estate loans.

The real money in real estate comes from acquiring good properties at attractive prices (or developing them at good yields) and then managing them efficiently. Owning mortgage REITs can be profitable, but they are best viewed as trading vehicles because of their high sensitivity to interest rates and mortgage market fluctuations. Accordingly, the great majority of top-quality REITs that investors want to invest in own real estate and do not make real estate loans. Throughout the rest of this book, then, the term "REIT" will refer to REITs that *own* real estate in one sector or another.

EXPANSION OF REIT PROPERTY SECTOR OFFERINGS

IN CHAPTER 1, we briefly mentioned some of the different sectors in which today's REITs own properties. This, too, is a story that is continually evolving. In the beginning and until 1993, REITs owned properties in a limited number of sectors: neighborhood strip malls, apartments, health care facilities, and, to a very limited extent, office buildings. If you wanted to invest in another sector, such as a major shopping mall, you were out of luck.

By the end of 1994, as a result of a huge increase in the dollar amount of initial and secondary public offerings, the REIT industry had mushroomed in size. According to The National Association of Real Estate Investment Trusts (NAREIT) statistics, the total dollar amount of offerings in those two years was $18.3 billion and $14.7 billion, respectively—about 117 percent and 46 percent of the total REIT market capitalization at the time. This trend continued in subsequent years, and by September 30, 1997, REITs' total book assets had grown to more than $123 billion, held by approximately 200 publicly traded equity and mortgage REITs.

The 1993–94 REIT-IPO boom changed the REIT industry forever. Today's investor has a choice of many well-managed REITs in many different sectors.

Each of these property sectors, which we'll discuss in the next chapter, has its own set of investment characteristics, including its individual economic cycles and particular risk factors, competition threats, and growth potential. Each sector might be in a slightly different phase of its own real estate cycle. Wise REIT investors will be fairly well diversified among the different property sectors, perhaps even avoiding those whose market cycles create an unfavorable risk/reward ratio. But for the long-term investor, investing in REITs with management that is knowledgeable, creative, and experienced in real estate will provide outstanding total returns over the years.

SUMMARY

◆ Most REITs are operating companies that own and manage real property as a business and must comply with certain technical rules that generally do not affect them as investments.

◆ The avoidance of "double taxation" is one of the key advantages to the REIT structure.

◆ Originally conceived as a tax-deferral device, the UPREIT structure has also become an attractive acquisition tool for the REIT.

◆ UPREITs and DownREITs are simply variations on REITs that enable property owners to "REITize" their existing property without incurring current capital gains taxes.

◆ The vast majority of today's REITs are in the business of
  owning and running real property rather than making real
  estate loans.
◆ The 1993–94 REIT-IPO boom changed the REIT industry forever. Today's investor has a choice of many well-managed
  REITs in many different sectors.

CHAPTER

Property
Sectors
AND THEIR CYCLES

CERTAIN THINGS ARE TRUE of all commercial properties: their value and profitability depend on location, maintenance, and tenancy, and such "macro" forces as the economy, interest rates, and inflation.

That said, they are all quite unlike one another. The owner of a large, luxury apartment complex, for example, has far different financial concerns from the owner of a neighborhood strip mall or a skyscraper office building. And those are just three of the more common property sectors.

You can invest your money in nearly any kind of real estate imaginable: apartment buildings, manufactured-home communities, malls, neighborhood shopping centers, outlet centers, offices, industrial properties, hotels, self-storage facilities, hospitals, golf courses—even prisons.

The chart on the following page, based upon data compiled by NAREIT, provides a glimpse of the diversity within the world of REITs.

The point is, the choices are as numerous as the differences among various property sectors. Before selecting a particular REIT, it's necessary to understand the specific investment characteristics that set each kind of property apart. While REIT investors need not be *experts* on apartments, malls, or any other specific sector, they need to know some of the basics.

UPS AND DOWNS

BEFORE WE EXAMINE the individual sectors of REIT properties, let's first look at the general nature of real estate. Real estate prices and profits move in cycles, usually predictable in type but not always in length or severity. If you're a long-term,

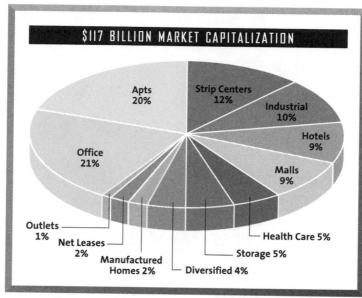

$117 BILLION MARKET CAPITALIZATION

- Apts 20%
- Strip Centers 12%
- Industrial 10%
- Hotels 9%
- Office 21%
- Malls 9%
- Outlets 1%
- Net Leases 2%
- Manufactured Homes 2%
- Diversified 4%
- Storage 5%
- Health Care 5%

SOURCE: NAREIT, 9/30/97

conservative REIT investor, you might choose to buy and hold your REITs even as their properties move through their inevitable ups and downs. Nevertheless, you should understand and be aware of these cycles since they can dramatically affect a REIT's funds from operations (FFO) and dividend growth. If you consider yourself more of a short-term market timer, you will want to plan your REIT investments either in accordance with a general real estate cycle or with the cycle of an individual property sector.

The phases of the real estate cycle are depression, recovery, boom, and overbuilding and downturn.

THE REAL ESTATE CYCLES

◆ **Phase 1: The Depression.** Vacancies are high, rents are low, and real estate prices are down. Many properties, particularly the highly leveraged ones, are being repossessed or are in foreclosure. There is virtually no new construction. Properties are selling at prices well below replacement cost.

◆ **Phase 2: The Gradual Recovery.** Occupancy rates rise,

rents stabilize and gradually increase, and property prices stabilize. There is still little or no new building, but prices are firming up or rising slightly.

◆ **Phase 3: The Boom.** After a while, most vacant space has been absorbed, allowing property owners to boost rents rapidly. With high occupancy and rising rents, landlords are getting excellent returns. Property prices are rising to the point that new construction makes sense again. Developers start flexing their muscles. Investors and lenders feel that they must join the party and provide all the necessary financing. During this phase, the media begin to talk about why "this time it's different" and why this property sector is "no longer cyclical."

◆ **Phase 4: Overbuilding and Downturn.** After property prices have been rising rapidly, overbuilding frequently follows as everyone tries to get into the act. Vacancy rates rise, and rents soften. Eventually there is an economic recession. As the return on real estate investment declines, so too do real estate prices. Eventually, this downturn phase may turn into a depression phase, depending upon the severity of overbuilding or the economic recession. Now the cycle is complete and begins anew.

Why do these cycles occur? Commercial real estate is tied closely not only to the national economy, but also to the local economy. Years ago, for example, when the steel mills in Pittsburgh or the rubber companies in Akron laid off workers, the local economy, from retail to real estate, became depressed. The part of the country known as "Smokestack America" very quickly became "Rust Belt America." Families doubled up, with grown children moving in with parents. As the number of households declined, apartment vacancy rates rose.

Conversely, when the Olympic Committee decided to hold the summer games in Atlanta, or when Michelin Tires decided to build a plant in Greenville, South

Carolina, the entire local economy picked up. Business improved for all the local residents, from dentists to dry cleaners, and job growth expanded.

Sometimes cycles become even more extreme than is justified by the local economy, however, and the boom phase becomes truly manic. Of course, it's not just real estate that's cyclical. You've seen manic cyclicality in the stock market. During bull market conditions, investors often throw caution to the winds. New York City's shoe-shine boys and taxi drivers hand out stock tips, and cocktail party chatter and Internet discussion groups are replete with details of the latest killing on Wall Street—that is, until there's a change in the wind.

When real estate is booming, there is—shall we say—"irrational exuberance," but the exuberance isn't limited to investors. When real estate prices, rents, and operating income are rising rapidly, developers, syndicators, venture-fund managers, and even lenders want a piece of the action. The traditional debt leveragability on real estate investments only exacerbates the situation. This was the scenario that commenced in the mid-1980s. Investors were buying up apartments at furious rates—individually, through syndications, and through limited partnerships. Developers were building everywhere. The banks and savings and loans were only too eager to provide the necessary liquidity to drive the boom ever higher. Even Congress got into the act, passing legislation to encourage real estate investment by allowing property ownership to shelter income tax and allow faster depreciation write-offs.

Eventually and not surprisingly, apartments, office buildings, shopping centers, and other property types all over the nation became overbuilt, and property owners had to contend with depression-like conditions for several years thereafter.

While we can always hope that greater discipline and more accessible information will help to moderate these cycles, as we'll discuss later, the bottom line is that some cyclicality is inevitable. In such times, investors must just repeat to themselves, "This, too, shall pass."

THE PROPERTY SECTORS

THERE'S SUCH AN assortment of "REITized" properties that it's hard to know where to begin. There are apartment buildings, shopping centers, industrial parks, factory outlet centers, health care facilities, and—you name it; it's out there. All these properties are owned by REITs and all have specific advantages, risks, idiosyncrasies, and cycles that set them apart from the others. The difficulty for the investor is deciding how much weight to give to each factor when trying to evaluate them. The pie chart at the beginning of this chapter shows the percentages of the REITs' aggregate market value represented by the different sectors of REIT properties as of December 1997. As you'll see, there's a veritable *feast* of offerings.

APARTMENTS

RECENT HISTORY HAS been witness to a virtual explosion in the number of publicly traded apartment REITs. Before the 1993–94 binge of new REIT public offerings, there were 4 major apartment REITs: United Dominion, Merry Land, Property Trust of America, and South West Property Trust. By late 1996, that number had grown to at least 30 major equity REITs, each with a market cap of over $100 million. These REITs own and manage apartment buildings in geographical areas throughout the United States. Some have properties located only in very specific areas, while others own units scattered across the country. Some managements have specialized development skills that enable them to build new properties in healthy markets where rents and occupancy rates are rising quickly or where profitable niche markets exist.

WHAT IS A "CAP RATE"?

A CAP RATE, generally speaking, refers to the unleveraged return expected by a buyer of an apartment building or other property, expressed as the anticipated cash-flow return (before depreciation) as a percentage of the purchase price. For example, paying $1 million for a 9 percent cap rate property should produce an initial unleveraged cash return on the investment of $90,000 per year.

Well-run apartments have, over the years, been able to generate 6–10 percent yields for their owners, and many such investments offer the prospects of substantial property value appreciation. Today, most "cap rates" range from 7 to 9 percent, depending upon location and property quality.

Apartment owners do well when the economy is expanding because of the resulting new jobs created and the rise in the formation of new households. Another very important factor for apartment owners is the rate of construction of new units in the local area. Such competing properties, if built when demand for apartment space is slowing, can force the owners of existing units to reduce rents or offer concessions, and often result in lower occupancy rates.

Inflation also determines an apartment owner's economic fortunes, since inflation can cause higher operating expenses for everything from maintenance to insurance to loan interest. But inflation is a double-edged sword. It can hurt on the way up, as expenses escalate. However, if markets are healthy, new buildings charge higher rents because of inflated construction costs, and owners of existing units can then, as new buildings become fully occupied, raise their own rents. Eventually, however, as inflation further increases, new construction may no longer be profitable; interest rates rise, the economy slows, and the process has run its course.

The housing market may be changing. For many years, apartments were mostly for young couples just starting out. It was the SFR, or single-family residence—the house with the white picket fence—that was the American dream. While the availability of affordable SFRs still provides plenty of competition for apartments, it is often an overstated threat, particularly in major metropolitan areas where today's young couples often prefer to live close to work, restaurants, and theaters.

Apartment REIT investors need to be mindful of certain risks. Even if the national economy is doing fine, the regional or local economy can drop into a recession, or worse, causing occupancy rates to decline and rents to flatten. Overbuilding can often occur, especially where land is cheap and available to developers. Poor management can result in the general deterioration of the REIT properties.

Fortunately, these adverse developments rarely occur overnight, and vigilant apartment REIT owners will usually be able to spot negative trends early enough to react to them without significant financial damage.

As an additional safety measure, the well-diversified REIT owner will normally own several apartment REITs, in order to spread the risk over several geographical areas and managements.

During the late '80s and early '90s, earning reasonable returns on apartment communities was difficult. The loan largesse of the banks and S&Ls and the real estate limited partnerships and other syndications had sharply accentuated the boom phase. Hapless investors had put large amounts of capital into new construction, only to have many buildings fall into the hands of the Resolution Trust Corporation (RTC).

RESOLUTION TRUST CORPORATION (RTC)

THE RESOLUTION TRUST CORPORATION is a public corporation organized by Congress in response to the banking and saving and loan crisis of the early '90s, for the purpose of acquiring and reselling real estate and real estate loans from bankrupt and near-bankrupt lenders.

Rents flattened—and even fell in many areas. Occupancies declined, and market values diminished.

Finally, from 1993–94, the supply-demand imbalance began to right itself as the economy strengthened, and very few new units were built. By 1995, rents were rising once more, and, by the end of the following year, occupancy levels were back over 90 percent.

Assuming a reasonably healthy economy, apartment ownership looks as though it will still be rewarding for at least a few more years, depending on the region. New construction has been increasing, but generally remains below the levels of the '80s, and only a few markets are facing an overbuilt situation. Apartment owners in most areas should be able to get annual rent increases of at least 3 percent without having their expenses rise comparably. If management is good, apartment ownership and operation will continue to be a good business.

RETAIL

The different retail-sector REITs behave differently from one another, and each retail sector must be considered separately.

◆ **Neighborhood shopping centers.** For many years, before the advent of major regional shopping malls, shoppers bought everything locally at the small stores on Main Street or in downtown shopping areas. That was then; this is now. Over the last 20 years, major malls have sprung up from Maine to California, equipped with piped-in music, elevators, and enclosures to ward off the elements. These malls offer puppies, furniture, shoes and apparel, CDs and software— just about anything a shopper might wish for. In an even more recent trend, discount megastores, such as Wal-Mart, K-Mart, Target, and Costco, started spreading across the country. Although the neighborhood shopping center has lost a lot of business to these megacompetitors, Americans still love their conveniences, and proximity is a great convenience. For certain run-in-and-run-out errands, such as grocery shopping, movie rental, dry cleaning, and shoe repair, most people don't want to be bothered with a mall.

The neighborhood shopping center is usually "anchored" by one or two major stores—usually a supermarket and a drugstore—and contains a large number of additional stores that offer other basic services and necessities. As a result, these centers tend to be "recessionproof" and not significantly affected by national or regional slowdowns. The property owner charges a minimum rent to the tenants and the lease is often structured to contain fixed "rent bumps" that increase the rental obligation each year. In addition, or in lieu of fixed rent bumps, the lease may contain "overage" rental provisions, which result in increased rent if annual sales exceed certain minimum levels. Often "triple-net" leases are signed, which make expenses like real estate taxes and assessments, repairs, maintenance, and insurance the responsibility of the tenant. In these leases it may even be incumbent upon the tenant to restore the property in the event of casualty or condemnation.

Many real estate investors believe that retail properties are overbuilt and in the declining phase of their cycle. Such astute REIT watchers as Milton Cooper (Kimco Realty Corporation) and Steven Roth

(Vornado Realty Trust) observed in early 1995 that retail stores were rapidly becoming overbuilt, and recent events have borne them out. Within the last two years a significant number of major retailers have either filed bankruptcy proceedings or otherwise closed stores. These problems have been particularly severe in the apparel sector. Consumers don't seem to want to shop as they did in the 1980s. As a result, retail store owners must contend with the prospects of rising vacancies and minimal rental increases. Even in March 1996, *Barron's* reported an observation made by Norman Kranzdorf, CEO of Kranzco Realty Trust: between 15 and 20 percent of the space in neighborhood shopping centers was obsolete.

So why would investors want to buy any REITs that specialize in this sector?

The answer to this question demonstrates an important irony of REIT investing:

Throughout many—if not most—periods in REITs' history, very strong property markets have proved difficult while poor markets have proven a boon.

This is because strong markets can eventually lead to overbuilding—which heightens competitive conditions and depresses operating income for up to several years into the future. Weak and troubled markets, conversely, depress the market prices of existing properties. Because most REITs have far better access to reasonably priced capital during weak markets than do other prospective buyers, they have the ability to buy properties with good long-term prospects at bargain-basement prices. The quality of a REIT's management and its access to capital, while always important, are particularly critical during times of overbuilt markets or depressed economic conditions.

◆ **Regional malls.** If neighborhood shopping centers provide the basics, large regional malls provide greater choice and luxury. From sofas to chocolates, the mall has almost anything you can imagine. The concept of going to the mall is that shopping is not necessarily related to need; it is an activity in itself.

The economics of malls are very different from those of neighborhood shopping centers. Rent payable by the tenant is higher, but so are the dollar volumes of sales per square foot. Even with higher rent, a retailer can do very well in a mall because of the high traffic and larger sales potential per store. Because of higher overhead, however, stores that can't generate strong sales can quickly run into trouble, and so there is a premium on the mall owner's finding and signing leases with the "hottest," most successful retailers. Some mall REITs own nationally renowned malls, where rental rates are high (close to $40 per square foot) and sales per square foot approach $400. Others emphasize smaller malls, which are usually located in less densely populated cities, where rental rates are in the low $20s per square foot and sales per square foot don't get much above $200–$250. In spite of the other activities they now offer, malls are truly in the retail business. Their success depends upon leasing to successful retailers who can attract the fickle and demanding customer, and upon the overall strength of the national, regional, and local retail economies.

Mall REITs are relatively new, and were unavailable to REIT investors until 1992.

Prior to 1992, malls were owned only by large real estate organizations and by institutional investors; there was no way a REIT investor could own a piece of the great "trophy" shopping properties of America. However, between 1992 and 1994, the large shopping-mall developers such as Messrs. Taubman, Simon, and DeBartolo "REITized" their empires by going public as REITs. There are now 12 REITs that own and operate regional shopping malls, almost all of which have gone public just since 1992.

Are malls and the REITs that own them good investments? Before we tackle this question, let's first take a quick look at some mall history. The 1980s were the golden years for the regional mall. Women were launching their careers in record numbers, and they had to buy clothes for the workplace. Baby boomers were spending their double incomes like giddy teenagers. Tenant sales rose briskly, the major retailers *had* to have space in all the malls, and mall owners could increase rental rates almost at will. Malls were truly attractive investments, and most large property-investing institutions wanted to own them.

By the early 1990s, however, this great era of consumerism ended, hastened by the same recession that knocked President Bush out of office and created waves of corporate restructuring. Wage gains were hard to come by, fears of layoffs were rampant, and consumer confidence declined. "Deep discount" became the American consumer's rallying cry. Further, on a longer-term basis, the baby boomers suddenly began to consider the prospect of their own retirements and decided that investing in mutual funds was more important than accumulating Armani suits.

These developments have taken their toll on mall owners and their tenants. Apparel sales, for years the stock-in-trade of most mall retail establishments, have been in the dumps for quite some time, and no one is predicting a major rebound in the near future. This has been a significant problem for mall owners. In fact, after years of healthy sales growth, malls' same-store sales have been sluggish since 1990.

Another problem for mall REITs has been the lack of good external growth prospects. There simply have been few opportunities for them to grow, either by acquisition, since few malls have been on the market, or by development, since there has been little need for additional malls. As a result, mall REITs have had to rely primarily on revenue improvements within each mall (*i.e.,* increasing tenants' rents, increasing occupancy levels, and replacing underperforming tenants) in order to create meaningful FFO growth.

Because of all of these factors, mall REITs have not, until recently, been very popular with investors, and their investment returns until 1996 were lackluster. Should investors therefore forget mall REITs altogether and look for better prospects elsewhere?

Not so fast. Reports of the malls' demise have been greatly exaggerated, and they are not without comeback potential. Since the cost of building a new mall can amount to $100 million or more, overbuilding within a given geographical area has not been a major concern. This factor alone gives malls a substantial edge over most other sectors.

Another advantage of mall ownership is that most major retailers continue to rely on malls for most of their total sales. It's significant that, despite the widely heralded problems of most retailers over the last several years, malls' occupancy rates have been holding steady and recently have even been increasing. While the apparel retailers' poor performance in recent years has had a negative effect on overall mall sales, such events are not unusual in the mall business. Mall owners historically have been able to reconfigure retail space to meet changing consumer demands.

Simon has been very active in adding entertainment locations to many of its malls. DeBartolo (prior to its merger with Simon) set up an "entertainment leasing division," with the intention of attracting such new tenants as theaters, "lifestyle" restaurants, family entertainment, and other special attractions. Mills has been developing new forms of shopping malls that emphasize food and entertainment.

These strategies may now be working. Sales of

home accessories, gifts, and children's clothing at Taubman Centers increased by 44 percent over the past six years, compared to 1 percent for apparel sales; the former represented 37 percent of revenues in 1995, up from 29 percent six years earlier (according to *Forbes*).

To the extent that the mall owners are successful in these endeavors, mall traffic will increase, and so therefore will tenants' sales—and rents. Somewhat surprisingly, as older leases have come up for renewal, most mall owners have been able to increase rents despite sluggish same-store sales. Occupancy rates will continue to improve with successful tenant repositionings, and rents from the newly leased space will flow almost directly to the bottom line. It's quite possible that investors who have dumped mall REITs in the expectation they do not have much income growth potential will be proven wrong, and that the better-managed mall REITs, aided by selective acquisitions and developments, will be able to report 6–9 percent FFO growth—pretty much in line with the long-term FFO growth of the entire REIT industry. Mall REITs could be solid performers in the years ahead.

◆ **Factory outlet centers.** If neighborhood strip malls provide the necessities, and malls provide luxuries and lifestyle, what's left? A trend that has picked up over the past several years has been factory outlet centers. These centers' tenants are major manufacturers, such as Bass Company, Van Heusen, Polo, Jones New York, Geoffrey Beene, and London Fog. The centers are normally located some distance from densely populated areas, primarily because the manufacturers don't want to compete with their own retail customers, such as the malls.

While most of these companies are manufacturers who normally sell to the major retailers, factory outlet centers also sell directly to the public at cut-rate prices. The theory is that they sell overstocked goods, odd sizes, irregulars, or fashion ideas that just didn't click. The goods, priced at 25–35 percent below retail, usually move quickly.

The outlet industry has been around for a long time but only recently has seen significant growth.

Industry sales have more than doubled from 1990 to 1995, and at the end of 1997 exceeded $12 billion. From January 1988 to December 1997, according to *Value Retail News,* the industry's GLA (gross leasable area) increased from 13.9 million to 55.4 million square feet. Whereas 15 years ago they averaged approximately 50,000 square feet, now the average size is close to 180,000 square feet. By December 1997, according to *Value Retail News,* there were more than 300 outlet centers in the United States where more than 500 manufacturers were operating more than 13,000 individual stores. While this sector has already experienced considerable growth, there is still room for more: outlet industry sales represent only about 3 percent of U.S. general merchandise sales, and outlet square footage represents only about 1 percent of the 45 million total U.S. retail square footage available.

While sales per square foot at outlet centers are very close to those at the malls, occupancy costs have been estimated at only 8–9 percent of sales, compared to about 12 percent for regional malls. These are very favorable numbers and help to explain the appeal of the outlet centers to the manufacturer-as-retailer.

Five major developer-owners of outlet centers went public between May and December 1993 to very enthusiastic receptions, since investors were expecting these new REITs to grow much faster than the REITs owning neighborhood strip malls and regional malls. Early in 1994, however, the shares of these REITs began to run into some rough weather.

After a bumpy beginning, outlet center REITs have left investors wondering whether this sector is comprised of misunderstood growth companies that will deliver outstanding total returns—or accidents waiting to happen.

It's certainly true that outlets face particular challenges. Typically they have no anchor tenants, and in many cases the land they're built on usually has little value for any other use. These properties are normally bought and sold in the private real estate market at cap rates significantly higher than other retail properties, indicating a higher level of risk. Same-store sales, as in other retail sectors, have generally shown little improvement during the last three years. One problem could be the perceived quality of the merchandise. Another, in some areas, is overdevelopment; reflecting this problem, only 7 new centers were developed in 1997, down from 22 in 1995. There is also the question of their location. Now that the novelty of the outlet center is beginning to wear off, will shoppers still be inclined to travel some 60 miles out of their way?

Finally, there is the problem of new competition from the regional malls, which run "sales" much more often, and from the new "Mills-type" retail format pioneered by Mills Corporation. The latter's formula is to offer not only the traditional outlet stores, but also "category-killer" retailers like T. J. Maxx or Burlington Coat Factory; discount department stores like Saks Fifth Avenue's Off Fifth or Neiman Marcus's Last Call; and entertainment centers with multiscreen theaters, water slides, and other novelty attractions.

These factors may all play a part in the number of new stores opened and the number of manufacturers participating in this sector, making the outlet center REITs controversial investments. Yet the outlets do have certain advantages. Their current small market share means there is still room for additional development, should the concept of outlet centers prove to be a valid long-term trend. The centers have impressive sales-per-square-foot and rental-rate-per-sales ratios, occupancy rates frequently over 95 percent, and a high tenant-retention rate. Finally, they are able to increase rents on new leases being signed, which seems to augur well for future demand.

What investors should look for in an outlet REIT investment is management that emphasizes leases with high-end manufacturers as tenants, together with excellent locations.

Quality tenants can draw shoppers looking for good value on "designer" products. Names such as Polo, Barneys New York, Burberrys, and Donna Karan come to mind. Equally important is finding outlet REITs that locate new centers close to densely populated areas or major tourist attractions. Such properties will be more likely to have intrinsic value as real estate, and will, because of zoning, discourage competition from building competing retail stores.

Outlet center REITs appeal to the contrarian and value-oriented REIT investor, since, like the mall REITs until 1996, they are an unloved sector selling at cheap prices. The key to making money in these stocks

---

OCCUPANCY COST AS PERCENT OF SALES

A VERY IMPORTANT MEASURE of a retail store's operating costs and a key factor in determining that store's profit margins is *occupancy cost as a percent of sales*. The lower the figure, the more of each of the sales dollar is available to pay other operating costs or to bring down to the bottom line.

is to determine whether or not consumers will continue to find outlet centers an attractive place to shop. If they do, the factory outlets will report increasing same-store sales, and the stocks of the outlet REITs will do well.

OFFICES AND INDUSTRIAL PROPERTIES

OFFICE BUILDINGS AND industrial properties are often grouped together in REIT discussions. While many of their economic characteristics are very different, they are the primary types of properties leased to businesses that do not cater to individual consumers. In that respect they are very different from apartments, retail stores, self-storage facilities, or even health care institutions. In addition, many of the REITs in this sector own both office buildings and industrial properties.

◆ **Office buildings.** Office buildings have had their own set of problems in recent years. As much as overbuilding was a problem for apartments in the late 1980s, it was far worse for offices, with vacancy rates rising catastrophically to over 20 percent in some major markets. This sector has taken longer to turn around than apartments—the situation having been exacerbated by the corporate downsizings of the 1990s. If all that weren't enough bad news, there is also the fact that office leases normally have fixed rental rates, with perhaps a small annual rental step-up, tied to something like the Consumer Price Index. These leases run for much longer terms than do apartment and retail leases. As a result, the problem of declining market rental rates is late in making itself known. During the last few years, as older, higher-rate leases have expired, many building owners have seen their cash flows diminished by the newer and lower lease rates, even apart from losses due to higher vacancy rates. Due also to periodic bouts of overbuilding, the office property sector has been a deeply cyclical one.

A problem unique to the office sector is the long lag time between obtaining building permits and final completion. Once the development process has begun, even if the builder or lender realizes that there is no longer sufficient demand for yet another office building, it is often too late to stop the process.

A troubling trend for big-city office building owners is the office population's drift to the suburbs, rural areas, and even to states not known for their central business districts. Tenants have been lost to such "hot" areas as Oregon, Utah, Arizona, North Carolina, Tennessee, Florida, and some parts of Texas—not only to improve the executives' and employees' quality of life, but also to take advantage of lower taxes, lower operating costs, and cheaper labor. Another concern, albeit a minor one so far, is the rising trend toward telecommuting. Not a pretty picture.

But should we give up on office REITs altogether? Not at all. Mitch Ellner, REIT specialist at E&Y/Levanthal, says that "office buildings in 1995–96 did not look good, but now, even in Southern California, such REITs as Arden and Kilroy are doing very well." Rental space and the prices that can be charged for it are, like most things, governed by the laws of supply and demand. Even during the 1990–91 economic slump when office jobs declined, net office space absorption nationwide was positive. Thus it's pretty clear that the problems in the office building sector resulted primarily from an oversupply of space. There has been very little development of new office buildings over the last few years, and rents in many markets started to rise in 1994, initiating a new cycle that looks as though it will continue for several years.

The prior bad news notwithstanding, office properties appear to be early in the recovery phase of their real estate cycle.

If a desirable building is located in a strong business market, has attractive amenities, is well maintained, and is not subject to competitive building by developers, both occupancy and rental rates can rise steadily and generate very healthy returns for the building owner.

For example, the office building occupancy rate in the "research triangle" around Raleigh and Durham, North Carolina, was approximately 93 percent as early as the end of 1995, and rents have been scaling up nicely. Major central business district markets such as Boston, New York, and San Francisco have also been very strong, commencing in late 1996.

Office REITs owning properties in vibrant cities and desirable suburban areas and having access to attractively priced capital can make profitable acquisitions, and therefore have excellent growth prospects. While office markets continue to improve across the board, there does seem to be a trend for businesses to relocate to suburban areas. Vacancy rates in suburban office buildings have been declining faster than for many offices located in metropolitan areas. However, at least in the near term, office markets seem to be recovering almost everywhere. Another trend to watch is increased market concentration, as some REITs, such as Spieker Properties and Equity Office Properties, are acquiring a dominant presence in many markets. This could enhance their ability to increase rental rates.

Investors should remember, since the sector is very cyclical, that they should keep a close eye on potential overbuilding.

◆ **Industrial properties.** An industrial building can be freestanding or situated within a landscaped industrial park, and can be occupied by one or more tenants. It has been estimated that the total square footage of all industrial property in the United States is approximately 9.5 billion square feet, of which about half is owned by the actual users. Ownership is highly fragmented, and the public REITs own only about 1 percent of all industrial real estate. Industrial properties include:

◆ Distribution centers
◆ Warehouses
◆ Service centers
◆ Light-manufacturing facilities
◆ Research and development facilities
◆ Small office space for sales and administrative functions.

Ownership of industrial properties has generally provided stable and steady returns, particularly in relation to office properties. According to *Industrial REIT Peer Group Analysis,* a research report published in June 1996 by Apogee Associates, LLC, approximately 80 percent of tenants renew their leases, and default rates are low. The report goes on to say that demand for industrial space has, since 1981, exceeded the demand for office space. Rents have generally grown slowly but steadily at a rate equal to or better than office properties, having declined, overall, only during the early 1990s, when this sector had its own overbuilding problem. Vacancy rates, according to the report, have historically been lower than those of office properties. The long-term norm for industrial property vacancy is approximately 7 percent.

The industrial-property market has had a good track record, in developing and building, of being able to stop quickly to shut down the supply of new space as soon as the market becomes saturated.

One big advantage of the industrial-building sector is that, since it doesn't take long to construct and lease these units, there is a faster reaction time than in some of the other sectors, and consequently there generally has not been excessive overbuilding. Most new space is built not on "spec," but in response to demand by new users. "Built-to-suit" activity has thus been an important contributor to new development in this sector.

Since this sector is currently well along in the recovery phase of its real estate cycle, investors do need to watch out for signs of overbuilding in some markets. Other major risks here include declining local economic and business conditions, dependence on the tenants' financial health, and, once more, overbuilding. While the $2–$10 million cost of developing an industrial property is not insignificant, it is low enough that "merchant developers" might be attracted to this type of speculative activity.

A key advantage the industrial-property sector owner enjoys is that unlike the office, apartment, or retail sectors, this sector does not have a great need for ongoing capital expenditures to keep the buildings in good repair.

REITs that specialize in industrial-sector properties can be very good investments, particularly if their managements have longstanding relationships with major industrial-space users and if they concentrate on economically expanding geographical areas.

HEALTH CARE

HEALTH CARE REITS specialize in buying and leasing various types of health care facilities to health care providers. Such facilities include nursing homes, "congregate"- and assisted-living facilities, hospitals, medical office buildings, and rehabilitation/trauma centers. These REITs don't generally operate any of their properties themselves and thus maintain a very low overhead, generating strong returns for their shareholders over the years.

Health care REITs were launched in the late '80s and, except for a few rough spots, have enjoyed a strong track record.

Health care REIT properties are, in most cases, bought by the REIT and leased back to health care companies who use the facilities for patient care, although many REITs also provide mortgage loan financing. New property development has been very limited, and the REITs' revenues come from lease payments from the operators. There is generally a base rent payment or, for mortgage loans, an interest payment, and there are additional payments if revenues from the facility exceed certain preset levels or are based on an inflation index, such as the CPI. In this respect, the leases (or mortgages, as the case may be) are similar to percentage rent on retail properties.

The most widely respected health care REITs have easy access to the capital markets, which allows them to increase their investments by buying additional health care facilities or making additional mortgage loans. As lease and mortgage income received by the particular REIT exceeds its cost of funds (whether debt or equity), each new facility adds to FFO and enables the REIT to increase dividends.

In recent years, with banks shying away from health care lending, the health care REITs have been strong competitors in this business, and they've used that advantage well.

The highest-quality health care REITs have well-diversified geographical locations and lessees, a large number of which are public companies. Tenant defaults are much less common than with other equity REITs, because in this sector—unlike, for instance, office buildings—supply and demand have been pretty much in balance over the last ten years. The health care industry is relatively recession resistant and has not had a problem with overbuilding, for the most part, because, at least with respect to nursing homes, states usually require a "certificate of need" before approving a new facility.

The area investors need to be somewhat more careful of is assisted-living and congregate-care facilities, which cater to healthier senior citizens. These facilities are not nearly as regulated as nursing homes and generally do not require certificates of need before being developed. Manor Care and Marriott, as well as several smaller companies that have recently gone public, are building assisted-living facilities quickly in response to rapidly increasing demand. Although this bodes well for assisted-living investments, investors must nevertheless be aware of the overbuilding risk.

Investors in health care REITs need to watch out for federal budget restrictions in Medicare. The current political environment of cost containment can put the squeeze on some health care providers.

Health care facilities have yet another idiosyncrasy the investor needs to be aware of: health care providers rely on government reimbursement programs to cover their costs and enable them to earn a reasonable profit. Such profits, of course, allow providers to make lease or mortgage payments to the REIT. Medicaid payments from the states and, to a lesser extent, Medicare payments from the federal government, are a big factor since most patients in such facilities are neither covered by private insurance nor can they personally afford the care, which runs in the neighborhood of $35,000–$40,000 annually per patient.

Inadequate state reimbursement policies have been a problem in the past, but, since Congress passed the

WHAT TO LOOK FOR IN HEALTH CARE REITS

◆ Conservative balance sheets (which facilitate additional capital raising at rates that will generate profits from new investments)
◆ An emphasis on stable sectors, such as nursing homes and related facilities, including congregate care and assisted living
◆ Diversification in both facility operators and geographical location
◆ Good record of growth in funds from operations (both internally and externally)
◆ Good record of adherence to conservative dividend-payout ratios
◆ Stable, motivated, and capable management teams

WHAT TO LOOK OUT FOR IN HEALTH CARE REITS

◆ Adverse reimbursement legislation
◆ Single-use facilities with questionable land values
◆ Overbuilding in assisted-living facilities
◆ Increasing competition from lenders

Boren amendment in 1981, nursing home operators have had the ability to file lawsuits against states on the grounds of inadequate reimbursement. Medicaid reimbursement rates have also risen in recent years after a number of health care service providers won court victories against the government. Nevertheless, investors must be mindful of the fact that, to a large extent, the REITs and the providers are dependent upon federal and state government policies.

The long-term prospects for health care REITs depend on the stability and growth prospects for the U.S. health care industry, and in particular the segments served by their lessees.

SELF-STORAGE FACILITIES

AS ANYONE WHO'S ever lived in one knows, there's one universal problem with apartments. It's stuff. *Where* do you put your stuff? Generally, there's no attic, no basement, and no private garage—and that means no storage. Well, that's where self-storage facilities come in. Usually they're built on the edge of town, perhaps near the railroad tracks, or next to an industrial park. The units normally range from 5 x 5 feet to 20 x 20 feet. These facilities were developed experimentally during the 1960s and they are rented by the month, allowing renters to store such items as business and personal files, furniture, and even large RVs and boats.

According to the 1995–96 *Self-Storage Almanac,* an industry publication, private individuals rent approximately 70 percent of the available space; commercial users account for about 20 percent; and the balance is comprised of students and members of the armed forces.

Self-storage was a mediocre investment in the late 1980s because of the same overbuilding problems that so bedeviled apartment, office, and other real estate owners at that time. The industry's health, however, has recovered substantially since 1990, and occupancy and rental rates have improved significantly.

The reasons are twofold: fewer new units have been built, and the facilities are becoming more popular. From a longer-term perspective, these properties may also be benefiting from recent trends, such as a more mobile workforce and businesses' attempts to cut costs by reducing file storage in expensive office areas. According to the *Self-Storage Almanac,* occupancy rates nationwide have increased from 78 percent in 1987, to 81 percent in 1990, and to 91 percent as of April 1998. Monthly rental rates for the typical 10 x 10-foot storage space have also improved steadily over that time, from $45.07 in 1988, to $51.70 in 1990, to $54.49 in 1997. The self-storage industry appears to be rather late in the recovery phase of the real estate cycle, moving toward equilibrium. While we are seeing new storage developments, absorption of space has been very steady in this sector.

The investing public has been offered investments in self-storage facilities for many years, either through limited partnerships or small REITs closely related to the Storage Equities organization. However, the industry gained substantial credibility with experienced REIT investors only recently, when four new, high-quality REITs were formed between February 1994 and June 1995. In chronological order, they are Shurgard, Storage USA, Storage Trust, and Sovran Self-Storage. Public Storage, the former Storage Equities organization, is now the largest self-storage REIT. Public Storage became a REIT in 1980, and in 1995 completed a complicated reorganization, which has greatly simplified its corporate structure.

Notwithstanding the entrance of these major players, the industry is still highly fragmented and is dominated by many "mom-and-pop" owners. This, of course, presents substantial opportunities to the sector's publicly held REITs, which have more sophisticated management and greater access to capital for new acquisitions. Not only can the REIT managements acquire properties at attractive returns, but the acquiring REIT can also target particular metropolitan markets to increase its marketing effectiveness. These REITs are, in fact, taking full advantage of the situation. Storage USA, for example, has bought 116 properties for an aggregate of $370 million, just in the period between the March 1994 date of its IPO and December 31, 1995.

What about cycles? This sector is less affected than others by economic cycles, and many operators, as a matter of fact, were able to *increase* rental rates even during the 1990–91 recession.

There.is a good case to be made for self-storage facilities being recession resistant since, in a recession, individuals as well as businesses cut costs by reducing the space they occupy. A reduction in living or office space means an increased need for storage space.

Still, as with any other investment, self-storage REITs aren't a sure thing. The largest risk, once more, is overbuilding, which hurt this sector when all real estate was hurting, in the late 1980s. Costing only $3 million to $5 million apiece to build, self-storage facilities are not expensive, and, for this reason, supply could exceed demand within just a few years, depressing rents and increasing vacancy levels. Another risk is that investors could become such aggressive buyers that they push up property prices to the point that it becomes difficult to make acquisitions at attractive prices.

That being said, well-managed self-storage REITs that have good capital access should continue to do well. Internal and external growth prospects are favorable, and national or regional economic recessions may be much less of a problem for this industry than others. As always, however, investors should avoid paying a price for a REIT's stock based upon estimated future growth rates that are overly optimistic.

OTHER PROPERTY SECTORS

OTHER PROPERTY SECTORS, ranging from hotels and manufactured-housing communities to golf courses and even fast-food franchises, can also generate attractive total returns. REIT investors should also be on the lookout for new sectors, such as prisons and movie theaters, to name a couple of the most recent public offerings.

◆ **Hotel REITs.** Hotel REITs have been star performers

over the last two years. Mitch Ellner, a partner at E&Y/Kenneth Levanthal and a REIT specialist, says, "Hotels, after being down in 1993–94, are now basking in the sun, as are office buildings and industrial properties." This sector has recovered well following the horribly overbuilt '80s. Room and occupancy rates have been rising steadily since 1991, and finally, in 1993, hotel companies returned to profitability. Between August 1993 and the end of September 1996, 10 hotel REITs have gone public, raising almost $1.1 billion, and follow-on offerings have raised significant additional proceeds. Nevertheless, while the prospects continue to look good for this property sector, some observers are now concerned about overbuilding, especially in the "limited-service" subsector, where some properties are being bought at prices exceeding replacement cost, and where large numbers of new properties are being built. A major concern regarding hotel real estate is that its cycles can be very deep and violent since room rates and occupancy levels can be very volatile, and overbuilding has often been a problem. While most hotel REITs have been doing well and may continue to post strong growth rates, they are not investments for the faint of heart.

Another difficulty for investors in this area is finding hotel REITs without major conflicts of interest. Operating a hotel is a very management-intensive business and the owner's success comes, in large part, from the popularity of the hotel with business and individual consumers—it must be operated properly. However, REITs are not allowed to receive income from operations because of their legal restrictions. This means that the hotels must, in most cases, be leased to a third party, which provides the management services. The management company, or lessee, will receive substantial fees that "leak" from the pockets of the hotel owners. Aside from "leakage," there may be conflict of interest issues. A REIT's owners might prefer the lessee to be an entity in which one or more affiliates of the REIT's management is actively involved, in order to have more control over the operations; such a situation creates obvious conflicts of interest between the REIT management's obligations to the REIT's shareholders, and its ability to earn substantial management fees outside the REIT.

Two companies, however, have arrangements designed to avoid these leaks and conflict issues. Starwood Hotels & Resorts is structured through a "paired-share" arrangement, which allows the REIT to own the hotel properties, and a sister corporation—whose shares are owned by the REIT's shareholders—to manage the hotels. Patriot American Hospitality has recently acquired another corporation, which, like Starwood's predecessor, has been "grandfathered" the right to operate on a paired-share basis. Patriot, like Starwood, may now manage its hotels through a sister corporation. These two REITs are much larger than their REIT peers, emphasize luxury and upscale hotels, and will also be of interest to investors who would like to participate in the hotel sector but are wary of the potential leakage and conflict of interest issues. As we'll see in Chapter 11, however, pending legislation could affect the advantages of paired share REITs.

◆ **Manufactured-housing REITs.** A number of years ago, an enterprising landowner brought a number of trailers, together with their owners, to a remote spot out in the boondocks, semi-affixed them to foundations, and called the project a "mobile-home park." Many of today's modern "manufactured-housing communities," however, bear little resemblance to yesterday's mobile-home parks. The homes are now manufactured off-site, rarely leave their original home sites, and generally have the quality and appearance of site-built homes. According to "No Laughingstock," an article that appeared in the January 6, 1997, issue of

Barron's, these units accounted for more than one-third of all new single-family homes sold in the United States in 1996 (up from 25 percent in 1991). About 370,000 manufactured homes were shipped that year, amounting to $14 billion in total sales.

In view of rapidly rising home prices and apartment rents in some parts of the United States, manufactured homes clearly help to satisfy America's need for affordable housing.

The quality manufactured-home community today looks something like a blend of a single-family-home subdivision and a nice apartment building. A unit's average price is about $40,000, compared with a nationwide median price of $120,000 for a site-built home. The residents own their own homes but lease the underlying land, typically at $150–$300 per month, from the owner of the community. The home-owners have amenities such as an attractive main entrance, clubhouse, pool, tennis courts, putting greens, exercise room, and laundry facilities. Most of the communities have catered to both elderly and younger couples. According to the Manufactured Housing Institute, there are now more than seven million manufactured homes in the United States, in which more than 18 million people reside.

Owners of manufactured-home communities enjoy certain advantages not available to owners of apartment buildings. First of all, the business is very recession resistant, in large part because of the low turnover rate. Next, the community owner's capital expenditures are limited to upkeep of the grounds and common facilities and do not entail any maintenance on the units themselves. What is particularly advantageous is that, because of the difficulties of getting land zoned for this type of property and the long lead time involved in filling a new community with tenant-owners, overbuilding has rarely been a problem.

Problems of owners and operators of manufactured-home communities include the periodic pressures for rent control in some areas and the difficult and time-consuming nature of developing or expanding communities.

Investors in manufactured-housing REITs should expect higher than average safety, dividend yields of close to 6 percent, and steady profit and dividend growth.

Because of low turnover and low maintenance, rental increases, even at 3–4 percent annually, together with modest debt leverage, provide healthy growth in operating income. Furthermore, because of the fragmented nature of manufactured-home-community ownership throughout the United States, recurring acquisitions can add an additional avenue for growth.

SUMMARY

◆ It's possible to invest in nearly every kind of real estate imaginable: apartment buildings, retail, office/industrial, self-storage facilities, hotels, assisted-living homes, golf courses—even prisons.

◆ The phases of the real estate cycle are depression, recovery, boom, and overbuilding and downturn, and these cycles can affect REITs' performance.

◆ Some apartment REITs own units in specific geographical areas, while others have holdings throughout the United States.

◆ The different retail-sector REITs behave differently from one another, and each retail sector must be considered separately.

◆ Mall REITs are relatively new on the investment scene; they are very much in the "retail business."

◆ What investors should look for in an outlet REIT investment is management that emphasizes leases with high-end manufacturers and chooses good locations for its properties.

◆ All the bad news of the early '90s notwithstanding, office properties appear to be early in the recovery phase of their real estate cycle.

◆ Because the office sector is so cyclical, investors need to watch for signs of overbuilding.

◆ The industrial-property market has had a good track record of reacting quickly and shutting down the supply of new space as soon as the market becomes saturated.

◆ REITs that specialize in industrial-sector properties can be very good investments, particularly if their management teams have longstanding relationships with major industrial-space users and concentrate on economically expanding geographical areas.

◆ Health care REITs were launched in the late '80s and have mostly enjoyed an excellent track record.

◆ Investors in health care REITs need to watch out for federal budget restrictions in Medicare. The current political environment of cost containment can put the squeeze on some health care providers.

◆ Self-storage was a mediocre investment in the late 1980s because of overbuilding. The industry's health, however, has recovered substantially since 1990, and occupancy and rental rates have improved significantly.

◆ There is a good case to be made for self-storage facilities being recession resistant since, in a recession, individuals as well as businesses cut costs by reducing the space they occupy. A reduction in living or office space means an increased need for storage space.

◆ Hotel REITs have been very good performers for the last few years, but they represent aggressive investments because of their cyclicality and volatile room and occupancy rates.

◆ Investors in manufactured-housing REITs should expect higher than average safety, dividend yields of close to 6 percent, and steady profit and dividend growth.

◆ Self-storage REITs, health care–facility REITs, and manufactured-housing REITs are fairly recession resistant.

HISTORY

And Mythology

PART

I

CHAPTER

REITs
MYSTERIES
AND MYTHS

HERE'S NO QUESTION about it: In spite of their growing acceptance, there *have been* lingering mysteries and myths that REITs haven't been able to shake off. This chapter addresses these misconceptions and lays the fading myths to rest once and for all.

CHANGING ATTITUDES TOWARD REITS

FOR MANY YEARS, REITs were regarded as somehow "different" from traditional investments. Even their name—REIT—implied that the standard criteria applicable to most investments didn't apply to them. Bruce Andrews, the very astute CEO of Nationwide Health Properties, noted that the term "trust," as in real estate investment *trust,* implies that REITs are somehow mysterious, that they are not like "normal" companies.

Standard & Poor's still will not admit even the largest REIT into the S&P 500 Index. One of the main reasons that REITs were suspect for so long is that many people who traditionally invested in real estate didn't really understand the stock market, while most people who invested in the stock market were uncomfortable with real estate. REITs just didn't fit into either category and therefore fell between the cracks.

All this is changing now, of course. There are those who believe (like Richard Rainwater, for example, who has some $425 million tied up in Crescent Real Estate Equities) that 10 years from now the value of REITs will top $500 billion—and that in 15 years, it will hit $1 trillion. "There's still a tremendous amount of real estate in private hands that will eventually come into the public market," observes Rainwater in *Business Week* ("The

New World of Real Estate," September 22, 1997).

With talk like that, you'd think that the day might come when there would be no private ownership of major properties and that most of the real estate in the country will be owned by REITs. If that were true, say the experts, some of the cyclicality would be eliminated from real estate, leading to a lot more stability.

However, some big private investors and developers, like Manhattan's Douglas Durst, for instance, say they think REITs will get into trouble. Do they *really* think that, or are they just keeping a poker face in a high-stakes game? Time will tell, but opinions like this are definitely in the minority. Andrew Davis, manager of the Davis Real Estate Fund, says, "We are watching what could be the biggest asset class in the country— bigger than the Treasury or bond market—begin to go public."

THE BIAS OF TRADITIONAL REAL ESTATE INVESTORS

TRADITIONALLY, MOST REAL ESTATE investors have chosen to put their money directly into property— apartment complexes, shopping centers, malls, office buildings, or industrial properties—and not in real estate securities like REITs. That's bricks and mortar, not pieces of paper. Direct ownership historically has provided the opportunity to use substantial leverage, since for many years lenders would lend 60 to 80 percent of the purchase price of a building. Leverage is a wonderful thing—when prices are going up.

Since the Great Depression, real estate values pursued a profitable upward road, even if there were a few potholes along the way. Appreciation of 10 percent on a building bought with 25 percent cash down would generate 40 percent in capital gains. In addition, owning a building directly provided the investor with a tax shelter for operating income. As a result, real estate continued to appreciate and provide easy profits, and most real estate investors tended to focus on what they knew—direct ownership.

Many of these individual real estate investors har-
bored a distrust for public markets (REITs included),
which they saw as roulette tables where investors put
themselves at the mercy of faceless managers—or
worse, speculators and day traders whose income
depended on volatility. These investors saw REITs as
highly speculative and wouldn't touch them.

Then there was institutional investment in real
estate. Originally, institutional and pension funds
"earmarked" for real estate were invested in properties either directly (where their own property managers and investment managers were retained), or
through "commingled funds" in which big insurance
companies used funds provided by various institutional investors to buy portfolios of properties. Who
managed these properties, supervised their performance, and answered for their results? The same sort
of real estate investors who, of course, didn't trust the
stock market.

Since REITs are classified as common stocks, the
result was—catch-22—that a decision to invest in
REITs could be made only by the "*equities* investment
officer" rather than the "*real estate* investment officer"
of the institution or pension fund. The institutions'
common-stock investment funds were placed and
monitored elsewhere. Furthermore, various "investment guidelines" often precluded the equities investment officers' investing in REITs—even if they knew
about them and wanted to pursue this sector of the
market. Why should they have bothered?

A further discouragement has been volatility. Real
estate investors have complained that REITs, even
though less volatile than the broader stock market,
nevertheless, do fluctuate in price. However, to be
fair, any asset fluctuates in price. With illiquid assets
that were held, not traded (and by relying upon occasional appraisals), the private-fund managers could

maintain the illusion that the values of their assets were "steady as a rock," despite the continuous ebb and flow of the real estate markets. Any asset fluctuates in price, but the owner is sometimes unaware of the price fluctuations unless he or she is trying to sell the asset.

Finally, institutions buy and sell stocks in large blocks, and it's been only recently that REIT shares have had sufficient liquidity to attract institutional types. In fact, one of the most oft-quoted reasons why pension funds have been reluctant to invest in REITs is their "lack of liquidity." The REIT market was so thinly traded prior to 1993–94, when the size of the REIT market began to expand geometrically, that it would have been extremely difficult for an institution to accumulate even a modest position without disrupting the market for any particular REIT.

THE BIAS OF COMMON-STOCK INVESTORS

WHAT STOPPED COMMON-STOCK investors from buying REITs? The flip side of the coin is that REITs' only business is real estate and stock investors didn't invest in *real estate;* they focused primarily on product or service companies. Real estate was perceived as a different asset class from common stock. This problem was particularly acute in the institutional world.

In addition, the public perception—wrong as it was—was that REITs were high-risk but low-return investments. There were also many investors who had bought construction-lending REITs and limited partnerships in the late '60s and early '70s and gotten badly burned in the late '80s. These investors did not take the trouble to distinguish between these ill-fated investments and well-managed equity REITs.

Also, for years investors had been told that companies that paid out a high percentage of their income in dividends did not retain much of their earnings and therefore could not grow rapidly. Since, to most common-stock investors, growth is the hallmark of successful investing, they didn't want to invest in a company that couldn't grow. Finally, some of the blame for lack of individual investors' interest in REITs can be laid at the feet of brokers.

REITs for a long time were perceived as stocks by real estate investors, and as real estate by stock investors.

Until the last few years, most major brokerage firms did not even employ a REIT analyst. And, since individual investors generally bought individual stocks only when their brokers recommended them, that was the end of that story. A lot of people were buying mutual funds, but only a handful of mutual funds were devoted to REIT investments—and those did not advertise widely. The few investors who did their own research and made their own investment decisions quite likely felt that REITs were too much of an unknown territory for them to venture into. Even income investors, for whom REITs would have been particularly suitable, invested primarily in bonds, electric utilities, and convertible preferred stocks.

REITs, of course, being the gems they are, were bound to be noticed sooner or later. They are gradually becoming the darlings of many real estate and common-stock investors, and REITs' long period of being neglected may already be ancient history.

THE MYTHS ABOUT REITS

IN ADDITION TO—and sometimes because of—the other obstacles REITs have had to overcome, some myths exist, myths that in the past scared off all but the bravest investors. Although these myths were based on misunderstandings of the investment characteristics of REITs, they discouraged many would-be investors. Let's confront them, one by one.

REITS ARE PACKAGES OF REAL PROPERTIES

THIS MYTH, WHICH probably sprang from investors' experience with the ill-fated real estate partnerships of the late '80s, may be the single most significant reason for REITs' failure in the past to attract a substantial investor following. Although REITs may have at one time been only collections of properties, they are much more than that today.

REITs are more than just packages of real properties.

Companies that merely own and passively manage a basket of properties—whether they be limited partnerships or another type—face several specific investment concerns. Management is generally not entrepreneurial, and thus is often unresponsive to little problems that can, if left unattended, develop into big problems. Also, management does not usually have its compensation linked to the success of the property, and therefore has no particular incentive to compete in today's environment. Often, there is no long-term vision or strategy for effective growth. Finally, inefficient management rarely has access to attractively priced capital, making it difficult for the entity to take advantage of "buyers' markets" or attractive purchase opportunities. An investment in such a company, although perhaps providing an attractive dividend yield, offers little or no opportunity for growth or expansion beyond the value of the original portfolio.

Conversely, a large number of today's REITs are vibrant, dynamic real estate organizations first, and "investment trusts" second. They are far more than collections of properties. Their management is savvy and highly motivated by their own ownership stake. They plan intelligently for expansion either in areas they know well or in areas where they believe they can become dominant players, and they have access to the capital necessary for such expansion. To categorize highly successful real estate companies, such as Avalon Bay, Equity Office, Kimco, Home, Post, Reckson, Simon DeBartolo, Security Capital Industrial, Spieker, United Dominion, or Weingarten, for example, as just collections of properties is to underestimate them seriously. Yet this myth still persists.

MYTH 2
REAL ESTATE IS A HIGH-RISK INVESTMENT

IT'S AMAZING HOW many people believe that real estate (other than one's own home, of course) is a "high-risk" investment where investors can be wiped out by tenant defaults or declines in property values. And, they surmise that if real estate investing is risky, then REIT investing must also be risky. Let's analyze risk here.

The three essential determinants of real estate risk are leverage, diversification, and quality of management.

◆ **Leverage.** Leverage in real estate is no different from leverage in any other investment: the more of it you use, the greater your potential gain or loss. Any asset carried on high margin, whether an office building, a blue-chip stock, or even a T-note, will involve substantial risk, since a small decline in the asset's value will cause a much larger decline in one's investment in it. However, because real estate historically has been bought and financed with a lot of debt, many investors have confused the risk of debt leverage with that of owning real estate.

Although real estate investments have often been highly leveraged, it is the high leverage rather than the real estate that is the great risk.

In fact, one could argue that, if lenders will lend a higher percentage of a real estate asset's value than the Federal Reserve will allow banks and brokers to lend on a stock investment, then real estate must be less risky than stock investments.

◆ **Diversification.** Again, the same rule that applies to other investments applies to REITs: diversification lowers risk. People who would never dream of having a one-stock portfolio go out and buy, individually or with partners, a single apartment building. Things happen—an earthquake, neighborhood deterioration, a recession—and all of a sudden the building is sucking up money like a sponge. Never mind that a similar apartment building in another location is doing well, or that an office building upstate is raking in cash. Diversification should be the mantra of every investor.

ONE COMMON MISCONCEPTION

WHEN ONE PROPERTY has difficulty, investors sometimes rashly conclude that real estate as an asset class is very risky. Yet no one would condemn the entire stock market just because the price of one stock had dropped.

◆ **Management quality.** Then, of course, there is the issue of management. Good management is crucial—but that is not only true in real estate. If you look around at major U.S. non-REIT corporations, you can see, for instance, the value of a Jack Welch to General Electric, or how Bill Gates's vision brought Microsoft to where it is today. Incompetent management can ruin a major corporation or a candy store. Real estate, like virtually all other types of investments, cannot simply be bought and neglected; it requires active, capable management. Despite this, many otherwise intelligent investors have bought apartment buildings, small offices, or local shopping centers and tried either to manage them themselves in their spare time or to give control to local managers who have no incentive to run the property efficiently. What happens? The building or strip mall does poorly, and the investor loses money and jumps to the wrong conclusion, that real estate is a high-risk investment.

MYTH 3
REAL ESTATE IS A ONLY A GOOD INVESTMENT WHEN THERE'S INFLATION

REAL ESTATE IS really nothing more than buildings and land, and, like all tangible assets (whether scrap metal, oil, or used cars), its value will ebb and flow with local, national, and even global supply and demand. However, inflation is only one factor that affects these market conditions; others are recession, interest rates, unemployment, consumer spending, levels of new personal and business investment, government policies, and even wars.

Part of the reason for the real-estate-as-inflation-hedge myth may come from the fact that real estate happened to do well during the inflationary 1970s, while stock ownership during the same period was not as productive. This, quite likely, was a simple coincidence. According to *Stocks, Bonds, Bills, and Inflation 1995 Yearbook,* published by Ibbotson Associates, equities have been very good inflation hedges over many decades. So has real estate. But the reality is that neither the real estate market nor the equity market is substantially better or worse than the other in this regard.

Yes, there are times when inflation *appears* to help the real estate investor by boosting the replacement cost of real estate, but such inflation can also significantly diminish a property's net operating income, and thus negatively affect its market value.

The value of a commercial building is determined essentially by two factors: the net operating income the

owner derives from the property, and the multiple of that income that the buyer is willing to pay for it. Both these factors fluctuate in response to various market forces, and inflation is only one of those forces.

High inflation can positively or negatively affect rent rates and net operating income. A positive influence resulting from inflation, at least in the retail sector, can come from the higher tenant sales that normally result from increased inflation and higher prices on goods sold to consumers. Although these higher sales can translate into higher rents for the property owner, this benefit will be short lived if the retailer can't maintain his or her profit margins. If the store is not returning a profit, it will be difficult to raise rents. Similarly, higher inflation can help apartment owners by increasing tenants' wages and thus their ability to afford higher rents, but only if wages are rising at least as rapidly as the price of goods and services.

When supply and demand are in balance, inflation may enable the owner to raise rents because, as the cost of new construction rises, rents in new buildings will have to rise to cover higher costs. If the demand is sufficient to absorb the new units that are coming into the market, owners of preexisting properties will often be able to take advantage of the new properties' "price umbrella" to charge higher rents. Real estate is not an effective hedge against inflation, however, when there is a large oversupply of competing properties.

Higher inflation rates can also have a negative effect on the value of real estate. The Federal Reserve acts as watchdog for inflation, and, when there is any perceived inflationary threat, the Fed will raise short-term interest rates. Higher interest rates are meant to slow the economy, but interest rates that are too high can strangle it, causing a recession. Once a recessionary economy exists, a property owner will have difficulty raising rents, and therefore will not be able to increase net operating income.

Now for the second part of the property-value equation: the multiples. If the price of a property is figured in multiples of annual operating income (or its reciprocal, the cap rate), why don't the multiples (or the cap rates) always stay the same? There is an argument that buyers will pay more for, or accept a lower cap rate on, real property during inflationary periods. Since investors view real estate as a hard asset, like gold and other commodities, they may be willing to pay a higher multiple for every dollar of operating income if they perceive inflation as accelerating. This is because future inflation will mean that investors can increase future rents, either enabling them to make greater operating profits or, because of higher multiples, to sell the property to the next buyer at a higher price.

Cap rates may indeed be influenced by inflation, but often in reverse. Higher inflation may drive up interest rates, which in turn will increase the "hurdle rate of return" demanded by investors in a property, and have the effect of increasing the required cap rate and *decreasing* the price at which the property can be sold.

If, for example, the demand for apartments in San Francisco exceeds the available supply of such units, rents will increase and the apartment building owner's net operating income will increase. Furthermore, if interest rates remain stable and investors believe that apartments' operating income will continue to increase for an extended period, the cap rate for similar buildings is likely to drop. If this seems technical, let's simplify it a bit.

Buyers will accept a lower yield on their investment and be willing to pay a higher purchase price for each dollar of operating income on properties in "hot" markets. In this scenario, the owner of the San Francisco apartment building will do well despite the lack of inflation. On the other hand, if the supply of apartment units in San Francisco exceeds the demand by renters, rents will not rise, nor will the building's value appreciate—even during inflationary periods. In that scenario, the owner's efforts to boost rents would merely result in his or her tenants' moving to another building, making it unlikely that the value of the building would rise, inflation notwithstanding.

Market factors like supply and demand are almost always more important than inflation in determining property value. Real estate investors should focus more on market conditions and management ability than on inflation.

MARKET TRENDS AND SMART MANAGEMENT

REAL ESTATE HAS at some times been a terrific investment and, at other times, a terrible investment. Right now, there appears to be no consensus as to whether real estate will be an exceptional investment through the rest of the decade and into the 21st century—or one that falls flat.

A favorite observation among stock traders, after a long bear market that has finally turned around and moved up strongly, is "The easy money has already been made." In the real estate markets, most sectors have rebounded very well from the depression-like years of the late 1980s and the early 1990s, and the *easy* money *has* been made here, too. As the 20th century draws to a close, it is likely that in many sectors of the real estate industry it will be difficult for property owners to generate investment returns significantly in excess of existing property cash flows.

The rapid industrialization and intense competition occurring today in North America, Europe, Asia, and Latin America seem to be major and perhaps long-lasting phenomena. U.S. companies must now go toe-to-toe with foreign competitors virtually everywhere in the world. This, in turn, requires U.S. businesses to be very cost efficient. Downsizings, restructurings, and layoffs have been the result. Companies are finding it difficult to raise prices, and employees are finding it equally difficult to get significantly higher wages. The bottom line for real estate owners is that, as long as these competitive trends continue, it will be difficult for rents and same-store net operating income to rise above the inflation rate.

All of this would make you think that, if there is a yellow warning light out for real estate, then the same caution must apply to REITs. Those REITs that are simply portfolios of individual properties will indeed be affected by the same market pressures that affect real estate. But others are organizations that are positioned to *take advantage* of the opportunities presented by challenging real estate environments, just as they take advantage of opportunities in favorable environments.

Great managements view difficult conditions as opportunities. REITs like United Dominion and Merry Land went on buying sprees during the apartment depression of the late '80s and early '90s. Nationwide Health, Health Care Properties, and LTC Properties bought defaulted nursing-home loans from the Resolution Trust Corporation (RTC) at 16 to 18 percent yields. Kimco Realty has bought poorly performing shopping malls and turned them into open-air shopping complexes occupied by thriving tenants. Several years ago, Weingarten Realty actually *increased* its occupancy rates during the Texas oil bust, as many tenants vacated half-empty locations and migrated to Weingarten's attractive shopping centers. More recently, Reckson Associates has been buying underoccupied offices in Long Island and refurbishing and retenanting them. These are but a few examples of how lemons can be turned into lemonade by imaginative and capable real estate organizations with access to capital.

Conversely, it can also happen that a great real estate market is *bad* for REITs. For example, many REITs ran into trouble in the mid-1980s, when real

estate prices were skyrocketing. Not only were properties simply not available at prices that would provide
acceptable returns, but owners were also facing competition from new construction. Before anyone realized what was happening, the cycle moved into the
overbuilt phase and funds from operations (FFO)
growth slowed markedly. Some investors worry that the
same conditions prevail in some markets and sectors
today, where cap rates have fallen dramatically.

To illustrate the point further, take a quick look at
the apartment sector. What would happen to apartment markets if a severe recession hit? Conventional
wisdom would dictate that markets previously in equilibrium would weaken, occupancy rates decline, and
rents stagnate. Market values of apartment buildings
would fall. Many apartment REITs would report flat or
even declining FFO, and their stock prices could fall;
dividends would be stagnant until recovery arrived.

But Equity Residential, Security Capital Pacific, and
a significant number of other quality apartment REITs
would then be out there buying apartments at exceedingly attractive entry yields, taking full advantage of
these difficult conditions. While FFO growth could
slow temporarily in response to difficult rental markets, these REITs' ability to buy sound properties at
cheap prices would allow FFO to grow quickly as soon
as market conditions began to stabilize again.

**The extent to which a well-managed REIT can
avail itself of the opportunities presented in a down market depends upon the amount and cost of available capital, the depth of the market weakness, and the buying
competition it faces.**

Some of the best investment opportunities arise
when a company or even an entire industry is overlooked or misunderstood by the great mass of
investors. Legendary investors Warren Buffett and

Peter Lynch made their reputations not by buying the growth stocks that everyone else was buying, but rather by taking advantage of solid companies with undervalued stocks. Buffett's investment in Wells Fargo Bank is a good example. While most investors and cocky short-sellers were predicting disaster for this California bank several years ago, Buffett knew that they were caught up in the fear of what looked like the impending collapse of the major banks. He was convinced that, because of fear, investors were unable to see Wells Fargo's real strengths and staying power, and he took full advantage of the situation.

The same principle applies to REITs. Investors' past fears and hesitations had, for a long time, left these lucrative investments largely undiscovered and, therefore, undervalued. That time is quickly passing.

SUMMARY

◆ For years, REITs have been shunned as "common stocks" by real estate investors and treated as "uninteresting real estate" by stock investors.

◆ The three essential determinants of real estate risk are leverage, diversification, and quality of management.

◆ Although real estate investments have often been highly leveraged, it is the high leverage, rather than real estate itself, that is the major risk.

◆ Real estate as an investment can be hurt as much as helped by inflation.

◆ Market factors like supply and demand and the existing and future strength of the economy are almost always more important than inflation in determining property value. Real estate investors should focus more on market conditions and management ability than on inflation.

◆ Even if the outlook for real estate is not good, REITs can still be very good investments since good management with access to capital find opportunities in bad times as well as good.

CHAPTER 6

A History Of REITs

AND REIT
PERFORMANCE

A S AN INVESTOR, you want to be equipped with as many analytical tools as possible. Knowing how a particular category of security has behaved in the past is a crucial yardstick in determining not only *whether or not* you want to buy it, but also *how much* of it you want to buy relative to other assets in your portfolio. How have REIT stocks behaved during the 35 years since they were conceived? Like a child, like a teenager, and like an adult, depending upon which stage of their development you examine. We'll take a look at those developments—specifically, how REITs performed in their infancy, how they created havoc in their wild adolescent years, and how they've matured into solid citizens of the investment world. We will also consider how REITs have behaved relative to different real estate and economic environments.

THE 1960s

INFANCY

THE REIT STRUCTURE was officially sanctioned by Congress and signed into law in 1960. It allowed individual real estate investors to "pool their investments" in order to enjoy the same benefits as direct real estate owners. Once the structure was created, it was only a few years until the first REITs were established, but these REITs were not "pretty babies" by today's standards.

According to a report by Goldman Sachs, *The REIT Investment Summary* (1996), only ten REITs of any size existed during the 1960s. Most of them were managed by outside advisers, and all property management functions were handled by outside companies. Many of these management companies were affiliated with the REITs' advisers, which presented an opportunity for significant conflicts of interest.

The REITs' portfolios were very small, ranging from $11 million for Washington REIT (one of the few survivors) to the $44 million REIT of America. Their total real estate investments were very small at the beginning, amounting to just over $200 million. (For comparison purposes, by the end of 1997, REITs owned assets of more than $200 *billion*.) These REITs were small in size, and their insider stock ownership was almost negligible—typically less than 1 percent.

Despite these weaknesses, the Goldman Sachs report shows that these early-era REITs turned in a respectable performance, aided by generally healthy real estate markets in the 1960s. "Cash flow" (the early version of today's funds from operations or FFO) grew an average of 5.8 percent annually, and the average dividend yield was 6.1 percent. The multiples of earnings (or cash flow) that investors were willing to pay for these early REITs remained steady, providing investors with an average annual total return of 11.5 percent. Not a bad performance, considering that from 1963 to 1970 the S&P 500's total annual return averaged only 6.7 percent. Thus, despite their many handicaps, these upstart investments performed quite well, some might say to the disadvantage of their better established common-stock brethren.

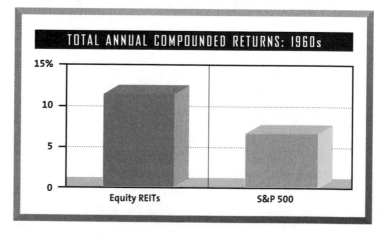

TOTAL ANNUAL COMPOUNDED RETURNS: 1960s

SOURCE: GOLDMAN SACHS, THE REIT INVESTMENT SUMMARY (1996)

THE 1970s

ADOLESCENCE AND TURBULENCE

THE 1970s WERE tumultuous times for the economy, for the stock market, and for REITs. Inflation, driven by the OPEC-led explosion in oil prices, roared out of control, as evidenced by the Consumer Price Index (CPI), increasing 6.3 percent in 1973, 11 percent in 1974, 9.1 percent in 1975, and 11.3 percent by 1979.

Not content with such external hardships, the REIT industry was busy creating problems of its own. Between 1968 and 1970, with the willing assistance of many investment bankers, the industry produced 58 new mortgage REITs. Most of these used a modest amount of shareholders' equity and huge amounts of borrowed funds to provide short-term loans to the construction industry, which, in turn, built hundreds of office buildings throughout the United States.

Such stalwart banks as Bank of America, Chase, Wachovia, and Wells Fargo got into the act, and it seemed no self-respecting major bank wanted to be left out in sponsoring its own REIT. Largely as a result of these new mortgage REITs, the REIT industry's total assets mushroomed from $1 billion in 1968 to $20 billion by the mid-1970s.

When the office building market—hammered by inflation-driven high interest rates—began weakening in 1973, the new mortgage REITs found that leverage worked both ways. Helped along by casual underwriting standards, nonperforming assets rose to an alarming 73 percent of invested assets by the end of 1974, and share prices collapsed.

As a result of their negative experience with mortgage REITs, investors of the 1970s became disenchanted with the entire REIT industry for many years thereafter.

Ironically, aside from these mortgage REITs, non-lending *equity* REITs didn't do badly during the decade of the '70s, since most real estate markets remained strong. Federal Realty and New Plan, among others, made their first appearances and these retail REITs did well for investors for many years. While asset growth slowed, operating performance was reasonably good. During that decade, ten representative equity REITs charted by the Goldman Sachs study turned in a 6.1 percent compounded annual cash-flow growth rate, with negative growth in only one year. As might be expected, those REITs with more than 5 percent insider stock ownership did much better than the others. These ten equity REITs also enjoyed an average annual compounded growth rate of 4.2 percent in their stock prices. This, when added to their dividend yields, produced a compounded total annual return of 12.9 percent during the '70s, which compared very favorably with the total compounded annual rate of return of 5.8 percent for the S&P 500 Index.

Nevertheless, as the decade drew to a close, REITs were still not accepted by much of the investment community, since investor sentiment focused on the debacle of the mortgage REITs. By then, most investors had come to disdain REITs, failing to distinguish between the slow, solid, equity REIT and its poor

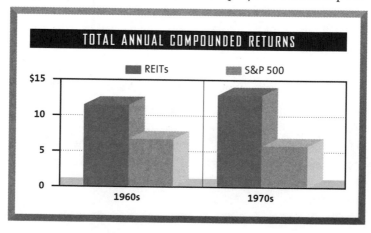

SOURCE: GOLDMAN SACHS

relation, the construction-loan–oriented mortgage REIT. There was virtually no pension money allocated to the equity REITs during this time, because they were unproven, illiquid, and still (in most cases) without independent management. Further, with only a few exceptions (notably Washington REIT, Federal Realty, and New Plan), few focused on specific property sectors in specific geographical regions. By and large, REITs were still suffering growing pains and were not widely respected.

THE 1980s

THE OVERBUILDING OGRE
REARS ITS UGLY HEAD

THE INFLATION OF the '70s had caused construction costs to mushroom, and, unless rents could be raised enough to provide a reasonable return on new investment capital, new construction would no longer be cost efficient. As occupancy rates rose, however, real estate owners (including, of course, the REITs) *were* able to increase their rents substantially, yet new building was, at least for the moment, deferred.

As the '70s drew to a close, investors, reacting to high inflation, were looking for "hard assets," such as gold, silver, and other commodities.

The extraordinarily high mortgage rates of the early '80s—ranging from 12.5 percent to 14.8 percent—substantially increased REITs' borrowing costs and eventually caused FFO growth to slow. According to the January 1996 *REIT Investment Summary*, per share FFO growth for Goldman Sachs's representative equity REITs ranged from 26.1 percent in 1980 to 4.4 percent in 1983. However, FFO growth in the first half of the decade averaged a very respectable 8.7 percent. During the six years from 1980 through 1985, the group's total annual rate of return to shareholders were truly eye popping, averaging 28.6 percent.

It says in Ecclesiastes, "To every thing there is a season. . . " and the good times, having had their season in the first half of the decade, were unfortunately no longer in season for the second half. Investors, both public and private, couldn't help noticing the outstanding returns achieved by real estate owners in the early '80s; they all just *had* to own real estate, and lots of it. What really put the icing on the cake, however, was when Congress passed the Economic Recovery Act of 1981, which created an attractive tax shelter for real estate owners. Authorizing property owners to use the vehicle of depreciation of their real estate assets as a tax shelter for other income prompted a real estate buying frenzy.

Almost immediately, major brokerage firms and other syndicators formed real estate limited partnerships and touted them as "can't-miss" investments, offering both generous tax benefits and capital gains. Of course, what happened was that the tax-shelter incentive inflated property prices to unsustainable numbers, and the properties could not possibly support themselves. REITs, offering greater stability but insignificant tax write-offs, were largely ignored. No one even considered the possibility that the tax laws might change (as tax laws always seem to do).

As megabillions poured into real estate, several unfortunate events occurred. First, REITs had to compete for capital with limited partnerships and private investors, who, in creating tax shelters, didn't have to show a positive cash flow. There was no contest: The latter could afford to pay a lot more for properties than the REITs could.

Second, as a result of all the buying frenzy, real estate prices escalated. Even if REITs could have raised the capital, properties were being priced at levels that precluded their earning an adequate return. Third, and worst of all, with such a hot market, the developers got into the act—without regard for the law of supply and demand—and began a great amount of new construction. Virtually every developer who had ever built anything (and many who hadn't) visited his or her friendly banker, laid projections and budgets on the table, shouted, "Construction loan time!" and walked away with 90 percent–plus financing.

Small wonder that within a few years the market, beginning to feel the effects of overbuilding, slowed considerably. As if that weren't bad enough, Congress then decided to take away the tax-shelter advantage that had been such an impetus for investment, and passed the Tax Reform Act of 1986. Investors who were left holding properties that had already been performing poorly now lost the last reason they had for owning real estate. By the late '80s, real estate was in big trouble.

During the 1980s, when investors were seeking the tax shelters offered by limited partnerships, real estate prices became inflated.

As early as 1985, year-to-year growth rates in FFO for most REITs were peaking or declining slowly. The growth rate for the representative group of REITs in the Goldman Sachs study dropped from 13 percent in the first half of the '80s to only 2.5 percent in the second half. Dividends continued to rise through the end of the decade, in most cases faster than FFO increased, and the payout ratios became extremely aggressive. The average ratio for Goldman's group rose from 72 percent in 1980 to 98 percent in 1986. Ironically, despite the problems encountered by the REITs in these lean years, their stocks didn't do badly. Total annual returns for Goldman's REIT group ranged from a high of 29.4 percent in 1985 to a low of 3.7 percent in 1988. They slightly underperformed the S&P

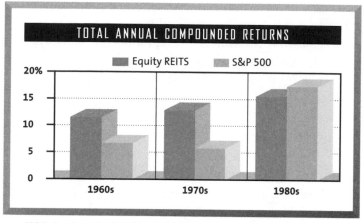

500 Index in 1985, 1988, and 1989, but bested it in 1986 and 1987. Nevertheless, these negatives, in 1990, would eventually catch up with REIT stock prices.

THE 1990s

THE REIT INDUSTRY COMES OF AGE

EMERGING FROM THE '80s' excesses, REITs did not begin the '90s well. REIT shareholders suffered through a bear market in 1990 that cut their share prices down to bargain levels not seen since the '70s. National Association of Real Estate Investment Trusts (NAREIT) statistics show that equity REITs' total return for 1990 was a *negative* 14.8 percent, making that the worst year since 1974, when their total annual return was a negative 21.4 percent. This was quite a shock to REIT investors, who had become quite spoiled; from 1975 through 1990, equity REITs had experienced only one year of negative total return—1987—when the figures were in the red by a scant 3.6 percent.

1990'S BEAR MARKET

REITS' BIG NEGATIVE NUMBERS in 1990 resulted from a number of factors: for office buildings and apartment houses, it was overbuilding, causing rising vacancies and stagnating or reduced rents; for retail, it was the

continued inroads made by Wal-Mart and other dis-
counters on the turf of traditional retailers. Dividend
cuts by several REITs, who had found their payout
ratios too high during such tough economic times,
didn't help matters. Although a general markdown in
real estate securities was warranted, investors overreacted, and share prices fell below reasonable levels.

Excellent REIT bargains had sprouted up by the
end of 1990, and these bear market lows set the stage for
a major bull market that thrived from 1991 through 1993
and ushered in the great IPO boom of 1993–94.

The opening of the decade had been rough for
REITs, but the investment vehicle itself by this time
had nearly completed its metamorphosis. REITs of the
late '80s and early '90s had come a long way from the
REITs of the '60s. Insider ownership increased and,
thanks to the Tax Reform Act of 1986, which liberalized the rules pertaining to REITs, many REITs termi-
nated their outside investment advisory relationships—and the major conflicts of interest that
accompanied them—and took over all their own leasing, maintenance services, redevelopment, and new
construction. By the end of 1990's bear market, several
REITs could boast strong management teams and
excellent track records. Among the stars were Federal
Realty, Health Care Properties, MediTrust, Nationwide Health, New Plan Realty, United Dominion,
Washington REIT, and Weingarten Realty. However,
it would not be until 1993 before a large number of
new, high-quality REITs would become available to
investors.

1991 TO 1993: THE BULL RETURNS

A COMBINATION OF FACTORS caused equity REITs to
do exceedingly well from 1991 through 1993. According to NAREIT data, total annual returns for 1991–93

averaged 23.3 percent. This outstanding performance was ample reward for the patient investors who had stuck with REITs through the bad times.

Why REIT stocks did so well following the tough years is easy to explain in hindsight. For one thing, investors overreacted terribly when they dumped REIT stocks in 1990; some of the gain came merely from getting prices back to reasonable levels. Perhaps a more important reason, however, was the bargain prices at which REITs were able to pick up properties in the aftermath of the depression-like and overbuilt real estate markets of the late '80s and early '90s. By 1991, many REITs were once again able to raise capital. They bought properties at fire-sale prices from banks that had foreclosed on billions of defaulted real estate loans, from insurance companies that wanted to reduce their exposure to real estate, from real estate limited partnerships that had crashed following the frenzy of the '80s, and, last but certainly not least, from the Resolution Trust Corporation (RTC), which had been organized by Congress to acquire and resell real estate and real estate loans from bankrupt and near-bankrupt lenders. REITs were once more able to pursue aggressive acquisition programs, raising funds from both loans and public offerings, at a cost far less than the initial returns on new acquisitions.

The rebound from the low, bear market prices, REITs' ample access to capital with which to make attractive deals, and lower interest rates were all factors in driving the REIT bull market onward from 1991 to 1993.

Between January 1991 and the end of 1993, the Federal Reserve Board incrementally lowered interest rates in an effort to ease what had become a long but shallow recession. In January 1991, the yield on three-month Treasury bills was 6.2 percent. By the end of

1993, it had fallen to 3.1 percent. High-yielding REITs presented an irresistible lure to investors.

Since REITs were giving such high yields, investors continued their romance with REIT shares during this period. Indeed, they were seen as an "antidote" to the puny, short-term yields available on CDs and T-bills. These investors may not have known much about REITs, but that didn't stop them from buying in with wild abandon. Individual investors and a few adventurous institutions alike flocked to REIT investing, not only for the hefty yields but also for the prospects of rich capital gains.

THE GREAT 1993–94 REIT IPO BOOM

ROBERT A. FRANK, a well-known REIT analyst for years, was quoted in *Barron's* on December 18, 1995, as saying that 1993 saw 93 REIT share offerings raise $12.6 billion, including $8.7 billion by 43 new REITs and $3.9 billion by 50 existing REITs. An additional $10.3 billion was raised in 1994, including 30 new REIT IPOs raising $6.4 billion and 53 follow-on offerings by existing REITs raising $3.9 billion. The offerings in 1993 alone surpassed the total amount of equity that REITs had raised during the previous 13 years, according to Merrill Lynch's August 1994 report, *Sizing Up the Equity REIT Industry.*

At the end of 1990, the estimated market capitalization of all publicly traded equity REITs was $5.6 billion. By the end of 1994, it exceeded $38.8 billion, thanks primarily to the REIT offering boom of 1993 and 1994. In contrast, while 71 REIT offerings were completed just two years later (1995), only $6.2 billion was raised, including 5 REIT IPOs garnering just $800 million.

Market cap =
  Number of shares outstanding x Market price

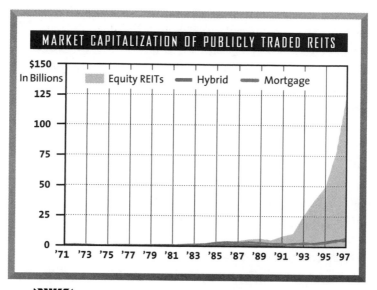

MARKET CAPITALIZATION OF PUBLICLY TRADED REITS

$150
In Billions — Equity REITs — Hybrid — Mortgage
'71 '73 '75 '77 '79 '81 '83 '85 '87 '89 '91 '93 '95 '97

SOURCE: NAREIT

While the 1994 slowing of the major bull trend in REITs' stock prices brought with it a subpar year for their investors, the IPO boom of the mid-1990s had a revolutionary effect on the REIT world: it was largely responsible for a huge increase in the number of REITs and property sectors in which investors could participate.

UNLIKE MANY SMALL-STOCK IPO frenzies that occur from time to time in U.S. stock market history, the REIT-IPO boom brought the public some of the most solid and well-respected real estate operating companies in the United States, including, to name just a few, Cali Realty, DeBartolo Realty, Developers Diversified, Kimco Realty, Post Properties, Simon Property Group, Taubman Centers, and Weeks Corp. Furthermore, the number of property sectors owned by REITs expanded widely. As a result of the success of these IPOs, these new sectors now included regional malls, factory outlet centers, industrial properties, manufactured-home communities, self-storage facilities, and hotels.

Why many of these companies went public has been the subject of much discussion. The cynics claim that, at some companies, insiders were taking the opportunity to cash out of some of their ownership at the expense of their new public shareholders, and, at others, opportunists were merely taking advantage of a hot IPO market. While these answers undoubtedly have some validity, there are more legitimate reasons to explain the phenomenon. In the early 1990s, the banks and savings and loan institutions had been so badly burned by nonperforming loans resulting from the real estate depression that they stopped providing the kind of real estate financing they had once routinely given. Cut off from their historical sources of private capital, many of these companies had good reason to seek access to public capital. Such public capital was expected to provide substantially greater financing flexibility. In addition, there was a growing perception in the minds of many managements that the "securitization" of real estate through REITs was becoming a major new trend and would help them to become stronger and more competitive organizations. A third reason might have been managements' desire to transform illiquid partnership ownership interests into publicly traded shares that could, from time to time, be more easily sold, transferred within the family, or used for estate-planning purposes. In this respect, these new REITs were not any different from other thriving enterprises that decided to go public as a way of solving financing, liquidity, and estate-tax issues.

The bottom line is that approximately 90 equity REITs did go public from 1992 through 1994, including some of the best real estate organizations in the country. As has been the trend recently through all industries, some have been taken over by or have merged with other REITs. Although there are mediocre performers among them, a large number of this new generation of REITs can make a legitimate claim to being outstanding real estate companies that should provide investors with excellent returns for many years into the future.

1994–95: THE REIT MARKET TAKES A BREATHER

EVEN BEFORE THE END of the IPO boom of 1993–94, the prices of many REIT stocks had cooled off considerably, particularly in the apartment and retail sectors. By the end of 1995, stocks of such outstanding REITs as Post Properties, United Dominion, and Weingarten were trading at prices well below their 1993 highs, and this was despite the continuing impressive FFO growth for 1994 and 1995. Post reported FFOs of $2.07, $2.25, and $2.53 in 1993, 1994, and 1995, respectively. Funds from operations thus increased by 22.2 percent from 1993 to 1995, yet Post's stock traded at $31 in October 1993 and had risen to only $31 $7/_8$ by the close of 1995. Another way of looking at this disappointing stock price performance is to compare P/FFO ratios. (FFOs and P/FFOs are explained in detail in Chapter 7.)

> P/FFO ratios consist simply of the stock price (P) at any given time, divided by the most recently reported (or estimated) FFO figures, on a per-share basis (P/FFO).

In October 1993, the P/FFO ratio for Post was 15.0; at the end of 1995 it was 12.6. Investors were therefore not willing to pay anywhere near as much per dollar of FFO in 1995 as they were in 1993. Post's experience was not unique; the same story applied to most of the apartment and retail REITs.

Other sectors did better, particularly in 1995. The prices as well as the P/FFO ratios of the industrial, office, and hotel REITs rose in response to investors' convictions that the overbuilt conditions plaguing these sectors from the late 1980s had dissipated, and that great acquisition opportunities were alive and well for those REITs with access to capital.

In all, although the average total return of equity

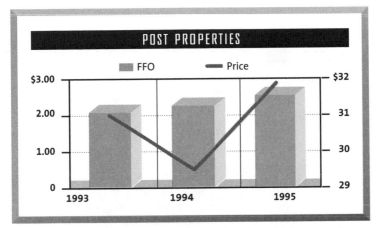

REITs was a disappointing 3.2 percent in 1994, according to NAREIT data, it recovered nicely in 1995, up 15.3 percent. While the equity REITs' 1994 performance was similar to that of the S&P 500 Index in 1994 (up 3.2 percent), it was outdone by non-REIT common stocks in 1995, when the S&P 500 Index rose by a whopping 37 percent *(see chart on the following page)*.

REASONS FOR THE REIT LULL

WHY DID MANY REITs fall out of favor in 1994–95, and why did the P/FFO ratios in the apartment and retail sectors decline so markedly? One of the benefits of being a historian is that causative events often become clearer with the passage of time. It might still be too early for us to understand completely what happened such a short time ago, but, even now, there are some contributing factors that can be seen.

First, lots of "hot money" was invested in REITs by non–real estate and non-REIT investors (such as individuals and mutual funds) in 1993 and early 1994, much of which was invested in the REIT IPOs of those years. Some of these investors were fickle "momentum traders," riding the uptrend in REIT prices but quick to take their money off the table when momentum slowed. Others, who were simply seeking higher yields than were available on short-term T-bills, sold their

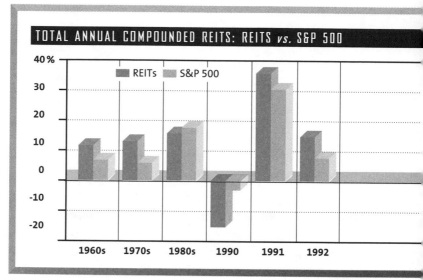

TOTAL ANNUAL COMPOUNDED REITS: REITS *vs.* S&P 500

REITs when interest rates rose in 1994.

Second, the REIT-IPO boom had overstayed its welcome, with supply eventually overwhelming the still limited demand for REIT shares by yield-oriented investors. This was particularly true in the apartment sector, where the number of REITs exploded from a preboom total of 5, to more than 28 only three years later.

Third, common-stock investors became so excited by the technology-led, major bull stock market of 1995 that they turned a cold shoulder to the 12 to 16 percent total returns historically provided by REITs, in favor of the potential for even greater appreciation in non-REIT stocks if the bull market continued.

Fourth, many new REIT investors had been misled by REITs' unusually high midteens FFO growth during the early '90s, and thus were unprepared in 1995 when the growth rate of many REITs, particularly in the apartment and retail sectors, returned to more normal levels of 5–8 percent annually. Their selling tended to retard the REIT stocks' continuing advance.

A final reason, at least with respect to the apartment and retail REITs, was that investors had become increasingly concerned about the prospect of supply-

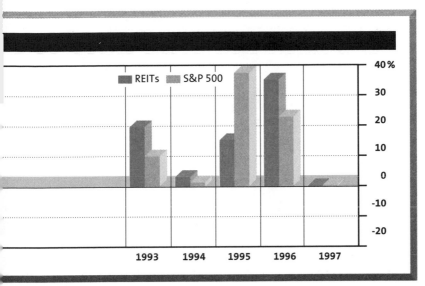

demand imbalances. In the apartment sector, new permits had been rising for quite some time, as the economics of apartment ownership continued to improve.
Some major cities were seeing supply catch up with
(and even exceed) demand, which led to lower occupancy rates and lower rent increases. In the case of the
retail sector, the news spread that consumers, suffering
from stagnant wages, were refusing to spend at the
malls and shopping centers, resulting in bankruptcy for
many retailers. Although these problems were temporary, investors don't like uncertainty, and their concerns quite likely contributed to the contraction of
P/FFO ratios in some sectors in 1994 and 1995.

**By 1996–97, securitization of real estate through
REIT offerings had become a major new investment trend.**

1996–97: THE NEW REIT BULL MARKET

THE YEAR 1996 was an exciting one for REIT
investors. NAREIT's Equity REIT Index logged in a
total return of 35.3 percent, comparing favorably with
a 23.0 percent total return for the S&P 500 Index.
While 1997 wasn't as spectacular, the NAREIT Equity

REIT Index nevertheless managed to turn a well above par total return of 20.3 percent. Why were REITs able to perform so well in these last two years? The following are some likely possibilities:

◆ **Faster growth.** REIT investors may have decided, based on what has been called our "Goldilocks economy" and REITs' "external" growth opportunities via acquisitions and developments, that REITs' future FFO growth would be significantly higher than previously anticipated. Whereas in 1995 folks might have thought that Beacon Properties, for example, would be able to increase FFO at 8 percent annually for the next few years, they might have concluded, as 1996 progressed, that 12–14 percent growth would be a "slam dunk." An upward revision in expected growth rates can cause a stock's price/earnings ratio (or, in a REIT's case, the P/FFO or P/AFFO ratio) to leap upwards, having a major positive effect on its price. When the projected growth rate for Bristol-Myers was being revised upwards by analysts in 1996, its "appropriate" price/earnings ratio went from 14 to 18. Similarly, to the degree that investors are willing to pay a substantially higher P/FFO or P/AFFO ratio for a REIT because of its more exciting growth opportunities, so will its price go up substantially. In fact, FFO growth in 1997 and into 1998 has been higher than previously anticipated. Sometimes the mere expectation of a stock's higher future growth rate will drive up its price.

◆ **Higher NAVs.** Those REIT investors who focus on net asset values (NAVs) when evaluating REIT stocks—in the belief that, in the final analysis, REIT values should be based on the value of their properties—may have been a bit chagrined by investors' enthusiasm for REITs in 1996. Why were investors willing to pay 35–40 percent premiums over NAVs for many REITs as 1996 drew to a close and 30 percent premiums well into 1997? The answer might be that the market was anticipating a decline in cap rates (a substantial increase in prices) for real estate, and the REIT market may have been discounting this decline.

As cap rates come down, the value of real estate goes up; the "hot" market for REIT stocks in 1996–97 may have discounted higher property values ahead.

Here again, the market has been proven correct, as cap rates have indeed declined in most real estate sectors. Lower cap rates can be justified by three possible explanations: first, the expectation of milder real estate cycles than in the past; second, a low-inflation and low–interest-rate environment brought about by the perception of competitive global markets and the end (for now) of government budget deficits; and third, the expected stable performance of high-quality real estate in an economy that continues to avoid the "next recession."

Real estate values may have been enhanced by:
— Milder cycles
— Low Inflation and interest rates
— Stable performance of quality real estate

◆ **Money flows.** Another possible reason for the recent bull REIT market, at least in 1996, is that, since REITs have now become liquid securities, they can thus compete with stocks and bonds for investors' attentions.

As the Dow soared and the long bond's yield fell to under 6 percent, investors may have decided that bonds and, to some extent, stocks, having provided double-digit returns for a couple of years, had gotten ahead of themselves, and that they should look elsewhere for value. REITs offer not only good value, but also reasonably good dividend yields and healthy FFO growth.

◆ **Institutional demand.** Another factor affecting the "great REIT bull market of 1996–97" was that increased institutional demand for REIT stocks drove prices relentlessly higher. Institutions are slowly but inexorably coming to the conclusion that the way to maximize the performance of their real estate investments is to invest in outstanding real estate companies, rather than to own real estate directly or through "commingled funds." While it's difficult to compare the performance of directly owned real estate with the performance of REIT stocks over the past 5, 10, or 20 years, the case can be made, anecdotally at least, that, since institutions are moving into REITs in a big way, direct real estate ownership becomes less attractive, and the volume of buying REITs increases.

Money managers and fund managers are now setting up new businesses devoted solely to the management of REIT portfolios. Institutional buying is having a major impact on the REIT market.

RECENT DEVELOPMENTS

AS 1997 DREW TO A CLOSE, several newer trends were becoming apparent to REIT investors: there was a significant pickup in REITs' merger-and-acquisition activity and in secondary offerings, and there was a significant rise in market caps, or market values, of outstanding shares for many REIT stocks.

Prior to 1995, REIT merger-and-acquisition activity was only an occasional phenomenon, but in that year things began to pick up; Wellsford Residential took over Holly Residential, HGI Realty took over McArthur/Glen, and BRE Properties took over REIT of California. These were significant transactions, but not earthshaking events.

Then, in 1996 and 1997, the merger-and-acquisition pace accelerated substantially. In 1996, Simon Property Group acquired another mall REIT, DeBartolo Realty, creating, at the time, the largest company within the REIT industry. Other noteworthy 1996 deals included Bradley's acquisition of Tucker Properties, Highwoods's purchase of Crocker, and South West's merger with United Dominion; these deals created much larger and more liquid REITs.

The rate of activity became even more frenzied in 1997. While there were many public REIT mergers (and acquisitions by REITs of private organizations) in that year, including the mergers of Columbus Realty, Evans Withycombe Residential, Paragon Group, ROC Communities, and Wellsford Residential, the largest and most interesting deals by far were Equity Office's acquisition of Beacon Properties, Starwood's winning the bidding contest for the huge ITT/Sheraton organization, and Patriot's merger deal with Wyndham Hotels (the latter two closing in 1998).

Another important trend for REITs in 1997 was the significant amount of funds raised in the equity capital markets, accelerating the pace of real estate securitization. There were close to 145 IPOs and secondary equity offerings completed by REITs in 1996, which raised a record $12.3 billion according to NAREIT. This was a significant increase from the $8.3 billion raised in 101 IPO and secondary offerings in 1995. However, these figures paled in comparison to 1997, when 266 IPOs and secondaries brought in almost $30 billion. These funds were used primarily for the continuing acquisition of commercial real estate from both individuals and institutions. The amount of commercial real estate acquired by REITs in 1996 set a record for the industry. Chris Lucas, NAREIT's former research director, has estimated that REITs now own approximately 30 percent of all equity in institutional-grade, commercial U.S. real estate, compared with just 10 percent at the end of 1993.

All of this activity has had the effect of significantly increasing the market caps of a large number of REITs. On December 31, 1994, there were only 4

REITs that had market caps over $1 billion. At the end of 1997, there were *47*.

The number of REITs with equity market caps of over $2 billion grew from 0 at the end of 1995 to 14 by the end of 1997.

A significant portion of the funds raised in 1996 was completed via "spot offerings," a new concept in the REIT industry. Because REITs' high payout ratio precludes their having enough free cash for additional acquisitions, the only way they can expand is by continually raising additional equity capital. A spot offering allows a REIT to file and maintain a "shelf" registration statement with the Securities and Exchange Commission (SEC), enabling the REIT to sell small offerings of shares "off the shelf." This type of financing mechanism should go a long way to satisfying REITs' continuing capital raising needs.

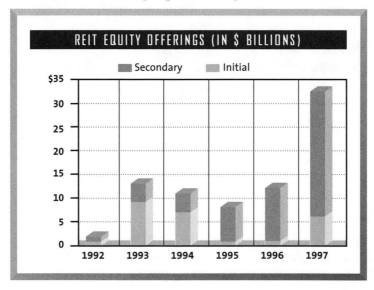

REIT EQUITY OFFERINGS (IN $ BILLIONS)

SOURCE: NAREIT

SUMMARY

◆ The first REITs, in the early 1960s, ranged from about $10–$50 million in size, their property management functions were handled by outside management agencies, and their combined assets were only about $200 million.

◆ As a result of their negative experience with mortgage REITs, investors of the 1970s became disenchanted with the entire REIT industry.

◆ During the 1980s, when investors were seeking the tax shelters offered by limited partnerships, real estate prices became inflated.

◆ REITs' performance improved in the early 1990s, because they were able to pick up property at bargain prices resulting from the bear market in real estate in the late 1980s.

◆ The IPO boom of the 1990s had a revolutionary effect on the REIT world: It was largely responsible for a huge increase in the number of REITs and property sectors in which investors could participate.

◆ As cap rates come down, the value of real estate goes up; the "hot" market for REIT stocks in 1996 and 1997 may have been discounting higher property values ahead as well as more rapid FFO growth.

◆ In 1996–97, institutional money managers started moving into REITs, and the trend of public securitization of real estate had become indelibly established.

◆ The number of REITs with equity market caps of over $2 billion grew from 0 at the end of 1995 to 14 by the end of 1997.

CHOOSING
REITs and
Watching Them
Grow

CHAPTER

REITs
HOW THEY GROW

THE SIGNIFICANCE OF FFOS

S AN ALL-STAR quarterback is to a football team, so are rising earnings to a stock, no matter what kind. Rising earnings are the sine qua non and the driving force behind the share price. Steadily rising earnings normally indicate not only that the REIT's rent roll is rising faster than its expenses, but also that it is making favorable acquisitions or completing profitable developments. Furthermore, higher income each year is a precursor of dividend growth, and, on a longer-term basis, this is what generally propels the stock price upwards.

Investors in common stock use "net income" as a key measure of profitability, but what is used in measuring a REIT is "funds from operations," or "FFO," since earnings and expenses of a REIT must be looked at differently from most non-REIT corporations. The Securities and Exchange Commission (SEC) has a blanket requirement that all publicly traded companies file audited financial statements. On a financial statement, the term "net income" has a meaning clearly defined under generally accepted accounting principles (GAAP). Since a REIT falls under the classification of a "publicly traded company," net income therefore appears on a REIT's audited financial statement. For a REIT, however, this figure is less meaningful as a measure of operating success than it is for other types of companies. The reason is that, in accounting, real estate "depreciation" is always treated as an expense, but, in the real world, not only have most well-maintained quality properties *retained* their value over the years, many have actually *appreciated*. In some cases, this is because of rising land values; in others, it is because of steadily rising rental income, property upgrades, or higher costs for new construction for competing properties. Whatever the reason, a REIT's net income, since it suffers from a large "depreciation" expense, is a less than meaningful measure of how the REIT's operations have actually fared. In the case of additional properties having recently been constructed or acquired, the depreciation expense—and thus also the distortion—is higher still.

Using FFO enables both REITs and their investors to correct the depreciation distortion, either by looking at net income before the deduction of the depreciation expense, or adding back depreciation expense to reported net income.

In using FFO, there are other adjustments that must be made as well, such as subtracting from net income any "income" recorded from the sale of properties. The reason for this is that the REIT can't have it both ways: In figuring FFO, it cannot *ignore depreciation,* which reduces the property cost on the balance sheet, and then *include the capital gain* from selling the property above the price at which it has been carried. Some REITs, in figuring FFO, have included an add-back of amortization charges on such items as IPO expenses, costs to "buy down" or cap the interest rates on debt, or amortized goodwill incurred in certain acquisitions. Furthermore, GAAP "net income" is normally determined after "straight lining," or smoothing out rental income over the term of the lease. This is another accounting device, but, in real life, rental income on a multiyear property lease is not smoothed out and often starts low but rises from year to year. For this reason, some REITs, when determining FFO, adjust "rent" to reflect actual rent revenue.

That mouthful of a definition is actually a significant step forward, since it enables investors to com-

FUNDS FROM OPERATIONS (FFO)

HISTORICALLY, FFO HAS been defined in different ways by different REITs, which has only exacerbated the confusion. To address this problem, NAREIT (The National Association of Real Estate Investment Trusts) has attempted to standardize the definition of FFO. In 1996, NAREIT declared that the term FFO, when used by REITs, should mean "net income" computed in accordance with GAAP, excluding gains (or losses) from debt restructuring and sales of property, plus depreciation of real property, and after adjustments for unconsolidated entities in which the REIT holds an interest.

pare the FFOs of different REITs.

Granted, the concept of FFO is superior to "net income," yet it is nevertheless flawed. For one thing, not all property retains its value year after year. There are some properties that actually depreciate, even considering the underlying value of the land. Adding back depreciation, then, to net income, in order to determine FFO, may provide a distorted and overly rosy picture of operating results.

The very term "depreciation" allows yet another opportunity for distortion when it comes to items that might fall more under general maintenance, such as, for example, an apartment building's carpeting. The cost of such carpeting often might not be expensed for accounting purposes; instead, it might be capitalized and depreciated over its useful life. When such "real-property" depreciation is added back to arrive at FFO, the FFO will be artificially inflated and thus give a misleading picture. Practically speaking, although carpeting, to use our example, really does depreciate over time, its replacement in a building does not significantly increase the property's value and its depreciation shouldn't be considered in the same way as depreciation on a physical structure.

Additionally, leasing commissions paid for the rental of offices or other properties are usually capitalized, then amortized over the term of the lease. These commission amortizations, when added to net income as a means of deriving FFO, can similarly inflate that figure. The same can also be said about tenant improvement allowances, such as those provided to office and mall tenants. Usually, these are so specific to the needs of a particular tenant that they do not increase the long-term value of the property.

Short-term maintenance expenses cannot be considered property-enhancing capital improvements, and they should be subtracted from FFO to give an accurate picture of a REIT's operating performance.

Unfortunately, not all REITs capitalize and expense similar items in similar ways when announcing their FFOs each quarter. With only FFO as a gauge, investors and analysts are still without an industry standard in terms of the way adjustments to net income are reflected. REIT portfolio manager Samuel Lieber agrees that "FFO is flawed as a performance measure because it allows many cash expenditures to be capitalized or amortized," and suggests that the REIT industry needs some standardization of its valuation terminology in order to maintain its credibility.

The term born of this need is "AFFO," or "adjusted funds from operations," which was coined by Green

ADJUSTED FUNDS FROM OPERATIONS (AFFO)

AFFO IS THE FFO as used by the REIT, adjusted for expenditures that, though capitalized, do not really enhance the value of a property, and adjusted further by eliminating straight lining of rents.

Street Advisors, Inc., a leading REIT research firm.

While FFO as a valuation tool is clearly more useful to REIT investors than net income under GAAP, NAREIT maintains that "FFO was never intended to be used as a measure of the cash generated by a REIT, nor of its dividend-paying capacity." Adjusted funds from operations, on the other hand, is by far the most accurate measure of a REIT's operating performance and is a much better tool to measure cash generation and the ability to pay dividends. Unfortunately, AFFO is normally not specifically reported by a REIT, and the investor or analyst must calculate it on his or her own by reviewing the financial statement.

Revenues *minus:*
- Operating expenses
- Depreciation & amortization
- Interest expense
- General & administrative expense   = NET INCOME

Net Income *minus:*
- Profit from real estate sales

plus:
- Real estate depreciation   = FFO

FFO *minus:*
- Recurring capital expenditures
- Amortization of tenant improvements
- Amortization of leasing commissions
- Adjustment for rent straight lining   = AFFO

In comparative valuations of two different REITs, then, it is important to remember to compare apples to apples and oranges to oranges. If, for one REIT, the valuation measurement you're using is price/AFFO (P/AFFO), then for the REIT you're comparing it to, you must not use price/FFO (P/FFO) or price/net income. In Appendix E, you'll find an explanation of how P/FFO or P/AFFO ratios can be determined, which includes two similar terms not specifically described here, FAD (Funds Available for Distribution) and CAD (Cash Available for Distribution); FAD and CAD are normally very similar to AFFO.

In valuing a REIT, forget "net income"; AFFO is the way to go—it is the most accurate means for determining a REIT's profitability.

Now that we have established the difference between these two important terms we will refer to both FFO—"funds from operations," and AFFO—"adjusted funds from operations."

When we discuss the price/earnings ratio of a REIT's common stock, we will use either the P/FFO ratio or the P/AFFO ratio, with the understanding that, although we are trying to be as consistent as possible, sometimes true consistency is not attainable, and we must therefore be aware of how these substitutes for net income are calculated for each REIT.

THE DYNAMICS OF FFO GROWTH

WHAT MAKES REIT SHARES so attractive compared with other high-yield investments like bonds and utility stocks is their significant capital appreciation potential and steadily increasing dividends. If a REIT didn't have the ability to increase its FFO, its shares would offer no more than a bond, and they would be bought only for their yield. Because of the greater risk, of course, their yield would always be higher than a Treasury bond's, but their price would correlate with their fluctuations of long-term interest rates and investors' perceptions of the REIT's ability to continue paying its dividend.

FFO should not be looked upon as a static figure, and it is up to management to continue to seek methods of increasing it.

We can sometimes find REITs that *do* trade as bond surrogates because of investor perception that they have very little growth potential. Some of these pseudo-bonds can be of high quality because of the stability of their stream of rental income, while others can be compared to junk bonds because of their high yields but uncertain flow of rental revenues. These "junk-bond" REITs may be traded, sometimes profitably, by bottom fishers and speculators, but such yield chasers are playing a dangerous game.

Long-term investors should be looking at REITs with dividends that are not just safe but also have good growth prospects. Wouldn't you rather own a REIT that pays a current return of 6 percent and grows 8 percent every year than one that pays 10 percent and doesn't grow at all?

Only once in a great while is it possible to get the best of both worlds—a 10 percent yield *and* 8 percent annual growth. But, with REITs, as with everything else, there's usually no such thing as a free lunch. A REIT that yields 10 percent almost always means that investors perceive very low growth or, even worse, a potential dividend cut.

All right, then, how does a REIT generate growth in FFO, and what should you look for? First of all, it is very important to look at FFO growth on a *per-share* basis. It does the shareholder no good if FFO grows rapidly because the REIT has issued large amounts of new shares. Such prosperity is meaningless—like a government printing up more money in times of inflation. Remember, also, that REITs, by definition, must pay their shareholders at least 95 percent of their taxable net income each year but, as a practical matter, most REITs pay out considerably more than this, as depreciation expense is also taken into account when setting the dividend rate. So, if REITs want to achieve external growth through acquisitions, where is the cash going to come from? They

must go to the capital markets, which means selling more shares, and such new capital is not always available—and can be very expensive. All of this means that internal growth—which can be accomplished without having to raise more equity or take on additional debt—is very important to a REIT and its shareholders.

FFO can grow two ways: externally—by acquisitions and developments—and internally—through a REIT's existing resources.

REIT investors and analysts need to understand exactly how much of a REIT's growth is being achieved internally and how much is being achieved externally. External growth, through new developments and acquisitions, may not always be possible, because of a lack of available, high-quality properties at attractive prices, inability to raise capital, or the high cost of such capital. Internal growth, on the other hand, since it is generated through a REIT's existing resources, is more under management's control.

INTERNAL GROWTH

INTERNAL GROWTH IS growth via an improvement in profits at the *property* level, through increased rental revenues (higher rents and occupancy rates) and reduced expenses at one or more of the specific properties owned by the REIT. Since it is not dependent on acquisitions, development, or outside capital, it is the most stable and reliable source of FFO growth.

Before we examine the specific sources of REITs' internal growth, however, we should review one of the terms that analysts use in reference to internal growth. The term is "same-store" sales—a concept taken from retail but also used in nonretail REIT sectors. In a retail operation, the term same-store sales refers to sales from stores open for at least one year, and excludes sales from stores that have closed or from new stores, since new stores characteristically have high sales growth.

Although the term "same-store" sales was originally a retail concept, it has been borrowed for use by other, nonretail REIT sectors to refer to growth that is internal, rather than from new development or acquisition.

Once you consider what the same-store concept means in retail, you can see how it might be applied to various REIT sectors. A REIT management entity often breaks down how much of its increase in FFO has been derived from same-store, rental revenue increases (and net operating income—or "NOI"—on a same-store basis), and how much from "new stores," *i.e.,* recent property developments and acquisitions. Same-store rental revenues, offset by related expenses, determines NOI growth, which presents a good picture of how well the REIT is doing with its *existing* properties.

Property owners, including REITs, use different tools to generate growth on a same-store basis. These tools include rental increases, upgrading the tenant roll, and upgrading the property. Those REITs that are more aggressive and creative in their use of these tools are more likely to achieve higher internal growth rates.

RENTAL REVENUE INCREASES

The most obvious type of internal growth, the ability to raise rental rates and revenue—regardless of property sector—is probably a REIT's most important determinant of internal growth.

RENTAL RATES CAN BE increased if the property is in demand by tenants, and higher occupancy rates can lead to even higher rental revenues. Nevertheless, raising rents is not always possible, and there are periods in the sector's cycle when such revenues actually fall rather than rise. Anyone who owned office buildings in the 1980s and early 1990s knows there's no guarantee the rent can be raised—or even maintained at the same level—when the lease comes up for renewal. Even if the rent is raised slightly, if the tenant demands too much in the way of property improvements, the lease may still not be profitable. In addition, unit rent increases can be wiped out by high vacancy rates and rental concessions. Similar problems were faced by apartment owners in the late '80s, when half-empty apartment buildings put the tenants in the driver's seat in negotiating rents on new leases. Many factors, such as supply and demand for a particular property or property sector, the current economic climate, and the condition of a property, can restrict rental revenue increases.

"Effective rents" =
Quoted rental rates minus Rental concessions

At the present time, the apartment sector is well along in its property cycle, and the recent pace of new construction has brought the level of available units into equilibrium with demand in most areas of the United States, with overbuilding a problem only in some cities in the Southeast and Southwest. With the exception of occasional problem areas, rental revenue growth for apartments should continue, although more slowly than the torrid pace of the last few years. Growth will come from mildly increasing rents rather than from occupancy gains. In the event of a recession, of course, projected absorption rates might prove to have been too optimistic. If apartment owners were to see some occupancy slippage, they would have difficulty raising rents until the economy recovered.

In retail, both malls and factory outlet centers have been able to raise rental rates modestly despite the poor retailing environment of recent years. In malls, tenants have signed new, more expensive leases to replace the leases signed during the years when sales volumes were lower than they are now. In the long run, however, rent increases will generally not be able to outpace the rise in same-store sales.

Self-storage facilities have shown similar steady success, although recently their growth has slowed just a bit. Their popularity, coupled with only moderate building over the past few years, has enabled owners of these facilities to increase rents frequently since 1991, and, even with a slight slowdown, they should still be able to do well. Hotels have likewise enjoyed increased room rates in recent years, and investors in hotel REITs expect this to continue, particularly in the full-service and some extended-stay subsectors.

In contrast, the owners of neighborhood shopping centers have had a more difficult time raising rents, since the supply of such centers has exceeded the demand, and same-store sales increases have been modest. Consumers' preference for "value retailers" such as Wal-Mart, Target, and K-Mart may also have had an influence on rental and occupancy rates.

Office rents, too, suffered years of softness in most areas of the country, but bottomed out in the mid-1990s. Now, office owners as well as owners of industrial property are getting significant rental rate increases when they sign new leases, and occupancy rates have been rising.

An advantage of health care–facility REITs is that, although in a *down* market they offer the protection of long-term leases with locked-in rents, in an *up* market they have lease clauses that enable them to share in profits. Base rents for these facilities should remain stable.

Although it may be an oversimplification, most real estate observers seem to think that owners of well-maintained properties in markets where supply and demand are in balance can continue to get rental revenue increases at least equal to inflation. We are talking here only about broad-based industry trends; some REITs—and their managements—are more adept than others at getting lease renewals and getting them at higher rates. Trying to determine *which* REITs and their properties have better than average potential rental revenue and NOI growth is the challenge—and the fun—of REIT investing.

HOW TO BUILD RISING FFO INTO THE LEASE

MANY PROPERTY OWNERS have been able to obtain above-average increases in rental revenues by using methods that focus on tenants' needs and their financial ability to pay higher effective rental rates. These methods include percentage rent, rent bumps, and expense sharing.

PERCENTAGE RENT

"PERCENTAGE-RENT" CLAUSES in retail-store leases enable the property owner to participate in store revenues if such revenues exceed certain preset levels.

A retail lease's percentage-rent clause might be structured so that if the store's sales exceed $5 million for any calendar year, the lessee must pay the landlord 3 percent of the excess, in the form of additional rent. The extent to which lessees will agree to this revenue sharing depends on the property location, the market demand for the space, the base rent, and the property owner's reputation for upgrading shopping centers to make them more attractive to shoppers. This concept carries over from retail to other areas, and health care REITs have structured most of their leases (and even their mortgages when the REIT provides mortgage financing) in the same way, so that the owner shares in same-store revenue growth above certain minimum levels; in some cases, the rent increases are "capped" at predetermined levels.

RENT BUMPS

"RENT BUMPS" ARE lease clauses that provide for built-in rent increases every few years. Office and industrial-property owners who enter into long-term leases are often able to structure the lease so that the base rent "bumps up" every few years, providing built-in rental rate increases and improving same-store NOI. The rent-bump device is also popular with owners of health care facilities, who use them in leases with their health care operators, and with retailers, who use them to match leasing costs with projected longer-term revenues from the stores' operations.

EXPENSE SHARING

"EXPENSE SHARING" OR "cost sharing" is a way in which owners have persuaded their lessees to share expenses that at one time were borne by the landlord, and have included "cost-sharing" clauses in their leases to increase rental revenues.

In the case of office buildings, the lessees might pay a portion of the increased operating expenses, including higher insurance, property taxes, and on-site management costs. Similarly, mall, factory outlet center, and other retail owners have, over the last several years, been able to obtain reimbursement from their lessees for certain common-area maintenance operating expenses, such as janitorial services, security, advertising, and promotion.

Many savvy residential property owners have put separate electric and water meters, or even separate heating units, into their apartments, with a twofold benefit. The owner is protected from rising energy costs, and the tenant is encouraged to save energy.

Cost-sharing lease clauses improve NOI, and thereby FFO, while tending to smooth out fluctuations from year to year. The degree to which they can be used depends on a property's supply-demand situation and location, as well as the property owner's ability to justify them to the lessee. Simon DeBartolo Group, for example, may, on the basis of its size and reputation for creative marketing, be able to get lease provisions a weaker mall owner could not.

OTHER WAYS TO GENERATE INTERNAL GROWTH

THERE ARE TWO WAYS to improve a property: One is by upgrading the tenants; the other is by upgrading the property, through renovation or redecoration. Both can be effective.

TENANT UPGRADES

CREATIVE OWNERS OF retail properties have been able to increase rental revenues significantly by replacing mediocre tenants with attractive new ones. Retailers who offer innovative products generate higher customer traffic and boost sales at both the store and the shopping center, and successful tenants can afford higher rents.

This ability to upgrade tenants is what distinguishes a truly innovative property owner from the rest. Kimco Realty, which boasts one of the most respected managements in the retail REIT sector, maintains a huge database of tenants that might improve its centers' profitability. This resource, along with the strong relationship Kimco has with high-quality national and regional retailers, allows it to upgrade its tenant base within an existing retail center on a continual basis. In the factory outlet center niche, Chelsea/GCA has been a leader in replacing poorly performing tenants with those who can draw big crowds, enhancing the value of the property and providing higher rent to the property owner.

Tenant upgrades are even more important during weak retailing periods. Late in 1995 and into 1996, many retailers, having been squeezed by sluggish consumer demand and inroads made upon them by Wal-Mart and other discount stores, filed for bankruptcy. Those mall owners who replaced poorly performing apparel stores with theaters, restaurants, and other unique retailing concepts prospered; those who did not encountered flat-to-declining mall revenues, vacancy increases, and declining or stagnating rental rates upon lease renewal.

PROPERTY REFURBISHMENTS

REFURBISHMENT IS A SKILL that separates the innovative property owner from the passive one. This ability can turn a tired mall, neighborhood shopping center, or office building into a vibrant, upscale center likely to attract good tenants and customers.

Successfully refurbishing a property has several benefits. The upgraded and beautified property attracts a more stable tenant base and commands higher rents and, for retail properties, more shoppers. On such investments, the returns to the REIT property owner can often be almost embarrassingly high.

Federal Realty, in particular, has had a long track record of completing successful property-refurbishing and tenant-upgrade programs in the retail sphere, often with excellent investment returns. Likewise, Kimco Realty's very imaginative management has successfully acquired and "demalled" older, poorly performing malls, turning them into more exciting, easily accessible, open-air shopping complexes. In the apartment sector, United Dominion and, more recently, Bay Apartment Communities and Home Properties, have been buying apartment buildings with deferred maintenance problems at very cheap prices, then successfully upgrading and refurbishing them. The lesson here for investors is that REITs with innovative management can create value for their shareholders through imaginative refurbishing and tenant-upgrade strategies.

SALE AND REINVESTMENT

SOMETIMES INVESTMENT RETURNS can be improved by selling properties with dim future rental growth prospects, and then reinvesting the proceeds elsewhere. REITs that own a number of properties should "clean house" from time to time and consider which properties to keep and which to sell, using the capital from the sale for reinvestment in more promising properties. This is still considered internal growth, since it is financed by the sale of existing properties and does not require new capital.

Truly entrepreneurial managements are always looking to improve investment returns, and sale and reinvestment is one conservative and highly effective strategy.

For example, a property might be sold at a 7.5 percent cap rate, and the net proceeds invested in another (perhaps underperforming) property that, with a

CAP RATE

"CAP RATE" IS roughly equivalent to the cash flow available to the purchaser, measured as a percentage of the purchase price, based on existing rental and occupancy rates.

modest investment of capital and upgraded tenant services, might provide a return of 10–11 percent or more within a year or two. This approach to value creation does not require significant use of a REIT's capital resources, since the capital to acquire the new property is created through the sale of the old property.

Again, as with tenant upgrading and property refurbishing, this is something to watch for. REIT managements are always alert for new opportunities and should have no emotional attachments to a property just because they've owned it for a while, or because it's performed well in the past. Post Properties and United Dominion Realty, two premier apartment REITs, have been selling off some properties with less than exciting future growth prospects and reinvesting the proceeds elsewhere. Another excellent apartment REIT, Security Capital Pacific, has sold a large number of apartment buildings in order to raise cash for its new apartment development program in higher-growth areas.

As we've seen here, REITs' internal-growth opportunities are as numerous as their property types. In the hands of shrewd management, these options can be maximized so that results pay off for both the REIT and its investors. However, internal growth isn't the only way REITs can expand revenues and funds from operations. There is another.

EXTERNAL GROWTH

LET'S ASSUME, FOR purposes of discussion, that the typical REIT can get average annual rental revenue increases equal to or slightly better than the rate of inflation, say 3 percent, and that expenses and over-head growth can be held to less than 3 percent. Let's assume further that with modest, fixed-rate debt lever-age, the typical REIT can increase its FFO by 4.5 per-cent. Finally, let's assume that the well-managed REIT can achieve another 0.5 percent annual growth through tenant upgrades, refurbishments, and prop-erty sales and reinvestments. How do we get from this 5 percent FFO growth to the 6–12 percent pace some REITs have been able to achieve for a number of years? The answer is through *external* growth, a process by which a real estate organization, such as a REIT, acquires or develops *additional properties* that generate profits for the organization's owners. Let's look at the ways in which this can occur.

External growth can be generated through attractive property acquisitions, development, and expansion.

ACQUISITION OPPORTUNITIES

THE CONCEPT OF acquiring additional properties at attractive initial yields and with substantial NOI growth potential has been applied successfully for many years by long-established and successful REITs, such as Federal Realty, New Plan Realty, Washington

---

ACQUISITIONS

"ACCRETIVE" ACQUISITIONS ARE dependent on a REIT's access to the capital market and the cost of such capital, the strength of its balance sheet, and the prevailing cap rates on the type of property it wants to acquire. Also, we cannot forget that it is crucial that the acquired properties have significant NOI growth potential, which, together with the initial yield, will provide internal rates of return equal to, or in excess of, the REIT's true weighted average cost of capital.

REIT, and Weingarten Realty, and has since been duplicated by most REITs.

For example, a REIT might raise $100 million through a combination of selling additional shares and medium-term promissory notes which, allowing for the dilution from the newly issued shares and the interest costs on the debt, might have a nominal capital cost of 8 percent. It would then use the proceeds to buy properties that yield 10 percent on their acquisition cost. The net result of such transactions would be an incremental "accretive" FFO increase equal to 2 percent of $100 million, or $2 million on day one. We must keep in mind, however, that obtaining an initial yield in excess of a REIT's nominal cost of capital, while important, is less meaningful than being able to find and acquire properties able to deliver longer-term internal rates of return that equal or exceed the REIT's true cost of capital.

A strong acquisition is simply not available to a REIT that cannot raise either equity capital (perhaps because of poor prior performance, unproved management, or limited growth prospects) or debt capital (when its balance sheet is already heavily leveraged). It's also unavailable if the REIT's nominal cost of capital, including both equity and debt, is higher than the yields that can be obtained from new acquisitions; dilutive acquisitions will not be popular with REIT investors.

The early '90s were a golden acquisition era for apartment REITs, which may be why so many of them went public during that time period. The best of them, like United Dominion, could raise equity capital at a nominal cost of 7 percent, and debt capital at 8 percent. They could then acquire apartment properties, in the aftermath of the real estate depression of the late '80s, that provided them with entry yields of 11 percent or more. (The sellers were troubled partnerships, over-leveraged owners, banks owning repossessed properties, or the Resolution Trust Corporation [RTC].)

Property Yields:

> = (Cash flow before depreciation and interest expense)
> ÷ Purchase price

At first glance it may seem odd that properties could become available at such substantial entry yields (*i.e.,* high cap rates), but, if a type of property in a particular location has few willing buyers but lots of anxious sellers, the purchase price will be low in relationship to the anticipated cash flow from the property, and entry yields to the property buyer will be substantial. At the bottom of property cycles we often see such supply-demand imbalances, since, with abundant foreclosures, not only are owners anxious to cut their losses, but property refinancings are unavailable, and confidence levels are low.

Outstanding acquisitions opportunities had waned for most apartment REITs by 1995—as entry yields on potential acquisitions declined to a rate just a bit above the REITs' nominal cost of capital—but are still alive and well in other sectors. The largest health care REITs have enjoyed profitable acquisitions for many years, and continue to do so today. Stubbornly high cap rates on office buildings, industrial properties, self-storage facilities, hotels, and neighborhood shopping centers have been driving excellent FFO growth for REITs making acquisitions in those sectors. While cap rates are now declining, property buyers (including, of course, the REITS) are expecting an offsetting advantage in the form of stronger NOI growth. How long this will continue is dependent upon the amount of new development and the strength of the economy. Mall REITs were unable to find attractive acquisitions until 1996, as mall cap rates have generally been equal to or lower than the mall REITs' nominal cost of capital. Until recently, there have been few sellers in this sector because malls, traditionally owned by major institutions and pension plans, have often been financed without leverage, and the good ones have produced such stable yields. Some malls were acquired at favorable cap rates in 1996 and 1997, but cap rates began to decline again at the end of 1997.

The importance of attractive investment opportunities to a REIT's FFO growth rate and stock price cannot be overemphasized.

It's crucial to understand that, for any REIT, the true measure of property acquisition goes far beyond the initial yield spread from "accretion." When professional real estate organizations like REITs take over a new property, they are often able to operate and manage it more efficiently and profitably than the prior owner did. Thus, not only can such a REIT earn additional FFO from the spread between the initial yield and the nominal cost of capital, but it can also obtain excellent *internal* growth from acquired properties by controlling expenses and spreading them over more units, even assuming no change in rents.

A final and very important point on acquisitions. When we talk about accretion to FFO, we are talking about the difference, or *spread,* between what the REIT can earn on its invested capital (for example, the cash flow that a newly acquired apartment will provide to the REIT buyer), and the REIT's nominal cost of capital. But just what is the REIT's "cost of capital"? The cost of *debt* capital is fairly straightforward—it is simply the interest that the REIT pays for borrowed funds. However, we should be careful not to use *short-term* interest rates, since drawdowns under a credit line are temporary and must be repaid relatively quickly. Calculations should be based on rates for debt that will be outstanding for seven to ten years, which will usually be higher than short-term interest rates. Using the short-term rate would distort the picture, making it seem that the REIT is able to borrow short term at 6 percent to buy 8 percent cap-rate properties—at times when the cost of long-term debt is actually 8 percent, a very attractive piece of fiction, but a fiction nonetheless.

What REIT investors need to remember on the issue of acquisitions is this:

◆ Investors should want a REIT to acquire properties that will offer sufficient growth prospects to generate total rates of return that will equal or exceed the REIT's blended true cost of capital. For most REITs, that cost is approximately 10 percent.

◆ A REIT whose shares trade in the market at a relatively high P/FFO ratio will generally have a lower nominal cost of equity capital (though not necessarily a lower true cost of equity capital) than a REIT trading at a lower ratio. A lower nominal cost of capital enhances the REIT's ability to find and make acquisitions that are, in the short term, accretive to FFO.

DEVELOPMENT AND EXPANSION

Some REITs can increase external FFO growth by developing entirely new properties, whether they are apartments, malls, outlet centers, neighborhood shopping centers, or any other property sector.

UNTIL THE REIT-IPO boom of 1993–94, very few public REITs had the capability of developing new properties from the ground up. To do that takes specialized skill and experience. Today, REITs with those attributes are not uncommon, and we see them in almost all sectors. A well-conceived development program requires capital as well as know-how. New properties require financing during the 12 to 24 months required to build them out and bring in the new tenants. Having development capabilities is a key advantage, for they allow REITs to grow externally when markets are "hot," a time when, because cap rates are low, finding attractive acquisitions is very difficult. Suc-

THE COST OF EQUITY CAPITAL

THE COST OF equity capital is a misunderstood concept. What does it really cost a REIT and its shareholders to issue more shares? The REIT must pay dividends on its new shares, so that's a cash outflow (even if it's not considered a "cost" under GAAP). But, because there will be more shares outstanding following the issuance, the value of the REIT (including its net assets and its stream of income well into the future) must be shared with more investors.

There are several ways to calculate such cost of equity capital. "Nominal" cost of equity capital refers to the fact that a REIT's current earnings (FFO or AFFO) and its net assets must be allocated over a larger number of common shares, while "true" or "long-term" cost of equity capital considers such dilution over longer time periods and gives credence to shareholders' total return expectations on their invested capital. This subject, though important, is an arcane one. What's important for investors, however, is that they focus not just on the initial "accretion" to FFO from an acquisition, but also upon the longer-term NOI growth potential from an acquired property. *(For more information on cost of equity capital, see Appendix E.)*

cessful developments can provide 10 to 12 percent returns on a REIT's investment, usually a much higher figure than returns on the acquisition of existing properties. Furthermore, the REIT's net asset value should be significantly enhanced, since, when lower cap rates are applied to newly developed and fully leased properties, extra property value is created, which, over time, may enhance the price of the REIT's stock. Some mall REITs, for example, have been able to develop new malls that provide 11 to 12 percent entry yields and could be sold at 8 percent cap rates.

Such capability also allows a REIT to capitalize on unique opportunities. For example, several years ago,

Weingarten Realty was able to obtain a parcel of property directly across the boulevard from Houston's Galleria, one of the premier shopping complexes in America, and build an attractive new center in that location. CarrAmerica Realty and Weeks Corp., similarly, were able to develop office and industrial properties, respectively, at yields not available to buyers of existing properties.

Although a REIT can contract with an outside builder to complete a development, it will not be as profitable because of the builder's need to generate his or her own profit. Furthermore, the REIT will lack full control over the project, thus increasing the risk.

All else being equal, it is better to own REITs with successful track records of property development, since they have yet another avenue for increasing per-share FFO growth.

Of course, property development does have a downside—the risks. What can go wrong? Plenty. Cost overruns can significantly reduce expected returns. The projected rents or anticipated occupancy might come in under estimates, a particular risk if the development occurs when a favorable property cycle ends abruptly. Overbuilding is a real danger to rental and occupancy estimates, and some analysts fear that this is an imminent event in certain apartment markets. If the national, regional, or local economy goes into recession, of course, the situation becomes even worse. REIT investors and managements alike *should* expect higher returns from development in order to be compensated for taking greater risks.

A parallel method of external growth closely related to new development is the expansion of existing successful properties. Some development capability is required here, but the risks are significantly smaller for two reasons: The existing property has proven itself, and the cost of adding space is less than developing property from scratch. Furthermore, while the *total* profit potential from an expansion may be less than that from an entirely new project, the *percentage* return from the expansion is often higher.

Nothing beats seeing a REIT announce it's adding "phase 2" or "phase 3" to an existing successful property. This generally indicates that the existing property is doing well, that management has had the foresight to acquire adjacent land, and that the risk/return ratio is favorable. Many well-regarded REITs in various property sectors have the ability to add expansion properties, sometimes even when they don't have full development capabilities.

SUMMARY

◆ Using FFO enables both REITs and their investors to correct the depreciation distortion.

◆ FFO should not be looked upon as a static figure, and it is up to management to continue to seek methods of raising it.

◆ AFFO is the most accurate means for determining REITs' income streams.

◆ FFO can grow two ways: externally, by acquisition and developments, and internally, through a REIT's existing resources.

◆ Internal growth is the most stable and reliable source of FFO growth since it does not depend on new capital or acquisitions, but only on reducing expenses and raising rental income at the property level.

◆ External growth can be generated through attractive property acquisitions, development, and expansion.

◆ The importance of attractive investment opportunities to a REIT's FFO growth rate and stock price cannot be overemphasized.

CHAPTER

Spotting the
BLUE CHIPS

As with any type of investing, a number of different selection approaches can be used depending on investment goals and styles. We can find companies of the highest quality, buy them, and hold them patiently over the long term. Or we can take a chance and go for the quick payoff. We can also try to pick up REITs that are down on their luck and watch for the turnaround. It's also possible to stress hidden value and search for the little-known gems. It's just a question of investment style.

INVESTMENT STYLES

SOME NON-REIT investors have done well by buying and owning the large, steadily growing companies with excellent long-term track records, such as Coca-Cola, General Electric, or Merck. Peter Lynch calls these stocks "stalwarts." Other investors have looked for companies growing at very rapid rates, such as Cisco or Microsoft. "Contrarian" or "value" investors buy shares whose prices are temporarily depressed by bad news that will eventually dissipate, or that might be relevant to much of the industry but not to that particular company. Some investors like to buy "small-cap" shares in growing companies most people have never heard of. All these approaches can work—for REITs as well as for other stocks—if the investor is disciplined and patient and exercises good judgment. There is no consensus as to which style works best, and a Warren Buffett–type guru of the REIT world has yet to emerge.

Most investors, but not all, will want to own blue-chip REITs. Those seeking quality and safety above all else certainly will. It is vital for *all* REIT investors to know what makes a blue-chip REIT different from the rest, since it's the blue chips that set the standards by which all others should be measured. Before we take on the blue chips, however, we'll examine a few of the others.

GROWTH REITS

GROWTH REITS ARE those viewed by investors as having the ability to increase funds from operations (FFO) much faster than other REITs. This growth potential may be because a specific sector is enjoying the boom phase of its property cycle when rental rates and occupancies are rising rapidly, or because their management's strategy is to implement a very aggressive acquisition or development program. This pattern of growth in a REIT requires a lot of new equity and debt capital to expand the business and property portfolio. If the newly raised capital is used to acquire properties that are cheaply priced and offer healthy rental and net operating income (NOI) growth prospects, management ends up looking very clever. If, however, management pays too much for the acquired properties (which, of course, can often only be determined with 20-20 hindsight) and the market then becomes overbuilt or takes a downturn, the REIT will be hard pressed to meet investors' lofty expectations and the stock of a growth-oriented company may have a long way to fall.

As long as a growth REIT can stay one step ahead of investors' expectations it can deliver exciting returns, but it's very important to know when the growth rate will be slowing significantly.

Several hotel REITs, for example, have been in a high-growth phase for the past few years. They have been enjoying above-average internal growth while acquiring billions of dollars in new hotels. Their FFOs have been increasing rapidly. Those who bought them in 1995, 1996, and into 1997 have seen their stock prices increase substantially. Growth-oriented REIT investors will seek out such opportunities and may, with good market timing, "beat the market." The key is knowing when to get out.

VALUE OR "TURNAROUND" REITS

IF YOU'RE A "value" investor, you always have a large choice of depressed REITs to choose from—these are REITs that are selling for very low relative valuations. This might be because they're below the radar screens of most investors, or because they own marginal properties, or because they have gotten into trouble recently. They might be excellent short- or even long-term investments if they're cheap enough or if you can get them just prior to a turnaround in their performance. CarrAmerica Realty is a good example. This office REIT was languishing a few years ago and had no access to capital to take advantage of the recovering office markets. The stock was selling at cheap prices despite excellent management. However, a short time later the savvy folks at Security Capital Group, a multi-billion-dollar real estate investment organization, agreed to acquire a controlling interest in CarrAmerica, and those who bought before the Security Capital Group transaction have been extremely well rewarded.

Investors can do very well buying a depressed REIT in hopes of a turnaround—but they should be aware of the risk. It's very difficult to differentiate between an investment that has bottomed out and one that's still on the way down.

Cheap REITs have potentially serious pitfalls that include questionable dividends, high debt leverage, and suspect managements. REITs like this can be compared to junk bonds—high risk *sometimes* brings high rewards. Proceed with caution, though, because these REITs don't usually have good access to capital. If they do manage to secure equity or debt capital, they may have to pay *so much* for it that they find it difficult to compete in the acquisition marketplace. Investors, therefore, will be faced with profitless growth.

Sometimes investors do very well with a turnaround REIT, but it's important to remember that some of these investments never make a comeback.

BOND-PROXY REITS

ANOTHER TYPE OF REIT that might be appealing to some investors is one that can be referred to as a bond proxy. It generates relatively slow FFO and dividend growth, but, because of its low debt and stable properties, it has a reasonably secure dividend, one that is usually higher than that of most REITs. Adjectives like "reliable" and "consistent" describe these REITs. They might include certain health care, retail, and apartment REITs that are not blessed with easy access to cheap capital for acquisitions. Tanger Factory Outlet Centers, for example, is a well-respected REIT, with moderate debt levels and with a substantial dividend that is well covered by its FFO. However, because of its sector's unpopularity with investors, it hasn't had easy access to attractively priced capital. Another in this category might be a "triple-net" REIT, one that is locked into leases with creditworthy tenants for long periods of time. Such a REIT, while very stable, is not expected to generate significant rent increases.

Bond-proxy REITs do provide high dividend yields, in the range of 7–9 percent, but they have less well-defined growth prospects compared with other REITs. It's a tradeoff.

These REITs might be quite suitable for those investors to whom stable, high income is more important than capital appreciation. However, most investors will do better to defer the reward of high current dividends in favor of the higher-potential, long-term total return of the blue-chip REITs, which have greater growth prospects.

THE VIRTUES OF
OF BLUE-CHIP REITS

SO FAR, WE'VE discussed growth, value, and bond-proxy REITs. Now we'll introduce the "king of the jungle"—the blue-chip REIT. Blue-chip REITs take you safely through the ups and downs in the sector's cycles and deliver consistent, rising, long-term growth in FFO and dividends. Because they are financially strong and widely respected, they will always have access to the additional equity and debt capital that fuels the growth engine. They will not always provide the highest dividend yields or even, in many years, the best total returns, nor can you buy them at bargain prices—but they should provide years of double-digit returns with a high degree of safety. These are the REITs least likely to shock investors with major earnings disappointments, and will provide very satisfying total returns.

The quality attributes of blue-chip REITs should be the standard by which all REITs are measured. Those qualities are:

◆ Outstanding proven management
◆ Access to capital to fund growth
◆ Balance sheet strength
◆ Sector and geographical focus
◆ Substantial insider stock ownership
◆ Low payout ratio
◆ Absence of conflicts of interest.

THE SUPREME IMPORTANCE OF MANAGEMENT

Strong management is the single most important attribute of blue-chip REITs.

IT IS WHAT separates mere collections of properties from superior growth companies whose stock-in-trade just happens to be real estate. Even if its management is mediocre, a REIT will do reasonably well when its sector is healthy; a rising tide lifts all boats. The rapidly rising rents and occupancy rates enjoyed during a sector's boom cycle will generate strong internal growth for the entire sector, such as was the case for the apartment REITs that went public from 1993 through 1994. Nearly all reported significant FFO increases through 1995.

The true test of quality is when difficult property markets return, which often brings excellent buying opportunities in their wake. That is when strong property-level management and good access to capital make the difference. When real estate is depressed, strong companies can retain their tenants while picking up sound, well-located properties cheaply—properties that can, with intelligent and imaginative management, be put back on track and produce excellent returns for shareholders. That is what is happening today in some apartment markets, and that is what has been happening in the office and hotel sectors for the last few years.

When shopping for solid blue chips, it's important to focus on REITs whose managements have been able to build a sound portfolio with only a modest amount of debt, and who can raise reasonably priced capital to take advantage of acquisition or development opportunities when they arise. These are REITs whose managements have been able to achieve internal growth by upgrading properties and tenant rolls, while maximizing rental revenues and reducing the rate of operating- and administrative-expense growth. Now all we have to do is learn how to recognize them.

FFO Growth in All Types of Climates

WE'VE DISCUSSED buying opportunities in depressed real estate sectors. But there are other advantages that superior managements offer: They can attract a good tenant who might be ready to move out of a slow shopping center into a livelier one. They make sure that the lease rates in acquired properties coincide with underlying real estate values, which enables them to find replacement tenants who can afford equal or higher rents if the original tenants don't make it. Superior managements will keep on top of tenant rosters, always looking to replace the weak with the strong and reducing the risk of tenant defaults. Defaults are disruptive to cash flow, not only because of lost rent but also because changing tenants midlease might require that expensive improvements be made for the new tenants.

Experienced managements will be continuously scanning for market weakness that they can use to their advantage.

One example of a REIT that's been able to take advantage of market weakness is Kimco Realty, a neighborhood-shopping-center REIT. Shopping-center owners have been facing a challenging real estate environment, due to overbuilding and changing consumer spending patterns. Capitalizing on these difficulties, Kimco bought a package of retail stores in early 1996 from a retailer, Venture Stores, that was trying to restructure its business. The stores were bought at prices well below market and leased to Venture at an estimated yield of almost 13 percent. Kimco's FFO has been growing at close to 9 percent annually, and transactions like these should help FFO grow at a similar rate in future years. Investors should look for blue-chip REITs, such as Kimco, that have the ability to do well even in difficult environments by making favorable acquisitions, upgrading tenant quality, continuing to generate good rental growth, and pursuing new business opportunities.

Extra Growth Internally

THERE ARE TIMES when attractive acquisitions are not available to a REIT *(e.g.,* when expected rates of return would be below the REIT's true weighted average cost of capital), and often there just aren't many development opportunities. This year, 1998, is an example of a time when there are simply very few attractively priced acquisitions. Robert McConnaughey, Managing Director and Senior Portfolio Manager of Prudential Real Estate Securities, says, "The low-hanging fruit has already been picked. We are no longer in an environment where anyone can find bargains, as we have been in a recovery mode for five years now." This is when the best REITs have the ability to increase FFO internally, in spite of the lack of opportunity for external growth. To accomplish this requires a competitive edge. Home Properties, for example, provides a "community" atmosphere at its seniors-oriented apartment buildings, which enables the tenants to feel that they're getting value for their rent dollars. One result is low turnover. Post Properties creates this through its "Post" brand name, which has come to mean a luxurious apartment environment and excellent tenant services. The brand-name recognition, the quality of the units, the extraordinary landscaping, and the service-oriented nature of on-site management have meant that Post has a significant advantage over other apartment owners. Equity Residential, yet another excellent apartment REIT, has been able to generate superior profits through highly efficient property management.

Kimco has also been able to build and maintain an extensive database of tenants' space requirements. As a result of its long-standing relationships with hundreds of national, regional, and local retailers, it has been able to refer to this database to fill vacant space quickly, whether in established properties or in new acquisitions.

We discussed earlier how a REIT is often able to charge higher rents for enhanced properties. There is no guidebook written on how to enhance property, nor on how to reduce operating costs, but innovative management will always find a way to generate above-average NOI growth at the property level, and this is a major contributor to rising FFO—regardless of prevailing market conditions.

External growth opportunities are important, but internal growth is more stable and dependable.

"The Art of the Deal"

ONE UNIQUE CHARACTERISTIC of a high-quality management is that, from time to time, it can make an unusual but very profitable real estate deal. A prime example of this is the 1995 Vornado coup involving Alexander's. Alexander's was a department-store chain in the New York City area that filed for bankruptcy in 1992. It owned seven department-store sites and a 50 percent interest in an adjacent regional mall. According to a Green Street Advisors' March 17, 1995 report, these sites were very valuable, including a full square block in midtown Manhattan. In March 1995, Vornado bought a 27 percent stock interest in Alexander's from Citicorp for $55 million, a purchase price 20 percent below the prevailing market price. Vornado also lent $45 million to Alexander's, at a weighted average interest rate of 16.4 percent. Alexander's has since become a REIT and Vornado is entitled to include, in its earnings reports, its proportional share of Alexander's FFO. Furthermore, Vornado structured the deal to earn fees for managing, leasing, and developing

Alexander's real estate. Green Street has estimated that this transaction has enabled Vornado not only to increase its future FFO significantly, but also to increase its per-share net asset value (NAV). Vornado continues to make unusually attractive real estate deals.

Other instances of what Donald Trump called "the art of the deal" include purchases of nursing-home mortgage loans from the Resolution Trust Corporation (RTC) by Health Care Properties and Nationwide Health in 1992 at interest rates exceeding 14 percent. Reckson Associates, an office REIT, has been able to buy defaulted mortgage loans, take control of the properties, and restructure and re-tenant them.

Investors should look hard for REITs with management teams that can add value by finding and making deals such as these.

Attracting the Best Tenants

A WELL-MANAGED REIT should not be entirely at the mercy of the quality and creditworthiness of its tenants. Even in difficult environments, it should be able to take space vacated by a financially troubled tenant and re-lease it at rates comparable to or better than before. Most retail REITs with good managements were not hurt in the last retail contraction of the late 1980s, nor have they been significantly affected by the 1995–96 wave of retail bankruptcies.

Nevertheless, a REIT's ability to attract a roster of high-quality tenants is very important, particularly in retail sectors such as malls, neighborhood shopping centers, and factory outlets. In a shopping center, having better tenants means higher traffic, which means higher sales—for all the stores. For the owner of the center, such retail prosperity means that the tenants will be able to afford their rent bumps and will generate the sales overages built into their leases.

A retail REIT's management wants to do everything possible to attract shopping traffic. More traffic means more sales, and more sales means less tenant turnover.

Better-quality tenants, whether in retail space, industrial properties, or office buildings, will usually be looking to expand, and, if a management enjoys good relationships with these tenants, they will turn to the REIT management when they're ready for additional space. For example, Security Capital Industrial Trust's business plan is for continual development of long-term relationships with America's major corporations, with the idea that this will lead to acquiring and developing additional properties for these companies.

The very best management teams perform well even when their tenants do not.

In the mid-1980s, when the downward spiral in oil prices sent Texas into a virtual depression, retail sales in Houston weakened considerably, and retail-store occupancy rates fell below 90 percent in the oil patch. However, Weingarten Realty, a blue-chip REIT, came out of the downturn completely unscathed, retaining occupancy rates of 93–95 percent. Weingarten was able to continue to do well, despite the horrendous economic conditions, by retaining excellent relationships with its tenants, owning centers in strong locations, and anchoring its centers with stores that catered to consumer necessities, such as drugstores and supermarkets.

Cost Control

IT HAS ALWAYS been axiomatic in business that the low-cost provider has an edge on the competition. That has never been more true than in today's highly competitive business environment. Outstanding REIT managements are likely to build a very cost-efficient internal property management team, while also keeping overhead costs—administration, legal, accounting, and so forth—under tight control.

We spoke about REITs' availing themselves of buying opportunities in a depressed market, but what about buying properties in a healthy market? Well, rich or poor, it's nice to have money. If the property-management team is highly efficient at keeping operating costs down, then it will be in a position to outbid competing buyers for high-quality properties and still generate highly satisfactory returns on those properties. For example, let's assume an attractive apartment building is available for $7 million. It has an annual rent roll of $1 million and would cost most property owners $500,000 in property-management expenses. That would leave the owner with an unleveraged return of $500,000, a return of only 7.1 percent ($500,000 divided by $7 million) on the asking price. Assuming that the bidder's nominal cost of capital is 8 percent, this is not a property that will attract many offers unless the property offers unusually high upside potential. But suppose that a REIT had a management team so efficient (aided, perhaps, by owning multiple properties in the same community) that it could manage the building at a cost of only $400,000 annually, providing $600,000 in annual operating income. At the same asking price of $7 million, the return would then be 8.6 percent, 0.6 percent above the assumed nominal cost of capital. This now makes the acquisition a do-able proposition.

But it isn't only property-management expenses that need to be kept under control; overhead must be kept down as well. Let's take a REIT that owns $10 million of properties that generate an unleveraged 9 percent yield, or $900,000 per year. If the overhead costs amount to 1 percent of assets, or $100,000 per year, the REIT's net return on its investments will be $800,000, or 8 percent. Compare this with a second REIT whose overhead costs amount to only 0.5 percent of assets, or $50,000. The second REIT will generate $850,000 in net operating income (NOI), providing an 8.5 percent return to its shareholders, half a percentage point over the first REIT.

Cost control is an often overlooked factor when evaluating managements, but over a significant time period the management that can contain its costs will have a substantial competitive edge.

Track Record of FFO Growth

PATRICK HENRY SAID, "I have but one lamp by which my feet are guided, and that is the lamp of experience." One of the most obvious but often neglected methods of determining the quality of management is to review the REIT's historical operating performance. Does the REIT have a long and successful track record of increasing FFO on a per-share basis? Does it have a history of steady, increasing shareholder dividends? How long has the REIT been a public company? Has its management found ways to turn in a satisfactory performance even when its local markets have been depressed or when it's had a lot of competition from new developments? How does it truly add value for its shareholders?

REITs have been around for more than 30 years, but we can count on just two hands the number of REITs that have established impressive track records of consistent and substantial growth of 7 or 8 years' duration, through a complete property cycle. These include, in the apartment sector, Merry Land and United Dominion; in the health care sector, Health Care Properties, Nationwide Health, and MediTrust; in the neighborhood-shopping-center sector, Federal, New Plan, and Weingarten; and Washington REIT (which owns several different property types). If they can be bought at reasonably attractive prices, REITs that like these have performed extremely well for investors over long periods of time should be seriously considered by conservative REIT investors. (We will discuss how to determine value in REIT shares in Chapter 9).

Fortunately, even if we want to go with the highest quality, we are not limited to the above-named old-timers, since some of the REITs that have gone public since 1991 are among the most outstanding names in the real estate industry, and most of them had operated successfully for many years as private companies prior to their IPOs. These are REITs with very capable managements and well-conceived growth strategies, but are less-established performers because of their shorter life as public companies.

In the apartment sector, REITs in this latter category include Bay Apartment Communities, Equity Residential, Home Properties, and Post Properties; in neighborhood shopping centers, Developers Diversified and Kimco; in shopping malls, Macerich, Simon DeBartolo Group, and Taubman Realty; in outlet stores, Chelsea/GCA and Tanger; in office/industrial, Reckson Associates, Spieker Properties, and Weeks Corporation; and in self-storage, Public Storage, Shurgard Storage, and Storage USA.

Though attractive, these newer REITs still have to prove they can maintain successful (long-term) track records as public companies as their older, blue-chip counterparts have through good cycles and bad.

ACCESS TO CAPITAL TO FUND GROWTH

IN DETERMINING WHICH REITs deserve the "blue-chip" label, we need to look next at access to capital. Since a REIT must pay out 95 percent of its annual net income to shareholders, it depends on access to capital to fund external growth like acquisitions and developments.

The better a REIT's track record, the more likely it is to have a solid balance sheet and the ability to earn a satisfactory return on new capital raised. As of February 1998, there were 169 publicly traded REITs with market caps of at least $100 million, and at least another 44 smaller ones. Of the top 125, probably only about 80 percent are able to raise capital through secondary offerings at reasonably attractive prices, although this percentage may be higher at times when REITs are particularly popular with investors.

The owner of a typical commercial property might expect that, when the market is in equilibrium, his or her property will generate increased annual cash flows only at the rate of inflation, say 2–3 percent, unless the returns are leveraged by taking on debt; this could get the internal growth rate to 4–5 percent. However, if the owner has access to additional equity capital, he or she will be able to buy additional properties, assuming a return exceeding the cost of capital, that will allow for significant external growth. Simply put, this is one of the principal reasons why many outstanding REITs will, over many years, be able to report FFO growth of 6–10 percent per year.

Access to capital is a key factor in separating the blue-chip REITs from the rest.

POSITIVE INVESTMENT RETURN

A POSITIVE INVESTMENT RETURN is essentially the positive difference between the true cost of capital and the long-term return expected from the use of that capital. In another kind of business, it would be the positive difference between the cost of producing the product (including overhead) and the revenues from the sale of the finished product.

The value of acquiring properties providing internal rates of return greater than the cost of capital has already been addressed. Similarly, in the case of new development, anticipated returns that are less than the cost of capital to finance that return is pointless. To make sense, the spread must be positive; thus the importance of low-cost capital.

Even though capital might *seem* expensive in absolute terms, if a REIT is able to buy properties at high enough returns or to create new developments that yield even more than the cost of the capital, the spread between capital cost and its ultimate return can still make the project attractive.

Mall REITs, for example, have often not had many attractive acquisition opportunities. At various times, their share prices have been valued at a discount to what their properties might have sold for in the private market. Simon DeBartolo Group, a well-managed mall REIT, has often seen its shares priced at an FFO yield of about 8–9 percent. Thus, Simon's "nominal" cost of equity capital has been about 8–9 percent during these periods. Borrowed funds would have been somewhat cheaper, but, since Simon, like most mall REITs, had already been carrying substantial debt, access to additional borrowed capital didn't mean much to them. It's often been difficult for Simon to buy good-quality malls at cap rates above 8–9 percent.

Think of getting lots of new credit cards in the mail; sure, you can use them, but sooner or later you still have to pay the bill—together with hefty interest charges along the way.

In addition, domestic mall REITs have had to deal with supersaturation in many of their markets. Attractive development opportunities have therefore been scarce.

For a brighter picture, let's look at LTC Properties, a health care REIT specializing in the ownership and financing of nursing homes and other health care facilities. LTC went public in August 1992, and has issued additional shares and convertible debentures several times since then. Because of the reputation of its management, LTC has always had access to capital with which to finance its growth. However, being a new REIT and specializing in an area that has not stirred investors' enthusiasm, LTC has been paying a fairly high price for its capital. At the time of its IPO, LTC sold convertible debentures yielding 9.75 percent. Shares were issued in March 1994 at an FFO yield of almost 10 percent. In addition to periodic share offerings, follow-on convertible debenture offerings were completed more recently, at rates often in excess of 8 percent. On an absolute basis, this is not cheap capital.

Nevertheless, because acquisition opportunities have often provided it with entry yields of about 10–11 percent, LTC, in spite of paying a lot for its capital, has had good acquisitions opportunities. Investors who bought LTC at its IPO price enjoyed an 80 percent increase in its share price by December 1996 (about 15 percent compounded annual growth), and have received annual dividend yields of between 7.5 and 10 percent, for a total annual return of 22.5 to 25 percent. This is a good illustration of how it's not just the cost of capital that investors need to look at, but the profitability resulting from the deployment of that capital.

BALANCE-SHEET STRENGTH

A THIRD FACTOR in determining a blue-chip REIT is its balance sheet. Property owners, probably since biblical days, have used debt to finance their acquisitions. At some times, such as when an individual buys a single-family residence, the amount of debt has dwarfed the amount of equity put into the property. Not too long ago, developers, too, were able to obtain 90–100 percent financing.

Debt leverage increases both the risks and rewards of owning real estate.

All property owners, including REITs, can justify a moderate amount of leverage to carry their properties and finance acquisitions. For this reason, several years ago, when Washington REIT boasted that it had reduced its debt to almost zero, knowledgeable investors were not impressed, since such low debt levels usually result in subpar FFO growth rates. What *is* impressive to investors is when a REIT can carefully manage a modest amount of debt in order to increase the rate of return on its properties and boost FFO, yet keep the balance sheet strong enough to take advantage of new opportunities.

A strong balance sheet enables a REIT to leverage ongoing business expansion by raising new equity capital and additional debt. Conversely, even in the best development or acquisition climate in the world, a REIT with excellent management will nevertheless be shut out of the capital markets and find itself unable to take advantage of the opportunities if it has a weak balance sheet.

Debt Ratios and Interest-Coverage Ratios

WHAT DETERMINES A "strong" balance sheet? First, the total amount of debt relative to either its total market cap or to the total amount of its assets; and second, the coverage of the interest payments on that debt by operating cash flows. Let's talk about debt levels first.

♦ **Debt ratios.** On September 30, 1995, Highwoods Properties, an office/industrial REIT, had 23.0 million total outstanding shares (including partnership units convertible into shares) when the market price was $26 3/8 per share. It had no preferred stock, but it had total indebtedness of $181.7 million. The debt/market-cap ratio can thus be determined by dividing debt

($181.7M) by the sum of the equity cap (23.0M x $26⅜ = $606.6M) and the debt ($181.7M), resulting in a ratio of 23 percent.

Debt/Market Cap Ratio =
Total Debt / (Common Stock Equity + Preferred Stock Equity + Total Debt)

Some analysts, such as Green Street Advisors, prefer using a ratio based on the asset values of a REIT, instead of the debt/total-market-cap ratio. For example, if a REIT had $100 million in debt and total asset values (an estimation of the fair market values of its properties) of $300 million, its debt/asset-value ratio would be $100 million divided by $300 million, or 33 percent. This method, which thus focuses on the *asset value* of a REIT rather than its *share valuation* in the stock market, has two advantages: It is more conservative (since most REITs trade at market valuations in excess of their NAVs), and it avoids fluctuation (since a REIT's share price bounces around from day to day). Advocates of this formula feel that a REIT's leverage ratio should not be adversely affected by a temporary decline in its stock price if the decline has nothing to do with operations or property values. Nevertheless, the debt/asset-value ratio is less frequently utilized than the debt/total-market-cap ratio.

Just what is the "right" amount of debt leverage for a REIT? First, let's look at some averages. At the end of 1995, Robert Frank, then chief REIT analyst with Alex. Brown and now with Legg Mason, estimated that REITs' median debt/total-market-cap ratio was 30 percent and the average was 34 percent *(Barron's,* December 18, 1995). This percentage is only slightly higher today. Some sectors use more debt than others. Mall REITs, for example, have been using more leverage than other sectors, which is justified by the stability of their lease income from national retailers.

Financial leverage means that, if things go well, you've increased your profits; if things go badly, you've increased your losses. Under adverse economic conditions, a high debt level can be a time bomb waiting to explode. Mall owners have been able to use substantial leverage because their business has generally been very steady and predictable; most national retailers have always needed to be located in malls, and so mall rent rates have moved steadily upward. If this situation should change, yesterday's reasonable leverage and manageable debt might be tomorrow's overly aggressive leverage and crippling debt. The reverse may be true in the office/industrial sectors, where conditions have been improving substantially. Several years ago, a 35 percent debt/market-cap ratio may have been too high for such property owners, whereas today (and for the next few years) they may be safely able to take on a higher amount of debt.

The answer to the debt/market cap or debt/asset value question is that there is no answer. There is no universally appropriate debt ratio, which, if exceeded, would make a REIT "overleveraged." It depends on the REIT's sector, the properties' locations, the exist-

DEBT/MARKET-CAP-RATIO GUIDELINES

SOME GENERAL GUIDELINES regarding a debt/market-cap ratio:

◆ Anything over a 50 percent debt/total-market-cap ratio is frequently dangerous and can mean that a REIT, if it has access to capital at all, will pay dearly for it.

◆ A ratio under 25 percent is almost always conservative and means a REIT with a good track record and sound investment strategies is likely to have access to reasonably priced capital.

◆ If competition is heating up or there is a danger of overbuilding, even a 40 percent ratio might be risky.

ing and prospective business conditions, and the supply-demand situation for the REIT's properties. Each situation must be analyzed on its own merits.

◆ **Interest-coverage ratios.** Another way to determine whether debt levels are reasonable or excessive is to look not at the *aggregate amount* of debt, but rather at the amount by which the debt's interest payment is *covered* by the REIT's NOI. (Net operating income is prior to interest payments, taxes, depreciation, and amortization.) This measurement is often expressed as the ratio of NOI, or "EBITDA," to total interest expense.

EBITDA means:
Earnings Before Interest, Taxes, Depreciation, and Amortization.

For example, if "Aggressive Office REIT" has annual NOI of $14 million and carries debt of $100 million, that costs it $9 million in annual interest expense, then its "coverage ratio" would be $14 million divided by $9 million, or 1.56.

Many analysts prefer to measure debt this way instead of looking at the debt/total-market-cap ratio or the debt/asset-value ratio, since this measurement gives a picture of how burdensome the debt service is in relation to current operating income. In other words, if the REIT is doing very well with its properties at a particular time and can obtain fixed-rate financing at reasonable rates, even though the debt level is high, the REIT may find it affordable. This measurement also avoids one obvious problem with the debt/total-market-cap ratio (but not with the debt/asset-value ratio), which is that, as a REIT's stock price declines, the debt/total-market-cap ratio rises.

However, advocates of interest-coverage ratios seem to ignore the fact that real estate markets do change over time, and managements don't always make perfect decisions. To use the interest-coverage-ratio method to the exclusion of either debt/total-market-cap or debt/asset-value ratio is to ignore the fact that a REIT's NOI may be *temporarily* high because of favorable economic or market conditions. If, because of, for instance, a recession or overbuilding, rent income declines and NOI is reduced, what might have been a sufficient coverage ratio will now be insufficient. Again, the risk is that the REIT will be forced to raise equity capital at the worst possible time—when investors are already nervous about future prospects.

A careful REIT analyst will look at both debt/total-market-cap (or, debt/asset-value) and interest-coverage ratios, in order to determine whether a REIT might be overleveraged or underleveraged.

Like debt/total-market-cap or debt/asset-value ratios, there is no magic-number cutoff that will tell us whether a REIT has taken on so much debt that inter-

INTEREST COVERAGE RATIOS

REIT SECTOR	INTEREST-COVERAGE RATIO	DEBT/ MARKET CAP
Apartments	3.9	32%
Neighborhood Shopping Centers	3.6	33%
Strip Malls	2.7	46%
Outlet Malls	2.7	51%
Manufactured Homes	3.7	29%
Health Care	4.4	23%
Hotels	7.9	32%
Office	4.4	31%
Industrial	4.6	25%
Self-Storage	13.0	10%
Net Lease	4.1	21%
Diversified	3.6	29%

SOURCE: REALTY STOCK REVIEW, PAINEWEBBER, AS OF 1/30/98

est expenses are too high in relation to current operating income. Generally speaking, an interest-coverage ratio of below 2.5 will often be cause for some concern, and blue-chip REITs will rarely have ratios that low.

To give you some reference point, the chart at left shows, as of January 30, 1998, the average interest-coverage ratios and the average debt/total-market-cap percentages for the various REIT sectors, as determined by *Realty Stock Review*.

Variable-Rate Debt

THE NEXT COMPONENT that we need to examine is variable-rate debt. Variable-rate debt subjects the REIT and its shareholders to significantly increased interest costs in the event that interest rates rise. Mike Kirby at Green Street Advisors has made the point that REIT investors normally like or dislike a REIT for its business and real-property prospects, and don't want to see what would otherwise be a good REIT investment spoiled because a REIT's management team guessed wrong on the direction of interest rates. Mr. Kirby is absolutely correct; it's clearly a negative for a REIT investor when the REIT is loaded up with variable-rate debt that exposes the REIT's FFO to the risk of rising interest rates. It's not that a good REIT cannot have *any* variable-rate debt; it's a question of how much is too much. Given the large portion of a REIT's total expenses that is comprised of interest expense, substantially higher interest costs could cause a significant reduction in FFO and even result in a dividend cut. Conversely, fixed-rate debt is a positive, since it allows REIT investors to be able to predict future FFO growth without having to guess whether rising interest rates will throw all forecasts askew.

Since a REIT's management strategy might be to inflate FFO growth by using cheaper, variable-rate debt, we have often seen it used excessively in prior years. Thus, the *quality* of a REIT's FFO and its growth

FIXED-RATE DEBT

THE BEST FORMULA for fixed-rate debt is set, by its own terms, at a specified interest rate. In addition, if the borrower is allowed to prepay the debt should interest rates fall substantially after the debt is incurred, the borrower should have the opportunity to reduce costs and, thus, increase FFOs. In recent years, many REITs have taken on a sort of semi–variable-rate debt in which the interest rate is capped at a level somewhat higher than the current rate. These caps can be expensive, their price depending upon the length of the cap and "width" of the interest-rate band. Generally, in spite of the cost, capped–variable-rate debt is worth paying for because it is an insurance policy against the possibility of inflation or an overheated economy's bringing interest rates to a much higher level. However, like term-life policies, the caps have termination dates.

rate are suspect when the REIT relies heavily upon variable-rate debt, and this quality—or lack thereof—should be reflected in the price multiples. Fortunately, we are seeing lower levels of variable-rate debt in today's REITs.

Before we decide to reject variable-rate debt altogether, let us just mention that for entities like REITs, which are constantly looking for additional capital, *some* variable-rate debt is inevitable. The typical pattern is for a REIT to establish a line of credit that can be used on a short-term basis and then paid off through either a stock offering or the placement or sale of longer-term, fixed-rate debt. Borrowing under such credit lines is almost always at a variable rate. The key is the *amount* of such variable-rate debt in relation to the REIT's NAV or its market cap. On January 27, 1997, a Green Street Advisors report noted that REITs' variable-rate debt, as a percentage of REITs' assets, then averaged 8.5 percent.

Look for variable-rate debt to be no more than about 8 to 9 percent of the value of the REIT's assets, or the REIT will be exposed to significant negative earnings surprises should interest rates start to rise.

A ratio in this neighborhood is usually fairly safe. However, 18 REITs in that report had ratios exceeding 10 percent, and 7 had ratios in excess of 20 percent. Needless to say, it would be hard for a REIT carrying such a high variable-rate–debt ratio to qualify as a blue-chip REIT.

Maturity of Debt

IT'S AXIOMATIC THAT real estate, being a long-term asset, should be financed with long-term capital.

Short-term debt (which must be repaid within one or two years) exposes the borrower to significant risk. When the loan comes due, if the lender for any reason is unwilling to "roll it over" or extend the loan to the REIT borrower, and if no other source of financing can be found, the REIT will be forced either to sell off assets at any price or to file bankruptcy proceedings. Second, if interest rates have risen in the meantime, the debt will have to be refinanced at the higher rate. Finally, the mere threat of a failure to extend financing can cause a severe drop in the REIT's stock price, thus precluding altogether its raising additional equity capital as an alternative to extending the debt, or, at the very least, making such capital prohibitively expensive.

Nationwide Health Properties, one of today's most highly regarded health care REITs, had this problem in its early years. Under its former management it took on a lot of short-term debt, which the lender was unwilling to roll over at its due date. The REIT (then known as Beverly Investment Properties) was required, unfortunately, to sell off significant amounts of assets and to reduce its dividend.

Accordingly, REIT investors must be mindful of the maturity dates of a REIT's debt. Some analysts look at the average debt maturity, and intelligent investors prefer that most of a REIT's debt not mature for several years. They like to see long-term financing (of at least seven years' average duration), at fixed interest rates.

Wise REIT managements will refinance debt well before maturity and seek as long a maturity as possible.

The above-cited Green Street report notes that, among the REITs in Green Street's universe, the amount of short-term debt (defined as cash less debt maturing within two years), as a percentage of asset value, averaged approximately 4.5 percent. Ten REITs, however, had ratios over 10 percent, a number which should raise a yellow flag with investors.

THE IMPORTANCE OF SECTOR AND GEOGRAPHICAL FOCUS

MANY YEARS AGO, some brokers and asset managers said that a healthy REIT is one that is well diversified in sector and in geographical location, since such a REIT diversifies the risks of owning real estate. We could not disagree more.

There are many idiosyncrasies in local real estate markets involving complex zoning and related regulations in different neighborhoods. Each property sector has its own unique set of characteristics. To buy, manage, and develop properties well requires a familiarity and experience with the properties' sectors and locations.

The investor should diversify—but by buying a number of REITs in different sectors and locations, not by trying to buy one REIT that is diversified within itself.

A good example of specialized REIT management is that of Bay Apartment Communities, which went public several years ago but has been an active developer and owner of apartments in northern California since 1970. It does not own other types of properties. Management has survived the depression-like conditions in California in the early 1990s, and has built an excellent track record in developing and refurbishing high-quality apartments. Until its recent forays into Southern California and the Pacific Northwest, this REIT had not owned a single apartment unit outside of northern California. No one knows the California apartment market better than Bay. Reckson Associates, which acquires, redevelops, and manages office buildings and industrial properties in New York, Connecticut, and New Jersey, is another good example of such specialization.

Such local, specialized knowledge gives a REIT several advantages in its markets. Its management will be more likely to hear of a distressed seller who must unload properties. It will therefore be able to take advantage of the opportunity, and similarly, it may be able to close a deal before it's put out for competitive bidding. If it has development capabilities, it will know the best and most reliable contractors and will be familiar with the ins and outs of getting zoning permits and variances. It will be very much aware of local economic conditions and which neighborhoods the city or region's growth is heading in. If it is a retail REIT, it will have good access to the up-and-coming regional retailers. The bottom line is that highly specialized REIT managements have a significant edge in the competitive business of buying, managing, and developing real estate.

If it's important for a REIT to concentrate on a specific geographical area, it is even more important to specialize in one property type. In the late 1990s and into the next century, successful real estate ownership will be no slam dunk. Each type of commercial real estate has its own peculiar set of economics, and it's far more likely that a management familiar with its sector's idiosyncrasies and supply/demand issues will be better able to navigate through rough waters than a management that tries to adjust to the shifting economies of several different property types.

For all these reasons, most blue-chip REITs will be specialized in both sector and location. Of course, there are exceptions in both general and individual cases. Health care REITs, for example, should *not* seek geographic concentration; since nursing homes depend on state reimbursement regulations, having too many properties in one state means exposure to the vagaries of that state's reimbursement policies. Mall REITs, on the other hand, do not need geographic diversification, but neither will such diversification harm them. Mall economics are similar in most areas of the United States, and a large percentage of mall tenants are nationally known retailers. Even some self-storage REITs, such as Storage USA, have done well with a national market strategy.

To make matters more confusing, some other real estate sectors have been taking on a regional, or even national character. Thus, it can be advantageous for a retail, health care, or even an apartment REIT to have locations in several neighboring states, because of the importance of size and market dominance. Kimco Realty is a prime example. It operates in many Eastern states, and, because of an extensive database of retailer requirements and strong relationships with many good tenants, its geographical diversification is often an advantage.

In other cases, quality REITs simply outgrow their home base. Long known as the dominant neighborhood–shopping-center owner in Houston, Weingarten Realty recently has been entering new markets, such as Las Vegas, Kansas City, and Albuquerque. Weeks

Corporation, a "local sharpshooter" in Atlanta industrial properties, has expanded into parts of North Carolina, Florida, and other Southeast cities. Some
veteran REIT investors may decry such wanderlust, but
at some point a well-run and growing real estate
company like each of those just mentioned is going to
exhaust most of the opportunities in its local market. If
Weeks, for example, applies the same degree of care
and foresight to its new markets that it's applied in
Atlanta, investors need not be overly concerned.

Finally, we are now seeing the presence of "national
REITs," with a strong local presence in several markets throughout the United States. The key to the
success of these REITs will be the strength of their
management teams in each of their markets,
together with the ability of corporate headquarters
to walk the fine line between providing adequate
guidance and allowing for local incentives and cre-
ativity. While it is too soon to tell how successful these
national strategies will be, the early results being
delivered by the likes of Equity Residential, Equity
Office, CarrAmerica Realty, and Security Capital
Industrial, among others, are very encouraging.

**REIT investors should be careful about investing
in companies that are very spread out, whether by property sector or geographical location, unless they become
market leaders in their areas of concentration.**

Before we leave the subject of specialization *vs.*
diversification, let us address how an investor is to
diversify a REIT portfolio. This is far easier today than
it was before the 1993–94 REIT-IPO explosion. Now
we can buy a package of high-quality REITs, each specializing in a particular property sector and operating
in a particular geographical region. For example, if
you like apartments in the Sun Belt, consider Merry
Land, Gables Residential, or United Dominion; if you

like California and the Northwest, take a look at Bay, BRE, Essex, Irvine, or Security Capital Pacific. On the East Coast and in the Midwest, check out Avalon, Home Properties, or Charles Smith, among others. Investors can do the same thing in retail properties, office buildings, or industrial properties. While it's true that investors might have a hard time finding an apartment REIT operating only in the Great Lakes area or an office REIT with properties located exclusively in the Rocky Mountain states, the range of property types and sectors covered by blue-chip REITs is sufficient to allow the individual investor as much diversification as is needed. Another way for a small investor to diversify is through REIT mutual funds, which we discuss in Chapter 10.

INSIDER STOCK OWNERSHIP

FEW INVESTMENT TECHNIQUES exist upon which both academics and investors seem to agree wholeheartedly. After painstaking research, academics often come up with conclusions that contradict principles most investors hold dear. One exception, however, about which these opposites concur is insider ownership. Significant stock ownership in a company by its management usually has a strong bearing on the company's long-term success.

That profit is the best incentive is basic capitalism, and a management that has a high percentage of ownership in the REIT it manages will be making money for shareholders while it's making money for itself.

Why this is true is certainly no puzzle. What better incentive for success can there be than for the operator of the company to be an owner? Managements that have a large equity stake in their company are more likely to align their personal interests with public shareholders' interests and look for long-term appreciation rather than the fast buck. They will sacrifice short-term FFO increases, if necessary, in order to reach a long-term goal. They will avoid "goosing" FFO by taking on too much short-term, variable-rate debt, and will not buy properties with limited long-term growth prospects just to increase FFO in the current fiscal year. Furthermore, REIT managements with high insider ownership are likely to be more conservative about new development projects and less tempted by the occasional conflict of interest at the expense of the shareholders.

Fortunately for us, REITs have a much higher percentage of stock owned by their own managements than most other publicly traded companies. The 1998 Green Street report *REIT Pricing—An Update of Our Pricing Model* indicates that near the end of 1997, REITs' average insider ownership was 14.7 percent and the median was 10.8 percent—both figures significantly higher than in other public companies. The main reason for this is that a large number of REITs that went public during the last several years had been very successful private companies, and, as these companies became REITs, the insider owners continued to hold large stock positions in the public entity.

Needless to say, a high percentage of insider ownership will be a key criterion in determining which of the REITs can be considered blue chips. However, it's also important to realize that the percentage of insider ownership will decrease over time as the number of outstanding REIT shares are diluted by additional stock offerings, as those within management seek to diversify their own investment assets, and as younger professional managers are brought onboard. The chart on the following page includes the percentages of outstanding stock held by insiders at the 20 apartment REITs followed by Green Street Advisors, as of October 1997.

INSIDER OWNERSHIP FOR SELECTED APARMENT REITS

October, 1997

Irvine
Security Capital Atlantic
Security Capital Pacific
Town & Country
Post
Associated Estates
Summit
Charles Smith
Equity
Camden
Merry Land
Oasis
Gables
Bay
United Dominion
Avalon
Bre
Amli

0%   10%   20%   30%   40%   50%   60%

LOW PAYOUT RATIOS

A low dividend-payout ratio allows the REIT to retain some cash for external growth.

ANOTHER CRITERION FOR separating the wheat from the chaff is the REIT's payout ratio of dividends to FFO or adjusted funds from operations (AFFO). Since new equity capital is so expensive, the best-managed REITs prefer to retain as much of their operating income as possible for acquisitions, developments, and other forms of asset expansion; using their own capital is cheaper than borrowing or selling additional shares.

A low payout ratio is also good insurance against unexpected events that might cause a temporary downturn in FFO or AFFO. Although it would be nice if their earnings climbed higher each and every year, REITs operate in the real world and are subject to such surprises as higher vacancy rates or tenant defaults, lower rents because of overbuilding, or higher-than-anticipated operating expenses. If a REIT pays out too much of its AFFO in dividends, it may create investor concern about the possibility of a dividend cut and depress the stock price. Once confidence is lost, the REIT will find it much more difficult to raise funds through an equity offering.

Traditionally, REIT investors have been attracted to REITs for their high and steady yields. However, with the recent increase in REITs' popularity among institutional as well as individual investors, together with the increasing importance being placed upon FFO and AFFO growth, the importance of retained earnings and low payout ratios is now being recognized.

REITs with low payout ratios will frequently command higher price price (P)/FFO multiples and, thus, higher stock prices.

Just what should we be looking for in payout ratios? Let's begin with the premise that AFFO is superior to FFO in determining a REIT's free cash flow. If a REIT claims to have earned $1.00 per share in FFO but uses $.05 of that to add new carpeting and draperies to its apartment units each year, it really has only $.95 available for dividend distributions or for acquisitions. Further, if it pays out the full $.95 in dividends, it will have retained absolutely nothing with which to expand the business. Accordingly, the wise investor will look at a REIT's ratio of dividends to AFFO. If AFFO is $.95 and the dividend rate is $.85, the payout ratio would be $.85 ÷ $.95—or 89.5 percent.

Realty Stock Review regularly publishes the payout ratios of REITs in the different sectors, using AFFO.

REIT SECTOR PAYOUT RATIOS	
REIT SECTOR	PAYOUT RATIOS
Apartments	81.7%
Neighborhood Shopping Centers	84.3%
Regional Malls	86.5%
Factory Outlet Centers	67.5%
Manufactured Homes	74.3%
Health Care	82.8%
Hotels	74.3%
Industrial	74.1%
Office	76.3%
Self-Storage	71.7%

SOURCE: REALTY STOCK REVIEW, NOVEMBER 14, 1997

The chart above shows average payout ratios published in the November 14, 1997, issue, based on estimated 1998 AFFOs.

These are nice, tidy averages, but there are wide differences from REIT to REIT, with five companies having payout ratios of 100 percent or higher, and many others with over 95 percent. Ratios like these can severely limit growth and increase risk.

Let's look at some well-regarded REITs with low payout ratios. In the same issue of *Realty Stock Review,* 13 REITs had ratios of under 70 percent; Public Storage, Starwood Hotels & Resorts, and Bay Apartment had ratios of only 44.4 percent, 58.2 percent, and 61.3 percent, respectively; The Rouse Company, which is now converting into a REIT, won the prize for the lowest ratio, at only 43.7 percent. The laws applicable to REITs require that no REIT's payout may be less than 95 percent of its *net income.*

A few last words about payout ratios. There may be times in the REIT sector's economic cycle when acquisition or development just doesn't make sense. At such times, a higher payout ratio might be the most efficient use of the REIT's FFO. Also, there may be occasions when a REIT structured as an UPREIT or a DownREIT can acquire properties through the issuance of operating partnership (OP) units. Home Properties has been particularly successful at this. In these cases, it will be less necessary to use retained earnings for growth, since there will be less need to engage in costly equity financing; thus a low payout ratio will not be so important.

Finally, if your REIT investment goal is income rather than long-term growth, you *want* the REIT to have a high payout ratio. That's a different case entirely, and such investors should seek out REITs with high payout ratios. Most *blue-chip* REITs, however, have low payout ratios, which is likely to contribute to faster long-term growth.

ABSENCE OF CONFLICTS

CONFLICTS OF INTEREST between management and shareholders are inevitable in any company. The shareholders, for instance, might benefit if the company is acquired, but such a takeover would probably put management on the unemployment line. In some cases, management shareholders or passive insider owners even have the ability or the right to prevent such a takeover, regardless of the public shareholders' wishes. In another case, management might have a compensation plan that would motivate them to emphasize short-term profits over the long-term growth value that would better benefit shareholders. These are but a few possible conflicts of interest that might arise between management and public investors.

Unfortunately, REITs' format makes them particularly vulnerable to these and other conflicts. One of the worst kinds of conflict of interest happened quite regularly several years ago, when most REITs' charters did not prohibit officers or directors from selling the REIT properties in which they themselves had a financial interest. The property values of some of these sales were later determined to have been vastly inflated—with dire consequences for the REIT. Today most REITs prohibit such transactions, but there are other types of conflicts unique to REITs that must be watched carefully.

One conflict involves a change in a REIT's management when the new management sells a portfolio of properties to the REIT. This occurred in late 1995 when a new CEO was elected at Burnham Pacific Properties. This REIT agreed to buy a portfolio of existing properties, as well as properties under development, from the new CEO for approximately $200 million. What was at issue here was the fairness of the purchase price and the prudence of taking on additional debt to finance the acquisition. This was a variation on the conflict that existed when management could benefit by selling properties to the REIT but had contrary fiduciary duties to the shareholders.

Another type of conflict can arise when a REIT is "externally administered and advised." Some years ago when REITs had outside companies handling administration, property acquisitions, and property management, these outside advisers' fees were based not on the profitability of the REIT but on the dollar value of its assets. This gave the outside company an incentive to increase the amount of the REIT's assets simply as a basis for increasing their fees, but not necessarily for the long-term benefit of the REIT or its shareholders. Today, fortunately, the great majority of REITs are internally administered and managed, and managements' interests are aligned much more closely with shareholders' interests. Of course, a high percentage of stock owned by management can also alleviate the concerns of shareholders.

Unclear participation of high-profile insiders can sometimes be a problem as well. Sam Zell, the legendary and highly successful real estate investor, organized Manufactured Home Communities (MHC), a manufactured-housing REIT, several years ago. While his knowledge, expertise, and reputation were instrumental in bringing the REIT public, some investors felt that he was not as involved in its management as they had been led to believe. When this REIT encountered problems assimilating a major portfolio acquisition, these investors blamed Zell for not having spent sufficient time personally monitoring the transaction. Investors should ask questions regarding management involvement when they see a high-profile investor lending his name to a REIT.

A relatively new area of concern is that of potential conflicts created by the UPREIT format. As discussed earlier, an UPREIT is merely a type of REIT corporate structure in which the REIT owns a major interest in a partnership that owns the REIT's properties, rather than owning them directly. Other participants in the "operating partnership" will often include the senior management. Sometimes one of the properties owned by the REIT has reached its full profit potential and might best be sold in order to use the equity elsewhere. Such a sale is not a tax problem for the shareholders, but since, in an UPREIT, the partners are carrying their portion of that property on their books for the same price as before the REIT was formed, a sale may trigger a significant capital-gains tax to the partner-officers of the REIT.

Hotel REITs are subject to yet another type of conflict of interest. We discussed in an earlier chapter how, because of a REIT's statutory requirements, its income from non–property ownership sources is restricted. Because of this legal limitation, hotel REITs are particularly ripe for conflicts. With the exceptions of Starwood Hotels & Resorts, whose "paired-share" structure was permitted "under prior law," and Patriot American, which has become a paired-share REIT via acquisition, hotel REITs' properties must be managed

by an outside company in order to circumvent the pro-
hibition against receiving income from "nonproperty
sources." For this reason, the hotels must be leased
and operated by an outside entity, which will then
transform "management income" into "rental
income." Because hotel ownership is very management intensive and since the REIT's shareholders may
want the properties managed by the founders or top
management of the REIT, the REIT's hotels are sometimes managed or supervised by an entity controlled
by the REIT's senior management. This gives management carte blanche on how it handles its expenses
and is an arrangement investors need to be wary of.

Suppose you discover a conflict of interest in a REIT
that otherwise seems like a healthy investment. Does
that mean you don't want to own it? *Not necessarily.*
Just because there is an opportunity for mismanage-
ment doesn't mean that opportunity is going to be
acted on. But this is an area investors need to watch.
The blue-chip REITs, as a group, tend to have fewer
conflicts between management and shareholders, but,
nevertheless, *caveat emptor*—buyer beware.

**For most investors, owning a portfolio of mostly
blue-chip REITs—those with excellent growth prospects
and experienced and innovative management—will be
the best route to long-term financial success.**

SUMMARY

◆ Growth REITs might appreciate quickly, but you can't expect
   much in the way of income. Also, since some growth REITs
   haven't been around very long and investor expectations
   are high, there's more of an element of risk here than in
   most other types.

◆ The value or turnaround REIT is the "junk bond" of the REIT
   world. Such REITs usually pay high dividends and have a
   high-risk factor. Sometimes, they do manage to turn them-

selves around and appreciate in value, but these REITs must be watched closely as it's difficult to differentiate between an investment that has bottomed out and one that's still on the way down.

◆ Bond-proxy REITs provide high dividend yields—in the range of 7–9 percent—but they have less well-defined growth prospects compared with other REITs. It's a tradeoff.

◆ Blue-chip REITs may not yield as much as other REITs, but, when purchased at reasonable prices, they are usually the best long-term REIT investment for conservative investors.

◆ Qualities to look for in blue-chip REITs are: outstanding proven management, access to capital to fund growth, balance-sheet strength, sector and geographical focus, substantial insider stock ownership, a low dividend payout ratio, and absence of conflicts of interest.

◆ The very best management teams perform well even when their tenants do not.

◆ Access to capital is a key factor in separating the blue-chip REITs from the rest.

◆ A REIT with a relatively low payout ratio has more capital available for growth and can save on the expense of debt service and frequent sales of additional shares.

◆ Beware of conflicts of interest between management and shareholders. Because of their structure, REITs are particularly vulnerable to such issues.

◆ Investors should diversify—but by buying a number of REITs in different sectors and locations, not by trying to buy one REIT that is diversified within itself.

◆ For most investors, owning a portfolio of mostly blue-chip REITs—those with excellent growth prospects and experienced and innovative management—will be the best route to long-term financial success.

CHAPTER

9

THE Quest
FOR INVESTMENT
VALUE

UCCESS IN REIT investing will be determined, at least over the short term, by the availability of REITs at attractive prices. In this chapter we'll look at some yardsticks for determining the investment value of a REIT's stock. Sure, we want high quality and growth, but only at prices that makes sense.

THE INVESTOR'S DILEMMA: BUY AND HOLD *vs.* TRADING

ONE SCHOOL OF THOUGHT is that the key to investment success is to purchase shares of stock in the largest, most solid companies, or to buy index or mutual funds and to hold those stocks or funds indefinitely. The only time to sell, say the *buy-and-hold* advocates, is when you need capital.

The other school of thought—a more hands-on approach—says that, with hard work and good judgment, an individual investor *can* beat the market or the broad-based averages—either by stock picking or by market timing. Some advocates of this method point to investors like Peter Lynch and Warren Buffett as examples of what a talented stock picker can accomplish, while others in this group believe that certain signs—technical or even astrological—can indicate when either the entire market or specific stocks will rise and fall.

Advice for the buy-and-hold crowd is simple: assemble a portfolio of blue-chip REITs or buy a managed REIT mutual fund or index fund. Then, if you've chosen solid stocks or performing funds, you can go off to Tahiti, collect the steadily rising dividends, and not worry about price fluctuations, beating the competition, or any other such irrelevancies. If history is any guide, such an investor can expect to average 12 to 16 percent in total returns over a long time horizon.

Advice for the active trader is somewhat more complicated. First, you must have a way to determine when REITs are overpriced or underpriced, given their quality, underlying asset values, and growth prospects. Second, you must have a way to determine when REIT stocks as a group are cheap or expensive. Valuation of any stock is never easy, but there are guidelines and tools that can help determine approximate valuation.

Before examining REIT valuation methods in detail, let's take a closer look at the buy-and-hold strategy and the logistics of organizing a diversified portfolio of blue-chip REITs.

THE BUY-AND-HOLD STRATEGY

The buy-and-hold strategy has a number of advantages. Investors don't need to worry about FFOs, payout ratios, occupancy or rental rates, or asset values.

ALSO, SINCE THESE investors are not active traders, commission costs and capital gains taxes are far less. Finally, if the efficient-market theory is correct, it's not possible to beat the market anyway. In that case, an index-based, "buy-and-hold" REIT portfolio will slightly outperform a traded portfolio or an actively managed mutual fund.

However, buy and hold has some disadvantages. If mutual funds are utilized—whether indexed or actively managed—investors will pay an annual management fee and other expenses and, in some cases, a sales charge. And, unless bought in an IRA or other tax-deferred account, capital gains taxes will be due on all positions sold at a gain (although an indexed fund will have lower capital gains).

Investors who like the buy-and-hold approach to REIT investing but who don't want to go with a REIT mutual or index fund, should be careful to construct a portfolio consisting of a broadly diversified group of large blue-chip REITs. These REITs are likely to grow consistently in all economic climates and to have managements that can be counted on to avoid serious blunders. Such REITs can be compared to blue-chip, non-REIT stocks as Johnson & Johnson, Coca-Cola, General Electric, Merck, and Procter & Gamble. There are also many other excellent smaller REITs, not specifically mentioned in this book, that qualify as blue chips.

Of course, owning any one of these blue-chip stocks is no guarantee of investment success, since individual companies are subject to management mistakes, changing economic conditions, and a slew of other potentially negative developments. Furthermore, all stocks are subject to periodic bear markets.

REIT STOCK VALUATION

Active REIT investors will want to spend time analyzing and applying historical and current valuation methodologies to seek maximum investment performance for their portfolios.

INVESTORS WHO ARE not content with the buy-and-hold strategy and who want to buy and sell REIT stocks more actively, and take advantage of undervalued securities, will need to know how to determine value. After all, it doesn't make sense to overpay, even if you're buying blue-chip REITs.

How can we determine what a REIT is worth relative to other REITs? And how can we decide whether REITs as a group are cheap or expensive? Professional REIT investors and analysts all have their own approach; there is no general consensus as to which works best. There is no Holy Grail of REIT valuation, but there are proven methods and formulas that can provide crucial insight into a REIT's relative investment strengths and weaknesses, historical and prospective ranges of fair pricing, and, in particular, the timing of buying or selling a specific REIT.

REAL ESTATE ASSET VALUES

FOR MANY YEARS, investment analysts have thought it important to look at a company's "book value," which is simply the net value of a company's assets (after subtracting all its obligations and liabilities), based on the balance sheet. Whatever the merits of such an approach in prior years, today's downsizings, writeoffs, and restructuring charges have made this a much less popular method of determining a company's present investment merits. Furthermore, "intellectual capital" and "freelance value" are now deemed more important than the value of physical assets.

Book value has always been a poor way to value real estate companies because offices, apartments, and other structures do not necessarily depreciate at a fixed rate each year (reducing book value but ignoring the appreciation of the underlying land values).

Although some analysts and investors like to examine "private-market" or liquidation values rather than book values, the majority today focus on a company's earning power rather than its breakup value. Nevertheless, while most of today's REITs are operating companies that focus on increasing FFO and dividends and will rarely be liquidated, they do own real estate with value that can be assessed through careful analysis. Furthermore, these assets are easier to sell than, say, the fixed assets of a manufacturing company, a distribution network, or a brand name. Finally, most REIT investors have concluded that asset values comprise well over 50 percent of a REIT's total market value—and in many cases, closer to 100 percent.

REITs are much more conducive than other companies to being valued on a net-asset-value (NAV) basis, and many experienced REIT investors and analysts con-

sider a REIT's NAV to be very important in the valuation process, either alone or in conjunction with other valuation models.

One of the leading advocates of using NAV to help evaluate the true worth of a REIT's stock price is Green Street Advisors, an independent REIT research firm that has a well-deserved, excellent reputation in the REIT industry for its in-depth analysis of the larger REITs. Green Street's approach is first to determine a REIT's NAV. This is done by reviewing the REIT's properties, determining and applying an appropriate cap rate to the properties, and then subtracting its obligations as well as making other adjustments; fee-based businesses which provide services to others are valued separately. Recognizing that REITs vary widely in quality, structure, and external growth capabilities, it then adjusts the REIT's valuation upward or downward to account for such factors as franchise value, sector and geographical focus, insider stock ownership, balance-sheet strength, overhead expenses, and possible conflicts of interest between the REIT and its management or major shareholders.

The net result, under Green Street's methodology, is the price at which the REIT's shares should trade when fairly valued. The firm uses a comparative approach, weighing one REIT's attractiveness against another's. It does *not* attempt to decide when a particular REIT's stock is cheap or dear on an absolute basis, or to determine when REITs as a group are under- or overvalued.

Let's assume that, with this approach, "Montana Apartment Communities"—a hypothetical apartment REIT—has a NAV of $20, and, because of good scores in the areas discussed above, the REIT's shares "should" trade for a 30 percent premium to NAV. Accordingly, Montana's shares would trade, if fairly priced, at $26. If they are trading significantly below

FINDING NET ASSET VALUE

UNFORTUNATELY, A REIT'S NAV is not an item of information that can be readily obtained. REITs themselves don't appraise the values of their properties, nor do they hire outside appraisers to do so. Net asset value is not a figure you will find in REITs' financial statements. However, research reports from brokerage firms often do include an estimate of NAV; also, NAV estimates can be obtained by subscribing to a REIT newsletter, such as *Realty Stock Review*. Finally, the investor can estimate NAV on his or her own by carefully reviewing the financial statements and asking questions of management.

that price, they would be considered undervalued and recommended as buys.

This approach to determining value in a REIT has substantial merit. It combines an analysis of underlying real estate value with other factors that, over the long run, should affect the price investors would be willing to pay for the shares. Since REITs are rarely liquidated, investors might expect to pay less than 100 percent of NAV for a REIT's shares if it carries excessive risk or unreasonable debt leverage, is plagued with major conflicts of interest, or is merely unlikely to grow FFO even at the rate that could be achieved if the portfolio properties were owned directly, outside of the REIT. Why pay a premium if the REIT adds no value?

Conversely, investors have historically been willing to pay more than 100 percent of NAV for a REIT's shares if the strength of its organization and its access to cheap capital, coupled with a sound strategy for external growth, make it likely that it will increase its FFO and dividends at a faster rate than a purely passive, buy-and-hold business strategy.

At any particular time, the premiums or discounts to NAV at which a REIT's stock may sell for can be significant. Kimco Realty, for example, since going public in late 1991, has been regarded as one of the highest-quality blue-chip REITs, and its shares have always traded at a premium to its estimated NAV, regardless of how other REITs were trading. At the end of June 1996, for example, Kimco was trading at a premium of 35 percent to its estimated $20.75 NAV. Conversely, at the same time an apartment REIT called Town & Country was trading at a *discount* of almost 20 percent to its $15.50 NAV, because of concerns over its dividend coverage and its anemic growth rate. In this method of valuation, each investor should develop his or her own criteria for determining the appropriate premium or discount to NAV, taking into account not only the rate at which the REIT can increase FFO and dividends, but all the other blue-chip REIT characteristics we have discussed.

An advantage to this approach is that it keeps investors from getting carried away by periods of eye-popping, but unsustainable, FFO growth that occur from time to time. From 1992 to 1994, apartment REITs enjoyed incredible opportunities for FFO growth through attractive acquisitions, since capital was cheap and there was an abundance of good-quality apartments available for purchase at cap rates above 10 percent. Furthermore, occupancy rates were rising and rents were increasing, since in most parts of the country few new units had been built for many years. Since FFO was growing at phenomenal rates, analysts using valuation models based only on their FFO growth rates might have had investors buying these REITs when their prices were sky-high. As it happened, growth slowed substantially in 1995 and 1996 as apartment markets returned to equilibrium. Investors who bought stocks of apartment REITs trading at the then-prevailing high multiples of projected FFO never saw FFO growth live up to its projections, and, consequently, saw little appreciation in their share prices for quite some time.

Using a NAV model may also keep an investor from giving too much credit to a REIT whose fast growth is a result of excessive debt leverage. If only price (P)/FFO-type models are used, such a REIT might be assigned a growth premium without taking into account that such growth was bought at the cost of an overleveraged balance sheet. Essentially, a´ NAV approach that focuses primarily on property values is a good one and, if used carefully, can help the investor avoid overvalued REITs. We must, of course, remember to apply an "appropriate" premium or discount to NAV—"appropriate" being the significant word here—in order to give credit to the enterprise value of the REIT. Such enterprise value—the ability of creative management to add substantial value and growth beyond what we'd expect from the properties themselves—can substantially exceed the real estate values. Once assigned, these premiums and discounts (or enterprise values) will change from time to time in response to economic conditions applicable to the sector, to real estate in general, and to the unique situation of each REIT.

P/FFO MODELS

SOME INVESTORS REJECT the NAV approach as flawed, because a REIT's true market value isn't based only on its property assets, and a simple NAV approach ignores the REIT's value as a business. These investors argue that, since REITs are rarely liquidated, their NAVs are irrelevant. If investors wanted to buy only properties, they argue, they would do so directly. REIT investors are more like common-stock investors, who want to judge how much is too much to pay for these growing companies. If we use P/E ratios to value and compare regular common stocks, the argument goes, we should use P/FFO ratios to value and compare REIT stocks.

This argument has merit—much more now than it

did several years ago—since today more REITs are truly businesses and not just collections of real estate. Indeed, most brokerage firms today make extensive use of P/FFO ratios when discussing their REIT recommendations. Nevertheless, P/FFO ratios have major defects that make it difficult to use them as the sole valuation tool, in spite of their being helpful in comparing *relative* valuations among REITs. They are less helpful as a measurement of *absolute* valuations.

Since the various valuation tools do not always agree, they should be used only in conjunction with one another and only as a general indication of whether REITs are cheap or expensive at a specific point in time.

The P/FFO ratio approach works something like this: If we estimate Beauregard Properties' FFO to be $2.50 for this year, and we think that it should trade at a P/FFO ratio of 14 times this year's estimated FFO, then its stock would be fairly valued at 14 times $2.50, or $35. If it trades lower than that, it's undervalued; if it trades higher than that, it's overvalued, right? Well, it's not that easy. How do we decide that Beauregard's P/FFO ratio *should* be 14, and not 10 or 18? Beauregard's price history should be our starting point. We need to look at Beauregard's past P/FFO ratios. Let's assume that between 1990 and 1996, the average P/FFO ratio for Beauregard REIT, based upon expected FFO for the following year, was 13.

Let's assume further that Beauregard's management, balance sheet, and business prospects have improved modestly and that the prospects for its sector are better than what they have been earlier. That might justify a P/FFO ratio of 14 rather than 13, but we need to do more. If we think that the market outlook for REIT stocks as a group is more or less attractive than it has been, we can use higher or lower multiples; and, of course, we need to look at the P/FFO ratios of its peer group. We also need to factor in interest rates, which have historically affected the prices of *all* stocks. Perhaps a 1 percent increase or decrease in the yield on the ten-year Treasury note might equate to a similar adjustment in the ratio. But that's not enough. We should adjust our appropriate ratio in accordance with prevailing price levels in the broad stock market; if investors are willing to pay higher prices for each dollar of earnings for most other public companies, they should likewise be willing to pay a higher price for each dollar of a REIT's earnings.

We could go through this process with all the REITs we follow, assigning to each its own ratio, based on historical data, and making all the appropriate adjustments. Then we must compare the P/FFO ratio of each REIT against ratios of other REITs in the same sector and against the ratios of REITs in other sectors. We must take quality into account as well, including the balance sheet. A blue-chip REIT should trade at a higher P/FFO ratio than a weaker one. You pay more for a diamond from Tiffany's than one from Macy's.

Finally, as we discussed, adjusted funds from operations, or AFFO, is a better indicator of a REIT's true earnings than FFO, but, unfortunately, AFFO figures are not reported separately by most REITs. The investor has the choice of either digging through various disclosure documents filed with the Securities and Exchange Commission to construct a quarterly approximation of AFFO, or getting a brokerage report or REIT publication. Most brokerage firms that deal with REITs issue research reports on individual REITS, and industry publications like *Realty Stock Review* are another good source of current AFFO estimates.

After all adjustments have been factored into FFO or AFFO, the ratio valuation arrived at is, at best, still a subjective "guesstimate," because of the difficulty in determining what the appropriate ratio should be, even if we were able to predict FFO or AFFO to the penny. For example, to what extent are past ratios relevant in future investment contexts? How important are long- or short-term interest rates in stock valuation, and how should they be figured in? In months and years to come, how will the individual and institutional investor perceive the value of REITs relative to other common stocks? What about all these attempts at "fine-tuning" the ratios to decide what investors will be willing to pay—are they shrewd estimates or wild guesses? These are just a few of the questions that arise when using P/FFO and P/AFFO models.

In October 1993, the shares of United Dominion Realty, clearly a blue-chip apartment REIT, were trading at $16 (a P/AFFO multiple of over 20 times the estimated 1994 AFFO of $.79) in anticipation of rapid growth. That multiple certainly seemed fair at the time for such an outstanding REIT, yet, although United Dominion delivered outstanding AFFO growth over the next few years, eventually its growth rate slowed. When the P/AFFO ratio on its shares began to decline in October 1993, the increased AFFO in the future years was offset by the lower P/AFFO ratio, and the stock price stagnated, still trading at $16 in December 1996. Investors who had bought at the high more than three years earlier received nothing more than steadily growing dividends. Unfortunately, P/FFO and P/AFFO models can't really answer the key issue of the "correct" valuation of a REIT at any particular time, except in hindsight.

These problems and issues involving P/FFO or P/AFFO models shouldn't cause us to discard them entirely as useful tools, but we must understand their limitations. We don't want to sell too early in REIT bull markets, should REIT prices exceed our appropriate target P/FFO or P/AFFO ratios, but neither do we want to delude ourselves about inherent value by constantly adjusting ratios higher as prices rise, and play the "greater-fool" game. These models are most helpful as *relative* valuation tools, for determining whether one REIT is a better investment value than another at any given time. If we believe one REIT has a stronger balance sheet, better management, and better growth prospects than another, but the two trade at equal P/FFO or P/AFFO ratios, that's when the ratios come into play; they help us choose between the two. Concluding, however, that one is overvalued because it sells at 15 times estimated 1998 AFFO when our P/AFFO model says it should sell at only 14.2 times the 1998 estimated AFFO—well, don't bet the farm on that one. Another valuation tool is called for.

DISCOUNTED CASH-FLOW AND DIVIDEND-GROWTH MODELS

ANOTHER USEFUL METHOD of share valuation is to discount the sum of future AFFOs to arrive at a "net present value." If we start with current AFFO, estimate a REIT's AFFO growth over, say, 30 years, and discount the value of future AFFO back to the present date on an appropriate interest-rate basis, we can obtain an approximate current value for all future earnings. This method of valuation can help determine a fair price for a REIT on an absolute basis; however, discounting AFFO this way somewhat overstates value, since investors don't receive *all* future AFFO as early as implied by this method. Shareholders receive only the REIT's cash dividend, with the rest of the AFFO retained for the purpose of increasing future AFFO growth.

Several methods can be used to determine the assumed interest rate by which the aggregate amount of future AFFO is discounted back to the present. One way is to use the average cap rate of the properties contained in the REIT's portfolio. If the cap rate on a REIT's portfolio of properties averages 9 percent, we apply a 9 percent discount rate. This method has the advantage of applying commercial-property market valuation parameters to companies that own commercial properties, and allows a drop or rise in cap rates to translate into a lower or higher current valuation for the REIT. However, this type of method really is appropriate only for discounted dividend-growth models, as market-cap rates assume free and available cash flows from the properties. Also, cap rates do not assume the use of debt leverage that results in higher returns during healthy real estate markets.

A better method is to evaluate just how much we're willing to pay for the different degrees of risk for each REIT, and decide what kind of total return we demand from our investment dollars. If, for instance, we feel that, in order to be compensated properly for the risk of owning a particular REIT, we need a 12 percent return, we'll use 12 percent as the discount rate. A higher-risk REIT would dictate a higher total-return requirement. This method will produce more consistent valuation numbers, but it will be less sensitive to interest-rate and cap-rate fluctuations.

The discount rate we use will produce wildly varying results. For example, a REIT with an estimated first-year AFFO of $1.00 that is expected to increase by 5 percent a year over 30 years will have a "net present value" of $17.16, if we use a 9 percent discount rate. Applying a 12 percent discount rate will give us a "net present value" of only $12.35. Using a discount rate

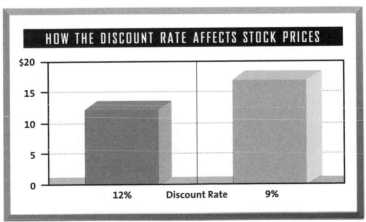

HOW THE DISCOUNT RATE AFFECTS STOCK PRICES

that approximates expected or required total return for a REIT investment (for example, 12 or 13 percent) provides a more realistic net–present-value approximation and will get us closer to what REIT stocks have *traditionally* sold for.

Because of the peculiarities of compound interest, there is little point in trying to estimate growth rates beyond 30 years; indeed, the contribution to net present value from incremental future earnings tapers off dramatically after even just 5 years, and thus it is the first 5 years that we really need to emphasize. A variation of this model might be to use only AFFO growth estimates for the next 5 years, and then to discount the expected value of the REIT's stock at that time at the same discount rate.

A variation of the discounted cash-flow growth model is the discounted dividend-growth model. It starts with the dividend rate over the past 12 months, rather than current FFO or AFFO, and projects the current value of all future dividends over, say, 30 years, based on an assigned discount rate and an assumed dividend-growth rate. A problem with this approach is that it penalizes those REITs whose divi-

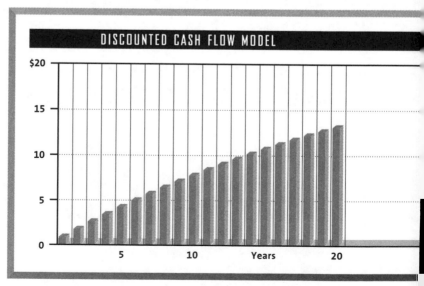

DISCOUNTED CASH FLOW MODEL

dends are low in relation to FFO or AFFO, unless the lower payout ratio is reflected in a higher assumed dividend-growth rate. A positive aspect is that it values only cash flow expected to be received in the form of dividend payments.

Both discounted cash-flow and dividend-growth models have their limitations. The net–present-value estimate is only as good as the accuracy of future growth forecasts; if we forecast 6 percent growth and get only 4 percent, our entire valuation will have been incorrectly based and therefore will be much too high. Another flaw in the net–present-value method is that it doesn't take into account either the *qualitative* differences among the various REITs or their NAVs. It takes into account only anticipated cash flow or dividend growth. Fans of this method should therefore adjust for *qualitative* differences by adjusting the total return required and thus the discount rate to be applied (*i.e.*, a riskier REIT will bear a higher discount rate) and by combining it with a net–asset-value model, a P/AFFO model, or other pricing model.

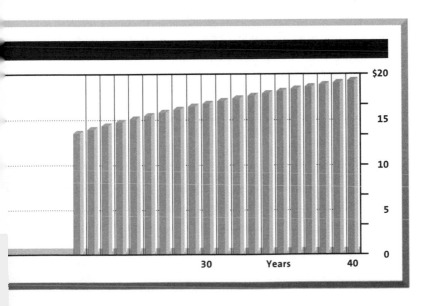

VALUING REITS AS A GROUP

NOW THAT WE'VE seen how individual REITs can be valued based on NAVs, P/AFFO ratios, and discounted cash-flow and dividend-growth models, what about determining whether REITs, *as a group,* are cheap or expensive?

Investors who bought REITs in the fall of 1993 learned, to their regret, that sometimes *all* REITs can be overvalued; if so, it may take a few years before REITs' FFOs and dividends grow into their stock prices. Although, fortunately, REITs pay high current returns while we wait, it still isn't much fun to watch the stock prices languish for a couple of years. In October 1993, New Plan Realty (NPR), at $23, was selling at 22.5 times its estimated 1993 FFO of $1.02. New Plan Realty's FFO has increased significantly since then, to $1.74 in 1997, but the stock price never rose above $24 until December 1996. Obviously the P/FFO ratio was much too high in 1993; its P/FFO ratio fell from 22 to less than 15 at the end of 1997.

It would have done us little good to have bought United Dominion (UDR) instead of NPR in 1993, despite its lower P/FFO ratio of 19.8, since UDR's P/FFO ratio also contracted, to 12.4 at the end of 1996, and its share price was still under $16 at that time, compared with $16.50 in October 1993. Meanwhile, UDR's FFO increased substantially from $.84 in 1993, to $1.35 in 1997. Admittedly, using the year 1993 (when P/FFO ratios were unusually high) may be extreme; nevertheless the message is clear.

No matter what product you're buying, it doesn't pay to overpay—even if you're buying blue-chip REITs.

If we use P/FFO ratios as our valuation method and a high-quality apartment REIT like Bay Apartment Communities (BYA) is selling at, say, 14 times expected FFO, and one of comparable quality, such as Security Capital Pacific Trust (PTR), is selling at 12.5 times expected FFO, we may conclude that PTR is *undervalued* relative to BYA. But this doesn't tell us whether they're *both* cheap or *both* expensive. Similarly, BYA may be trading at a premium of 15 percent and PTR may be trading at a premium of 5 percent over their NAVs, but this tells us nothing about what premiums over NAVs these REITs *should* sell for. Is there any way out of this dilemma?

The use of a well-constructed, discounted AFFO-growth or dividend-growth model may be of some help here. When the REIT market is cheap, the current market prices of most REITs will be significantly lower than the "appropriate" prices indicated by such a model. For example, if 60 of the 70 REITs that we follow come out of the "black box" of our discounted AFFO or dividend-growth models as significantly *undervalued,* this is likely to mean that REIT stocks are being *undervalued* by the market. Nevertheless, we cannot make such an assumption in a vacuum. It may be that these models have failed to take into account fundamental negative changes in real estate or the economy that will cause future AFFO- or dividend-growth rates to be significantly lower than we've projected in our models. If we believe that this is the case, we must revise our models, since it may be that REITs, as a group, are not undervalued at all.

How, then, do we get our bearings? Is there some lodestar by which we can determine our current valuations to what REITs *should* sell for? Unfortunately, no. Yet all is not lost—we do have history as a guide, imperfect though it might be. If we know that REITs have historically provided dividend yields slightly above the yields available on ten-year U.S. Treasury notes, we have at least one useful tool by which to measure current REIT valuations. It would also be useful to know whether REITs have historically traded at

THE RELEVANCY OF OLD STATISTICS

ALTHOUGH IT IS true that before 1992 there were few institutional-quality REITs in existence, these statistics are still relevant. They provide an accurate picture of the returns available to most investors who bought shares in such widely available REITs as Federal Realty, New Plan Realty, United Dominion, Washington REIT, and Wein-garten Realty, all of which have been public companies for many years. Furthermore, there's no reason to think that REITs' total returns should be lower after 1992. Indeed, due to the quality of many new REITs, one could make the argument that the pre-1992 statistics understate the kinds of total returns that REIT investors might reasonably expect, now and into the next decade.

prices above or below their NAVs and by how much, and what has happened to REIT prices when they were at a huge premium to NAV. A third method would be to compare REITs' current average P/AFFO ratios to their historical P/AFFO ratios.

THE T-NOTE SPREAD

GREEN STREET ADVISORS has published several graphs comparing average REIT yields to the ten-year Treasury note yield, going back to January 1990.

These graphs show *some* correlation between the two yields during certain time periods. Thus, between the spring of 1991 and the spring of 1995, the dividend yield on the average REIT tracked quite closely with that of the T-note. While the average yields ranged from 6 percent (5.5 percent for the T-note) to 8.5 percent during that time period, the yield premium of the average REIT to that of the T-note ranged from –10 percent to +20 percent.

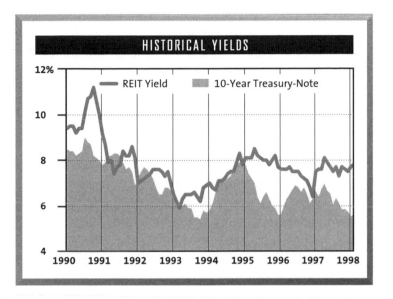

HISTORICAL YIELDS

Yield premium = $\dfrac{(\text{average REIT yield} - \text{T-note yield})}{\text{T-note yield}}$

The yield premium is the difference between the average REIT yield and the T-note yield, expressed as a percentage of the latter. For example, if the average REIT yields 6 percent and the T-note yields 5 percent, the yield premium would be the difference between 6 percent and 5 percent, *divided* by 5 percent, which would be 20 percent. However, it is interesting to note that the yield premium widened substantially in two periods: July 1990 to April 1991 (when it rose to almost 40 percent), and April 1995 to January 1996 (when it again hit 40 percent).

In these two latter periods, we must conclude that REITs, based on their dividend yields, were either inordinately cheap relative to the T-note or that investors were discounting a difficult period ahead for REITs. As it turned out, 1991 and 1996 were extraordinarily good years for REIT investors, as the National Association of Real Estate Investment Trusts (NAREIT) Equity REIT Index (on a total-return basis) was up 35.7 percent in 1991, and 35.3 percent in 1996. Thus we know, after the fact, that investors were either unduly concerned about REITs' future prospects from late 1990 to early 1991 and from April 1995 to early 1996, or that they had simply decided to ignore them as investments. To state it another way, the 40 percent premium was a strong "buy signal" for REITs. Near the end of 1997, the T-note was yielding approximately 5.8 percent, and the average REIT Green Street was covering yielded 6.0 percent, for a premium of 3.4 percent. By this measure, REITs were in the middle of the –10 percent to +20 percent band noted above, and thus were reasonably priced as we entered 1998.

There is a word of caution to keep in mind regarding this comparison with T-note yields. It's important to remember, in using this model with historical data, that many REITs have been reducing their dividend payout ratios in recent years. Thus, there may be a secular decline in REIT yields vis-à-vis FFO or AFFO, that could make the comparison with the ten-year T-note misleading as an indicator of relative valuation. Another factor that must be taken into consideration is that REITs are larger and stronger organizations today than they were even five years ago. This, too, can have a bearing on the comparison with T-note yields. So, many investors choose to compare T-note yields to REIT AFFO yields (rather than dividend yields). An AFFO yield is merely the inverse of the P/AFFO yield, $i.e.,$ a P/FFO ratio of 12 would mean an AFFO yield of $1/_{12}$, or 8.3 percent.

THE NAV PREMIUM

NOW LET'S CONSIDER another Green Street graph, which charts, since January 1990, the average REIT's stock price in relation to Green Street's estimate of its NAV. Between January 1990 and the end of November 1997, the average REIT traded at prices between 36 percent *below* NAV (October 1990) and 30 percent *above* NAV (December 1996 and August 1997); during most periods they ranged between a 10 percent discount and a 20 percent premium. Following the late 1990 period when the discount was unusually large, REITs' stocks mounted a furious rally, as indicated by their 1991 total return of 35.7 percent. Conversely, 1994 (the year following the first time REIT stocks reached a 20 percent premium to NAV level) was very disappointing; in that year the equity REITs managed a total return of only 3.17 percent.

What can we learn from this NAV approach to REIT industry valuation? Can this indicator tell us something despite its short sampling period? One obvious observation is that, when REITs traded at a significant discount to NAV (as they did near the end of 1990), they were extremely *cheap,* and when they traded at a premium of 20 percent over NAV, such as in 1993, they were quite *expensive* (as indicated by 1994's disappointing performance). However, following the first time they reached 30 percent (December 1996) they still managed to perform well, scoring a 20.3 percent total return in 1997. In this instance, the REITs' good performance in 1997 may have meant that the market at the end of 1996 was discounting a continuing

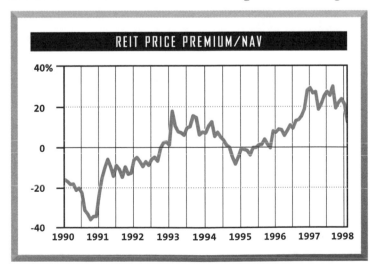

REIT PRICE PREMIUM/NAV

increase in property values generally, or REITs' NAVs in particular. Furthermore, as REITs are increasingly seen by investors as highly active business corporations (rather than as passive investments in real estate), NAVs may become less significant in the valuation process, at least with respect to the faster-growing REITs, or REITs in general might deserve to trade at higher NAV premiums.

P/FFO RATIOS

LET'S TAKE YET ANOTHER LOOK at historical *vs.* current valuations, this time from the perspective of P/FFO ratios. The 1992 Goldman Sachs report *REIT Redux* reviewed average price/cash-flow ratios for selected groups of REITs over long time periods. Assuming that Goldman Sachs's price/cash-flow ratios are approximately equal to P/FFO ratios, we see that they averaged 9.3 between 1963 and 1969, 7.6 between 1970 and 1979, 11.6 between 1980 and 1989, and 11.6 between 1989 and 1991.

In 1995, another Goldman Sachs report, *Real Estate Stock Monitor,* contained a graph showing REIT P/FFO ratios from 1980 to 1996. According to Goldman's data, the lowest P/FFO ratio was just under 8

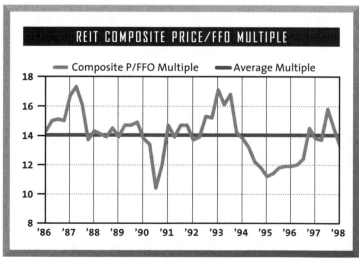

REIT COMPOSITE PRICE/FFO MULTIPLE

Composite P/FFO Multiple — Average Multiple

SOURCE: GOLDMAN SACHS

(between 1981 and 1982), and the highest was 19 (between 1992 and 1993). The average ratio over the entire time horizon of 1980 to 1996 was 13.0. My own analysis of a narrower list of arguably higher-quality REITs showed that P/FFO ratios averaged 14.0 between 1992 and 1996, with a high of 16.5 in 1993, and a low of 12.4 in 1995.

From the foregoing, except for the 1960s and 1970s when there was only a small total market cap of REIT stocks, we can determine that REITs have traded at average P/FFO ratios of between 13.0 and 14.0 over much of the last 15 years. If we average the 13.0 and 14.0 ratios, we can conclude that REITs have traded at an average P/FFO ratio of approximately 13.5 since 1980.

What are today's REITs' P/FFO ratios, based on current prices? Let's look at P/AFFO ratios as being more representative than P/FFO ratios since, although this will result in higher ratios, such ratios will be more representative of REITs' free cash flows. Using average P/AFFO multiples based on estimated 1998 AFFOs provided, as of November 14, 1997, by *Realty Stock Review,* we note the following:

SECTOR	P/AFFO RATIO
Apartments	12.5
Shopping Centers	11.7
Regional Malls	12.2
Factory Outlets	9.8
Manufactured Homes	13.5
Health Care	11.1
Hotels	12.1
Industrial	13.3
Office	16.1
Self-Storage	11.8
Diversified/Other	13.9
AVERAGE	12.5

Although we are using forward-looking P/AFFO ratios (the historical ratios were based on trailing FFO ratios), we can still see that at 12.5, REITs were well within their historical valuation zones at the end of 1997. Furthermore, the historical ratios would have been higher if P/AFFO ratios rather than P/FFO ratios had been used.

SUMMARY

◆ Buy-and-hold investors don't have to worry about FFOs, payout ratios, occupancy or rental rates, or asset values.

◆ Active REIT investors will need to spend a fair amount of time analyzing and applying historical and prospective valuation methodologies to achieve maximum investment performance for their portfolios.

◆ There are a number of tools to help us evaluate REIT stocks. These include NAV-based models, P/FFO or P/AFFO models, and discounted cash-flow (AFFO) and dividend-growth models—all of which have their strengths and weaknesses.

◆ REITs are more conducive than other companies to being valued on a net–asset-value basis, and many experienced REIT investors and analysts consider a REIT's NAV to be very important in the valuation process, either alone or in conjunction with other valuation models.

◆ Since the various valuation tools do not always agree, they should be used only in conjunction with one another and only as a general indication of whether a REIT is cheap or expensive at a specific point in time.

◆ Similar tools can help to determine whether REITs, as a group, are cheap or expensive at any point in time. These include REITs' dividend yields (or P/AFFO yields) in relation to the ten-year Treasury note, the premiums at which they trade *vs.* their NAVs, and their current P/AFFO ratio *vs.* REITs' historical P/AFFO ratios.

CHAPTER

10

Building a
REIT PORTFOLIO

I F YOU'VE READ this far, you're pretty interested in REITs. You already have some idea which sectors you like and whether you want to go for quality or chase high yields, but, before you call your broker, let's get a little perspective on REITs as investments.

HOW MUCH OF A GOOD THING DO YOU WANT?

EVERY INVESTMENT BOOK seems to talk about asset allocation: how much of your portfolio should be in stocks, how much in bonds, how much in cash, and how much in hard assets, like gold or real estate. Some experts say that, as you get older, you should shift more into bonds and have less in stocks, but others recommend that your asset allocation be adjusted according to the investment environment. Who's right?

The only right answer is that the proper asset mix depends on you, and the same answer applies to how much you should be investing in REITs. One of the most important factors to consider is how long you can wait before you'll need to sell any assets. A lot depends upon your investment goals. Are you a newlywed who's saving to buy a house? Perhaps you have a five-year-old who's just starting school and you think you need to start thinking about college tuition. Or maybe you're a baby boomer who is finally starting to think about retirement.

Before you make any decision on precisely what to invest in, you need to determine why you're investing—you need to define your investment goals.

ONE VERY IMPORTANT piece of advice comes from Geoff Dohrmann of *Institutional Real Estate Securities,* who reminds us that "if you're already a mutual fund investor, you want to look to see what your exposure [to REITs] already is, since many fund managers now include at least a few REIT issues in their portfolios." He advises that "any target allocation [10 percent of your equities portfolio, for example] should be adjusted to compensate for existing holdings in existing stock funds."

If you're going to need your nest egg in the next year or two, just sitting on it may be the best thing to do. Put it in the bank, maybe in a CD, where you know you'll have it when you need it. Investing—whether in stocks, bonds, or REITs—is still a speculative venture. It should be no surprise that the market is affected by such variables as Yeltsin's heart condition, the possibility of war with Iraq, Beijing's attitude toward Hong Kong, whether or not Alan Greenspan smiles at reporters on the way into the Congressional committee hearing, or some other event you can't even conceive of right now.

Nevertheless, let's assume you have $100,000 that you don't think you'll need for many years and you already have something set aside for a rainy day. The way you should divide the pie depends on your answers to four questions:

1 How aggressive an investor are you?
2 How comfortable are you with market fluctuations?
3 How depressed would you feel if you were holding a stock that declined substantially?
4 How much income do you need from your portfolio investments to supplement your business, salary, or other income?

AGGRESSIVE INVESTORS SHOULD BE LIGHT ON REITS

The aggressive investor seeking very large returns over a short time period should not put a high percentage of his or her assets into REITs.

WHILE IT'S TRUE THAT, on a total-return basis, long term, REITs have been competitive with the S&P 500 Index, in the short term, REITs are a singles-hitter's game. Very few REIT investments will enable an investor to score a 50 percent gain in one year or rack up a "ten-bagger," to use Peter Lynch's expression, within just a few years. Despite what many people believe, real estate ownership, as long as there is not excessive debt leverage, is a low-risk, steady-reward venture. Shareholders of even the fastest-growing REITs, as a matter of fact, will suffer continual dilution, as a result of the REITs' need to raise additional equity capital with which to expand the business. This alone prevents such REIT stocks from skyrocketing. Investors looking to double their net worth in 18 months had better look elsewhere.

REIT PRICES DON'T FLUCTUATE MUCH

ON THE OTHER HAND, if you don't like a lot of price fluctuation, you'll be quite comfortable with REIT shares, since their fluctuation is only a fraction of what you'll see with most other common stocks. On a big day, a $38 REIT stock, such as Mack-Cali, may be up or down $3/8$ of a point, or about 1 percent. Compare this with the 4 and 5 percent gyrations of such large-cap stocks as Sears, Motorola, or Lucent Technologies, not to mention such high-tech favorites as Intel, Microsoft, or Cisco Systems. Some people get queasy stomachs when their stocks' prices go up and down a lot. If you get sick when your stock's chart gets choppy, adding some REITs to your portfolio might be just what the doctor ordered.

If watching your stocks bounce up and down like a sailboat in a storm makes you a little queasy, you might be better off, psychologically and financially, owning a large portion of REITs to provide some ballast to your portfolio.

REITS CONTAIN LITTLE RISK OF MAJOR PRICE DECLINES

ONE NICE THING about REITs is that even those that turn out to be turkeys don't decline precipitously. From time to time, usually because of overleveraging, there have been some big declines among REIT stocks, but at least the declines have usually been gradual, giving investors a chance to react. The more sudden drops have mostly been because of significantly reduced dividends, but, even then, there are clues. For one thing, beware of an exceptionally high dividend. If it's too good to be true, it won't be true for long. In general, if you watch FFO or AFFO closely and compare it with a REIT's regular dividend, you can usually see a dividend cut coming and get out in time. Other

WHEN STABILITY IS WHAT YOU'RE LOOKING FOR . . .

"I DO BELIEVE REITS are unique," says Geoff Dohrmann of *Institutional Real Estate Securities*. No other sector of the stock market has cash flow based on a diversified portfolio of relatively stable, predictable, contractual revenues (rents) that in most cases are essential components in the ability of the customer (tenants) to continue to do business. Consequently, even though subject to the business cycle as any other corporation, REIT cash flows will tend to be more defensive than most other cash flows. REITs, therefore, offer relatively high, stable yields that—because of their stock market effect—adjust well to inflation, but that also tend to be defensive on the downside.

common stocks are far more sensitive to negative news, and, among such stocks, it's not at all unusual for a lost contract, an earnings "shortfall," a product-liability claim, or a new technology to decimate the price of a stock overnight.

REITS PROVIDE A HIGH CURRENT INCOME LEVEL

SOME FINANCIAL PLANNERS advocate a large common-stock weighting even for people near or in retirement. They argue that bonds don't protect retirees from inflation, and, over any significant period of time, common stocks have provided more appreciation than almost any other kind of investment.

It's hard to criticize the wisdom of investing in common stocks, but the problem with many investment theories is that they're based on recent stock market history, and recent stock market history is not the norm, not by a long shot. There are a lot of investors out there today who have never experienced a bear market, but there's *no* reason to believe they won't, in their lifetime, see such market conditions—perhaps even soon. Many investors at or near retirement must live off their investments; selling off a piece of their portfolios is not something they will want to do in a bear market. Owning REIT stocks provides a high level of current income and make it unnecessary to sell significant portions of stock investments to fund living expenses.

LOOKING FOR THE APPROPRIATE REIT ALLOCATION

THERE ARE TWO PARTS to the question of allocation. First, there is the weighting of REITs relative to other investments. Your answers to the above four questions will help you work out the optimal allocation of REITs in your portfolio; there are just too many variables to give you any rigid formulas.

REIT allocation plans must necessarily be different for every different investor, depending on the investor's financial goals, age, portfolio, and risk tolerance.

Even if, because of all their wonderful qualities, you absolutely love REITs, you still shouldn't put 50 or 75 percent of your portfolio in them. The most fundamental principle of investing is that, over time, diversification is the key to stability of performance and preservation of capital. You *might* have outstanding results if you put a huge portion of your assets in REITs, but nobody can foretell the future. Occasionally even George Soros zigs when he should have zagged.

Every investor must do what is appropriate in regard to his or her specific needs and investment goals, but there *are* some general guidelines to use as a barometer. If you're a fairly conservative investor and you're looking for steady returns with a modest degree of risk and volatility, a REIT allocation of somewhere between 15 and 35 percent of your portfolio should suit you. If the stock market seems overpriced, you might feel comfortable moving up toward 35 percent—and down toward 15 percent if the opposite market conditions exist. Of course, these are only very general guidelines—in investing, it's rare that "one size fits all."

DIVERSIFICATION AMONG REITS

ALL RIGHT, YOU'VE decided on what percentage of your portfolio should be allocated to REITs. Now comes the second part of the allocation question. Within your REIT allocation, what would be an appropriate allocation for the different sectors, investment characteristics, and geographical locations that REITs offer?

BASIC DIVERSIFICATION

MUCH DEPENDS, OF COURSE, on the absolute level of cash you have to invest. One way to diversify is through

REIT DIVERSIFICATION

WITH SIX REITS, a reasonable diversification would call for one REIT in each of six of the following eight sectors: apartments, retail, office, industrial, hotel, health care, self-storage, and manufactured-housing communities. Office and industrial might be combined in one REIT (*e.g.,* Spieker Properties).

REIT mutual funds, which we'll discuss later in this chapter. Here, we'll tell you how you should diversify when buying individual REITs.

For most investors, an absolute minimum of six REITs is necessary to achieve a bare-bones level of diversity of sector and location.

The problem is that, at some asset level—perhaps below $30,000—you just can't get enough diversification without getting beaten up on commissions. Suppose, for example, you have $6,000. If you invest $1,000 each in six different REITs and your brokerage firm has a minimum commission of $50 per trade, your 5 percent commission would cost you most of your first year's dividend. On the other hand, with $30,000 to invest in REITs, six trades would amount to $5,000 each, and the $50 commission would be only 1 percent of the purchase price on each trade.

Six different REITs would provide an *acceptable* level of sector diversification, but ten REITs would be *preferable*. If you're in a position to buy ten different REITs, a good allocation would be two each in apartments, retail, and office/industrial; and one each in health care, self-storage, hotel, and manufactured housing. With more funds, you might seek to widen your *geographical* diversification within each sector, adding an apartment REIT on the West Coast, for example, if you already own one in the Southeast and one in the Northeast. The same policy can be applied in other sectors, such as neighborhood shopping centers or office/industrial properties. An alternative is to buy two or three of the well-managed, diversified REITs that own several different types of properties within a single geographical location—such as Washington REIT, in the D.C. area; Colonial Properties, in the South; or Cousins Properties, in the Southeast.

OVERWEIGHTING AND UNDERWEIGHTING

ONE OF THE KEY ISSUES involving diversification is the weighting of REIT holdings for particular property sectors. There are many opinions on this topic, even among institutional REIT investors. Some money managers don't try to adjust their portfolios in accordance with how much they like or dislike a sector but simply use "market weightings." For example, if mall REITs make up 10 percent of all equity REITs, such investors, using a market weighting, will make sure that mall REITs comprise 10 percent of their REIT portfolio. The theory here is similar to that of buying the S&P 500 Index rather than trying to select individual stocks. Advocates of this approach would argue that all stocks, including REITs, are usually efficiently priced and it's unrealistic to assume that anyone can forecast with any accuracy which sectors will do better than others.

Other investors, frequently those oriented toward maximum short-term performance, think that they *can* figure out the best sectors to be in at any particular time. They will closely examine the fundamentals within the national real estate markets—and overweight or underweight their portfolios accordingly. They will seek the sectors where demand for space exceeds the supply, where rents and occupancy rates are rising fastest, where great acquisition opportunities abound, or where some other factor seems to make the outlook particularly favorable. Kenneth Heebner, a well-known fund manager, uses this approach in his relatively new but very successful CGM Realty Fund. CGM has been heavily invested in hotel and office/industrial REITs; retail REITs and health care REITs have been conspicuously absent.

Unless an investor is very confident in his or her knowledge of which sectors will do best over the next couple of years, a portfolio allocated according to market weighting makes the most sense.

Overweighting what you perceive to be the "right sectors" is tricky, since, if other investors have the same perceptions, that will already be factored into the price and you won't have gained anything.

DIVERSIFICATION BY INVESTMENT CHARACTERISTICS

ANOTHER APPROACH TO diversification is not to own different property sectors in different locations, but instead to own a package of REITs with different investment characteristics. This diversification-by-investment-style approach would have the investor assemble one group of high-quality, low-risk REITs that offer highly predictable and steady growth with

AUTHOR'S CHOICE

WITH RESPECT TO investment style, I prefer to put most of my REIT investment dollars in blue chips, add some that seem underpriced and misunderstood—perhaps with high yields and less well-defined growth prospects—and then add a few more that look as if they'll enjoy rapid growth. I'm wary of mortgage REITs since they've often been badly hurt by rising interest rates and other gyrations pertaining to the bond markets. Fortunately, the REIT industry is now so vast that the choice is tremendous.

little regard to sector or location; another group of "value" REITs with low valuations based on a narrow spread between the stock price and underlying net asset value (NAV) or a low P/AFFO multiple; a group of high-growth REITs; and, to round out the portfolio, a few bond proxies, with high yields and price stability but minimal growth prospects. Such an approach may help to insulate the portfolio from major price gyrations as institutional investors shift their REIT funds from one style of REIT investing to another.

TOWARD A WELL-BALANCED PORTFOLIO

WHICH APPROACH TOWARD diversification is best? By property type? By geography? By investment characteristics? Or by all of the above? There isn't any definitive statistical evidence that one approach is better than another. REITs' new popularity has been so recent that there's not enough history to guide us. While there's no agreement on *how* to diversify, there is almost universal agreement on the *need* to diversify.

Although REIT investors shouldn't ignore the concerns expressed by industry observers with respect to particular sectors, neither should they take them too seriously, particularly when investing in the blue chips, since REITs with excellent management teams can do well in good climates and bad. REIT investors thus needn't become terribly concerned if they find themselves overweighted in some sectors, as long as the quality is there.

Unlike most sectors, *geographic* diversification isn't a major issue with respect to mall REITs, health care REITs, and self-storage REITs, since detailed knowledge of the opportunities peculiar to local markets isn't nearly as important in these sectors.

The chart on pages 258–59 is just a sample of the kind of diversification that can be obtained within certain major sectors. Where relevant, the areas of major geographical focus are included. The table includes REITs with substantial equity market caps as of January 1998.

HOW TO GET STARTED

AS AN INVESTOR, you can choose from three very different approaches in building a REIT portfolio: you can do the research yourself; you can rely on a professional, such as a stockbroker, financial planner, or investment adviser; or you can buy a REIT mutual fund. Let's examine what's involved in each approach.

DOING IT YOURSELF

THE TOOLS REQUIRED to build and monitor your own REIT portfolio are (1) a willingness to spend at least a few hours a week following the REIT industry and your REIT portfolio, and (2) a subscription to a good REIT newsletter or research service.

The do-it-yourself approach is the most difficult and time-consuming method, but many investors find it the most rewarding. There are several ways to stay informed of what's happening in REITs. For example, *Realty Stock Review,* which is published bimonthly, covers the entire REIT world with thoroughness and candor, and provides vital REIT data, dividend, and financing news. In addition, it provides excerpts from various research reports and contains a model REIT portfolio. Most retail brokerage firms will also provide research reports on individual REITs. More information than ever before can be obtained on-line, and many individual REITs, as well as The National Association of Real Estate Investment Trusts (NAREIT), have established their own Websites.

Since REITs are not complicated and their business prospects do not change quickly, they are less data and research intensive than most other common-stock investments. With just a bit of outside help, a willingness to ask questions of management, and the disci-

PROPERTY TYPES, REITS, AND PRIMARY LOCATIONS

REIT	PRINCIPAL LOCATION
APARTMENTS	
Apartment Investment and Management	Nationwide
Avalon	East Coast/Upper Midwest
Bay, BRE, Essex, and Irvine	West Coast
Camden Properties	Nationwide
Equity Residential	Nationwide
Gables Residential	Texas, Tennessee, Georgia, and Florida
Merry Land and Summit	Southeast
Post	Georgia/Florida
Security Capital Atlantic	East Coast
Security Capital Pacific	Western United States
United Dominion	Southeast/Southwest
RETAIL: NEIGHBORHOOD SHOPPING CENTERS AND FACTORY OUTLET CENTERS	
Chelsea/GCA	East and West Coasts
Developers Diversified	Nationwide
Federal	Nationwide
Kimco	Eastern United States
New Plan	Eastern United States
Regency	Southeast/Midwest
Weingarten	Texas and Southwest
RETAIL: MALLS	
CBL	Southeast
General Growth	Nationwide
Macerich	Nationwide
Mills Corp.	Nationwide
Simon DeBartolo	Nationwide
Taubman	Nationwide
Urban Shopping	Ilinois, Florida, and California
Westfield America	Nationwide
HEALTH CARE/LONG-TERM CARE, MEDICAL OFFICE/REHABILITATION	
American Health	Not applicable
Health Care Properties	Not applicable
Health and Retirement Properties	Not applicable
MediTrust	Not applicable

REIT	PRINCIPAL LOCATION
National Health	Not applicable
Nationwide Health	Not applicable
Omega Healthcare	Not applicable

OFFICE

Arden	California
Boston	East/West Coast
CarrAmerica	Nationwide
Cornerstone Properties	Nationwide
Crescent	Nationwide
Equity Office	Nationwide
Highwoods Properties	Southeast
Mack-Cali	East Coast/Southwest
Prentiss	Nationwide
Reckson	Northeast

INDUSTRIAL

Duke Realty	Midwest
First Industrial	Nationwide
Liberty Property	Mid-Atlantic/Southeast/Midwest
Security Capital Industrial	Nationwide
Spieker Properties	West Coast
Weeks Corp.	Southeast

SELF-STORAGE

Public Storage	Nationwide
Shurgard	Nationwide/Europe
Storage USA	Nationwide

HOTELS

American General	Nationwide
FelCor Suites	Nationwide
Hospitality Properties	Nationwide
Innkeepers	Nationwide
Patriot American	Nationwide
Starwood	Nationwide

MANUFACTURED HOMES

Chateau Communities	Nationwide
Manufactured Home	Nationwide
Sun Communities	Midwest and Southeast

pline to review the information publicly available—
such as annual reports and various filings with the
Securities and Exchange Commission—most investors
can do a good job managing their own REIT portfolios. The table on pages 262–63 provides a general
description of some very good sources of information
for REIT investors. If you go through all of these and
are still hungry for more, just do a Web search on the
word "REIT."

The do-it-yourself approach has several advantages.
First, it saves on management fees and brokerage commissions, since, without the need for advice or management, you can use a discount broker. Second, the
realization of capital gains and losses can be tailored
to your own personal tax-planning requirements.
Third, as we discussed in previous chapters, a significant portion of most REITs' dividends is treated as a
"return of capital," and is not immediately taxable to
the shareholder. Owning REIT stocks directly allows
you to take full advantage of this tax benefit. Finally,
the knowledge and experience gained from managing
your own portfolio may well lead to good investment
results and a great deal of personal satisfaction.

USING A STOCKBROKER

**For investors who don't enjoy poring over annual
reports and calculating NAVs and AFFOs, the solution is to
find a stockbroker who is very familiar with REITs and
who has access to the research reports published by major
brokerage firms.**

MOST INVESTORS WOULD rather not spend their
spare time managing their own portfolios when they
could be playing golf, taking the kids to a baseball
game, or gardening. Not too many years ago, however, individual investors had no alternative, since it
was difficult to find a broker who knew much about

REITs. Today, such brokers are not only universally available, but they're not hard to find, either. REITs are gaining popularity. Now you read about them in personal-finance magazines and the business section of major newspapers, and most major brokerages employ one or more good REIT analysts. You should have no problem finding at least one REIT-knowledgeable registered representative in any good-sized brokerage office.

Assuming that you find a good broker, the advantages of this approach are lots of personal attention, the ability to decide when you want to take capital gains or losses, and the relief of not having to research and worry about such issues as AFFO, rental rates, and other REIT essentials. The brokerage commissions will be higher than for the do-it-yourself investor, but, if you're careful to avoid a lot of trading and you buy only those REITs consistent with your investment objectives, higher commissions may be a small price to pay for the service provided.

FINANCIAL PLANNERS AND INVESTMENT ADVISERS

TODAY, AS THE average age of the population increases, there are more people concerned about investing for a longer life expectancy and a retirement free of financial worry.

Financial planners can act in different capacities. Some manage and invest their clients' funds directly; others refer the client to an investment adviser. Some are paid on the basis of commissions from insurance or other investments, while others charge on a set-fee basis only.

Investment advisers, on the other hand, generally do little or no financial planning, and specialize in investing client funds in stocks, bonds, and other securities. Generally their only compensation is a commission of between 1 and 2 percent of the assets they manage. Thus, as the portfolio grows, so does the adviser's

INFORMATION SOURCES FOR REIT INVESTORS

SOURCES FOR THE DO-IT-YOURSELFER	WHERE TO FIND IT
America Online ("Motley Fool" Real Estate Board)	American Online; keyword, "Motley Fool"
Barron's **"Ground Floor"**	*Barron's* weekly magazine (available by subscription or on newsstands)
Brokerage firms throughout the United States	Contact the appropriate broker or registered representative
Green Street Advisors	Green Street Advisors; 567 San Nicolas Dr., #203, Newport Beach, CA 92660
Institutional Real Estate Securities	Institutional Real Estate, Inc.; 1475 N. Broadway, Suite 300, Walnut Creek, CA 94596
Korpacz Real Estate Investor Survey	Korpacz Company; 470 New Technology Way, Frederick, MD 21703
National Real Estate Index	KOLL; 2200 Powell St., Emeryville, CA 94608
Penobscott Group	Penobscott Group; 160 State Street, Boston, MA 02109
Real Estate Capital Markets	Institutional Real Estate, Inc.; 1475 N. Broadway, Suite 300, Walnut Creek, CA 94596
Realty Stock Review	Realty Stock Review; 179 Avenue at the Common, 2nd Floor, Shrewsbury, NJ 07702
The SNL REIT Weekly	SNL Securities; 10 E. Main St., P.O. Box 2124, Charlottesville, VA. 22902
Websites and home pages	Available from NAREIT (http://www.nareit.com) and numerous REITs

GENERAL DESCRIPTION

General on-line discussion of real estate and REITs

Frequently appearing columns on real estate

Research reports on REITs and related services

REIT research service (for institutional investors)

Newsletter containing articles and information on REITs and real estate investing

Information on institutional investment in real estate on a nationwide basis

Discussion and information on various real estate markets, including rental rates, cap rates, etc.

REIT research service (for institutional investors)

Newsletter containing articles and statistics regarding real estate financing and capital flows

Newsletter covering all facets of REITs and REIT investing

Newsletter containing condensed versions of REITs' press releases on earnings, deals, and financings

Data on individual REITs and the REIT industry available on-line

fee. Some advisory firms provide a great deal of personal attention and handholding, while others do not.
Some take great care to individualize a portfolio, taking into account their clients' personal tax situations
before making buy-and-sell decisions, and some buy
and sell solely on the basis of maximizing their clients'
investment gains.

Many investors find that using a financial planner or
investment adviser has its advantages: the similarity of
goals of the firm and its clients, the personal attention
given to clients, and the customizing of clients' portfolios based on their tax situations. For someone who is
interested in REITs, however, the advantages are not
so clear. It can be difficult to find a financial planner
or investment adviser who is experienced in REIT
investing, and fees often recur whether or not any
trades are made in the account. Also, many financial-
planning firms do not have good REIT research services available. Some of these problems may diminish,
of course, as REITs become better understood.

REIT MUTUAL FUNDS

AS RECENTLY AS five years ago, only about 5 mutual
funds were devoted to investing in real estate–related
securities such as REITs. Today there are over 30 such
funds. Most of them are very small in size, however,
according to the January 30, 1998 *Realty Stock Review,*
with only 18 of them having $100 million or more in
assets. The three giants, each with over $1 billion in
assets, were Cohen & Steers Realty Shares ($3.4 bil-
lion), Fidelity Real Estate ($2.5 billion), and Vanguard
REIT Index Fund ($1.3 billion). A list of the ten
largest REIT mutual funds, as of April 1, 1998,
together with relevant information, is included in
Appendix C. While some may scoff at the small size of
these funds, most have done quite well during their
relatively short histories. The Vanguard Group, which
has a market niche in index funds, has the Vanguard

REIT Index Fund, a REIT mutual fund indexed to the Morgan Stanley REIT Index launched at the end of 1994. The Morgan Stanley REIT Index, it should be noted, excludes mortgage REITs and health care REITs. These exclusions mean that this index could outperform or underperform a broader REIT index, such as the NAREIT index.

REIT mutual funds provide an excellent way for individuals to obtain sufficient REIT diversification.

To take a purely arbitrary number, if we assume that the REIT investor wants to put 20 percent of his or her assets into REITs, putting $30,000 into REITs implies a total portfolio of $150,000. In contrast, with the same or a smaller budget, you can get much more diversification through a REIT mutual fund, since most such funds own at least 20 or 30 different REITs.

What is perhaps even more important, however, is that, in a REIT mutual fund, the investor gets the benefit of professionals who, when they make their investment decisions, have access to detailed information because they have access to REITs' top managements. Even active investors might want to invest a minimum amount in some of these funds in order to benchmark their personal REIT investment track records and get a window on what the "big boys" are doing.

Despite their significant strong points, REIT mutual funds are not without disadvantages. While no brokerage commissions are payable when investing in no-load funds, management fees can be sizable, typically ranging from 1 to 1.5 percent of total assets. In addition, the investor pays—indirectly, through reduced dividend yields—for the fund's legal, accounting, and administrative expenses. Fund investors do not receive individual attention, nor do they have the ability to align purchases or sales with tax needs. All the gains or losses realized by the fund during the year are simply passed on to the individual investor. Finally, for the investor who trades in and out of the same fund, it may be difficult to keep a current and accurate record of his or her cost basis and tax-gain or -loss information.

For investors who don't have the resources to diversify REIT holdings adequately, do the advantages outweigh the disadvantages? Clearly—especially if the investor refrains from doing a lot of trading. REIT funds are especially good for IRAs, where neither tax gains and losses nor cost bases are relevant.

SUMMARY

◆ Before you make any decision on precisely what to invest in, you need to determine why you're investing—you need to define your investment goals.

◆ The aggressive investor seeking very large returns over short time periods should not put a high percentage of assets into REITs.

◆ REIT allocation plans must necessarily be different for each investor, depending on the investor's financial goals, age, portfolio, and risk tolerance.

◆ For most investors, an absolute minimum of six REITs is necessary to achieve a bare-bones level of diversity of sector and location.

◆ Unless an investor is very confident about which sectors will do best over the next couple of years, a portfolio allocated according to market weighting makes the most sense.

◆ Investors who want to be somewhat involved but who don't want to worry about weekly monitoring of their investments can use the assistance provided by the services of a knowledgeable stockbroker, financial planner, or investment adviser.

◆ Investors who prefer not to do any individual research can invest passively through different REIT mutual funds or even a REIT index fund. Both provide excellent ways for individuals to obtain sufficient REIT diversification.

RISKS AND
Future
Prospects

CHAPTER

What
CAN GO
WRONG

OW THAT YOU know all the good things about REITs, it's only fair that you also understand what can go wrong. Alas, no investment is risk free (except, perhaps T-bills, which don't provide much upside). In general, the risks of REIT investing fall into two categories: those that might affect *all* REITs, and those that might affect individual REITs. First we'll address the broad issues.

ISSUES AFFECTING ALL REITS

All REITs are subject to two major hazards: an excess supply of available rental properties and rising interest rates.

A SUPPLY/DEMAND IMBALANCE, with the excess on the supply side, is often referred to as a "renters' market," because, in such a market, tenants are in the driver's seat and can extract very favorable lease terms from property owners. Excess supply can be a result of more new construction than can be readily absorbed, or it can be a result of a major falloff in demand for space, but there's an old saying that it doesn't matter whether you get killed by the ax or by the handle. Either way, excess supply, at least in the short term, spells trouble for property owners.

Rising interest rates are another obstacle to property owners' profits. When interest rates skyrocket, REITs' borrowing costs increase, which can eventually reduce growth in FFO. But there is another implication here. Those rising interest rates can foreshadow a weak economy, which in turn is likely to reduce demand for rental space. Furthermore, rising interest rates mean that as investors chase higher yields available elsewhere—perhaps in the bond market—they may decide to sell off their REIT shares, thus depressing prices.

Although excess supply and rising interest rates aren't the only problems that can vex the REIT industry, they are easily the two most critical; let's talk about them in more detail.

EXCESS SUPPLY AND OVERBUILDING: THE BANE OF REAL ESTATE MARKETS

EARLIER, WE DISCUSSED how real estate investment returns can change through the various phases of a typical real estate cycle. When markets get "hot," as tycoon real estate investor Sam Zell likes to say, it's not long before the "construction crane" becomes an endangered species. We also discussed how overbuilding in a property type or geographical area can influence and exacerbate the real estate cycle by causing occupancy rates and rents to decline, which in turn may cause property prices to fall. Over time, of course, demand catches up with supply, and the market ultimately recovers.

While a recessionary economy sometimes results in a temporary decline in demand for space, the excess supply that is brought on by overbuilding can be a much larger and longer-lasting problem.

Overbuilding can occur locally, regionally, or even nationally; it means that substantially more real estate is developed and offered for rent than can be readily absorbed by tenant demand, and, if an overbuilt situation exists for a number of months, it puts negative pressure on rents, occupancy rates, and "same-store" operating income. Overbuilding can cause cap rates in the affected sector or region to increase, thus reducing the values of REITs' properties. To the extent that a REIT owns properties in an area or sector affected by overbuilding, the REIT's shareholders often sell their shares in anticipation of declining FFO growth, which, in turn, drives down the share price of the affected REIT. Despite a strong market for REITs in 1997, the stocks of some Southeast apartment REITs declined essentially for this reason. In extreme cases, the reduced prospects for a REIT may cause lenders to shy away from renewing credit lines, preventing a REIT from obtaining new debt or equity financing, perhaps even forcing a dividend cut. Not a pretty picture.

Of course, problems caused by excess supply vary by degree. Sometimes the problem is only slight, creating minor concerns in selected cities in just one property sector, such as what was beginning to happen to apartments in some cities in the Southeast and Southwest in 1996. Sometimes the problem is devastating, wreaking havoc for years in many sectors throughout the United States. We saw the effects of severe overbuilding in the late 1980s and early 1990s in office buildings, apartments, industrial properties, self-storage facilities, and hotels. A mild excess-supply condition will work itself out quickly, especially where job growth is not severely affected. Then, absorption of space alleviates the oversupply problem before the damage spreads very far. In these situations, investors may overreact, dumping REIT shares at unduly depressed prices and creating great values for investors with longer time horizons.

Investors must try to distinguish between a mild condition of excess supply and a much more serious period of significant overbuilding, in which case a REIT's share prices may decline and stay depressed for several years, eventually forcing the REIT to cut its dividend.

Overbuilding can be blamed on a number of factors. Sometimes overheated markets are the problem.

When operating profits from real estate are very strong because of rising occupancy and rents, property prices seem to rise almost daily. Everybody "sees the green" and wants a piece of it. REITs themselves could be a significant source of overbuilding, responding to investors' demands for ever-increasing FFO growth by continuing to build even in the face of declining absorption rates. Today there are many more REITs than ever before that have the expertise and access to capital to develop new properties, and those that do business in hot markets will normally be able to flex their muscles and put up new buildings.

In the past, a major cause of overbuilding has been legislation. In 1981, when Congress enacted the Economic Recovery Act, depreciation of real property for tax purposes was accelerated. The tax savings alone justified new projects. As we discussed in previous chapters, investors did not even require buildings to have a positive cash flow, so long as they provided a generous tax shelter. The merchandise was tax shelters, not real estate, and tax shelters were a very hot product. This situation was a major contributing factor to the overbuilt markets of the late 1980s. Similar legislation does not seem to be a danger today, but because REITs pay no taxes on their net income at the corporate level, it may still be said that Congress is "subsidizing" and "encouraging" real estate ownership.

While participation of investment bankers is essential in helping REITs raise the capital they need for growth, these same firms can sometimes be another source of trouble. When a particular real estate sector becomes very popular, Wall Street is always ready to satisfy investors' voracious appetites. But do investment bankers know when to stop? Some argue that too many investment dollars were raised for new factory outlet center REITs a few years ago, and the over-development created an excess of supply.

Strangely, even when it has become obvious that we

WILL THE "BIG BOXES" SURVIVE?

"BIG-BOX" RETAILERS, such as Wal-Mart, Ross, and T. J. Maxx have been doing well for a number of years, and investors have thrown a lot of money at them in order to encourage continued expansion. Today, some observers fear that big-box space is rapidly becoming excessive. On a smaller scale, this has been happening with large bookstores such as Crown, Borders, and Barnes & Noble. Only a few short years ago, a town that might have had one or two small bookstores now has several large ones. Can America support them all?

are in an overbuilding cycle, the building may continue. As early as 1984, it was apparent to many observers of the office sector that the amount of new construction was becoming excessive; nevertheless, builders and developers could not seem to stop themselves, and they continued to build new offices well into the early 1990s. Although some would explain this by the long lead time necessary to complete an office project once begun, it's more likely that there were some big egos at work among developers and that lenders were too myopic to detect the problem early enough.

Aside from apartments, where there always seems to be some excess supply in some cities, the only sector that has been suffering from excess supply in recent years is retail. The problem was described aptly several years ago by Milton Cooper, CEO of Kimco Realty, "Simply put, the USA is overstored. Many retailers are increasing their square footage without any regard for the relationship of space to the increase in population or disposable income." He predicted a significant increase in retailer bankruptcies, a prophecy that was borne out about two years ago. The usual effects of excess supply, declining occupancy rates, and rising cap rates occurred; more recently, however, rents have been stabilizing and even rising modestly in certain mall and outlet center properties, and while cap rates have recently been declining, vacancies are slowly but surely being filled. It remains to be seen whether the improving conditions in the retail sector will continue, since consumer spending has been very volatile.

The lingering problems in the retail sector and the pockets of apartment overbuilding notwithstanding, it does not appear that any sector will be ravaged by excess supply or severe overbuilding in the near future.

Today, the tax laws no longer subsidize development for its own sake. Lenders, pension plans, and other sources of development capital that were once burned are now demanding that their required rates of return be met by new projects.

Further, there is much more discipline in real estate markets today. The savings and loans, a main culprit of the 1980s' overbuilding, are no longer major real estate lenders. The banks, which often funded 100 to 110 percent of the cost of new, "spec" development during the last decade, have "gotten religion" and adopted much more stringent lending standards, which are still in effect today, often limiting construction loans to 70 to 80 percent of the cost of the project. They require significant equity participation from the developer—a factor, like insider stock ownership, that generally increases the success rate. Dan Dormer, executive vice president of Bank of America, observed, in the October 22, 1997, *Los Angeles Times,* "Now there is more equity cash going into transactions. Typically it is not unusual to see 15 to 30 percent, whereas in the '80s you could do it with zero." Lenders are also looking at prospective cash flows much more carefully, relying less on similar property appraisals, and requiring a prescribed minimum level of preleasing before funding a construction project.

REITs may eventually become the dominant developers within particular sectors or geographical areas, as has occurred with apartments in the Southeast. Should this trend continue, new building in a sector or an area may be limited by investors' willingness to provide REITs with additional equity capital. Furthermore, in view of the fact that managements normally have a significant interest in their REITs' shares, they will have no desire to shoot themselves in the foot by creating an oversupply.

WHITHER INTEREST RATES?

WHEN INVESTORS TALK about a particular stock or a group of stocks' being interest-rate sensitive, they usually mean that the price of the stock is heavily influenced by interest-rate movements. Stocks with high yields are interest-rate sensitive since, in a rising–interest-rate environment, many owners of such stocks will be lured into T-bills or money markets when those securities begin to yield more than their stocks are paying in dividends. Of course, a substantial number of shareholders will continue to hold out for long-term growth, but selling *will* occur—driving down the price of interest-sensitive stocks.

A sector of stocks might also be interest-rate sensitive for reasons other than their dividend yields. The type of business they're in, for instance, might be very dependent on borrowed funds. In that case, in a rising–interest-rate environment, the cost of doing business would go up, since the interest rates on their borrowed funds would go up. If increased borrowing costs cannot immediately be passed on to consumers, the sector's profit margins shrink. Some stocks are interest-rate sensitive for the first reason, some for the second reason, and some, such as utilities, for both reasons.

Whether their perception is correct or incorrect, if investors *perceive* that rising interest rates will negatively affect a company's profits, then the stock's price will have an inverse ratio with interest rates—rising when interest rates drop, and dropping when interest rates rise.

How, then, are REIT shares perceived by investors? Are they interest-rate–sensitive stocks? Is a significant risk in owning REITs that their shares will take a major tumble during periods when rates are rising briskly? Before we try to answer these questions, let's take a quick look at why REIT shares are bought and owned by investors, and how rising interest rates affect REITs' expected profitability.

Traditionally, REIT shares have been bought by investors who are looking for high total returns. "Total return" is the total of what an investor would receive from the combination of dividends received plus stock-price appreciation. Yields have traditionally made up about half of REITs' total returns. For example, a 7 percent yield and 7 percent annual price appreciation (resulting from 7 percent annual FFO growth and assuming a stable price P/FFO ratio) results in a 14 percent total annual return. Because the dividend component of the expected return is so substantial, REITs must compete in the marketplace with such income-producing investments as bonds and utility stocks.

For example, let's assume that in January "long bonds" (with maturities of up to 30 years) yield 6 percent and the average REIT yields 6 percent as well. If the long bond drops in price in response to rising interest rates, causing it then to yield 7 percent, the average REIT's price may also drop, causing its yield to rise to 7 percent. This kind of "price action" would preserve the same yield relationship then in effect between bonds and REITs. In the real world, REIT prices do not always correlate well with bond prices (in 1996, for example, there was no correlation whatsoever), but the reality remains that REITs *do* compete with bonds and other high-yielding securities to attract yield-hungry investors, and most REIT buyers and owners assume that REIT prices will fall in response to higher interest rates and vice versa. For this reason, REIT investors should *assume* that REIT prices, like the prices for all common stocks, will weaken in response to higher rates.

A second, related, and very important question is whether a rise in interest rates might cause significant problems for REITs by causing FFO to decline, weakening their balance sheets, diminishing their asset values, or otherwise affecting their merits as investments. This is a multifaceted analysis, and of course it also depends upon the individual REIT, its sector, its properties' locations, and its management, but let's consider the possibilities.

Higher interest rates are generally not good for any business, since they soak up purchasing power from the consumer and can cause recession.

Apartment REITs, then, or hotel, or retail REITs, which cater to individual consumers may be hurt more by higher interest rates than other sectors, if rising rates slow the economy and reduce available consumer buying power. However, even REITs that lease properties to businesses, such as office and industrial-property REITs, will be somewhat adversely affected, since businesses will also be affected by rising interest rates and a slowing economy. In general, property sectors that use longer-term leases (such as offices and industrial properties) will be hurt less by temporary recessions, since their lease payments will be more stable.

Interest is usually a significant cost for a REIT, since, like other property owners, REITs normally use debt leverage to increase their investment returns. The whole concept of variable-rate debt is that it allows the lender to adjust the rate according to the interest-rate environment. In a rising–interest-rate environment, then, the lender's rates will rise; the higher the amount of variable-rate debt a REIT is carrying, the greater will be the impact on its profit margins and FFO. But, even with fixed debt, REITs must be concerned with interest rates—when they are rolling over a portion of their debt and when they are taking on new debt.

Even when a REIT chooses to raise capital through equity offerings rather than debt financing, higher interest rates can have an adverse effect, since rising interest rates are likely to depress all share prices, thus raising a REIT's nominal cost of equity capital.

Another negative aspect of rising interest rates relates to a REIT's asset values. Although cap rates are influenced by many factors, it's almost intuitive that a major increase in interest rates will exert upward pressure on cap rates. All things being equal, property buyers will generally insist on higher real estate returns when interest rates have moved up; correspondingly, when interest rates have moved up, property values will tend to decline, which affects the asset values of the properties owned by REITs. Although a large number of REIT buyers focus on FFO rather than the asset value of a particular REIT, asset values are nevertheless very important in determining a REIT's intrinsic value, as we've seen in Chapter 9.

Any significant decline in the value of its underlying real estate properties could affect the share price of a REIT.

The foregoing discussion shows how rising interest rates can negatively affect a REIT's operating results, balance sheet, asset value, and stock price. However, we might also note that in one important respect REITs may actually be helped by rising interest rates. This relates to the overbuilding threat. New, competing projects, whether apartments, office buildings, outlet centers, or any other type of property, must be financed. Clearly, higher interest rates will increase borrowing costs and make developing new projects more expensive or, in some cases, too expensive. Higher rates may also affect the "hurdle rate" demanded by the developer's financial partners, again causing many projects to be shelved or canceled. Obviously, the fewer new competing projects that get built, the less existing properties will feel competitive pressure. Threats of overbuilding can rapidly fade when interest rates are rising briskly.

We should keep in mind, of course, that we are speaking in generalities here, and the extent to which rising interest rates will affect a particular REIT's business, profitability, asset values, and financial condition must be analyzed individually. On balance, however, rising interest rates are generally not favorable for most REITs. Combined with the tendency of all companies' shares, including REITs', to decline in response to rising interest rates, REIT investors need to be very much aware of the interest-rate environment.

HOSTILE CAPITAL-RAISING ENVIRONMENTS

SINCE REITS MUST PAY their shareholders at least 95 percent of their taxable income but most pay out more than that because of higher FFO and AFFOs, they are unable to retain much cash for new acquisitions and development and are, therefore, dependent on the capital markets. Their FFO growth, without new acquisitions and development, will then depend only on how much REITs can improve the bottom line on their income from *existing* properties.

As a result of this inherent limitation, investors must be mindful that even the highest-quality REIT may not always have access to additional equity capital. At some point there will be another bear market—for the broad market as well as for REIT stocks—and, when it comes, many REITs will find it difficult to sell new shares to raise funds for new investments. This, in turn, will retard FFO growth until such time as the markets return to "normalcy."

However, that is not the only circumstance in which REITs could find their flow of capital shut off. There is also the great specter of overbuilding that can only be beaten back but never eliminated entirely. In mid-1995, when a few apartment REITs owning properties in Southeast apartment markets tried to raise new equity capital by selling additional shares, there were few takers. Individual REITs with lackluster growth prospects, excessive debt, or conflicts of interests will also have problems attracting potential investors. Attracting new capital is the lifeblood of healthy, growing REIT organizations. External and even internal events over which managements may have little or no control may cut a REIT off from this essential new capital and thus affect its rate of FFO growth, which in turn affects investor sentiment and the REIT's stock price. This is one reason investors will pay a premium for those REITs whose quality and growth prospects are perceived as being most likely to attract additional equity capital, even in a bear market.

LEGISLATION

IF THE CYNIC'S VIEW that "no man's life, liberty, or property is safe when Congress is in session" is correct, we must recognize that what Congress giveth, Congress may also taketh away. But it is highly unlikely that Congress would enact legislation to rescind REITs' tax deduction for the dividends paid to their shareholders, thus subjecting REITs' net income to taxation at the corporate level.

There are several public-policy reasons for this.

First, because of REITs' high dividend payments to their shareholders, they probably generate at least as much income for the federal government as they would if they were conventional real estate corporations that could shelter a substantial amount of otherwise taxable income by increasing debt and deducting their greater interest payments. (It's just that the taxes are paid by the individual shareholders rather than the corporation.) Second, property held in a REIT most likely provides more tax revenues than if it were held, as it typically has been, in a partnership. Finally, REITs have shown that real estate ownership and management can be quite profitable without using excessive debt leverage, which, if not for the REIT format, would be the way real estate would probably be held. Excessive debt can be a very destabilizing force in the U.S. economy, and it's unlikely that Congress would want to contribute to that.

Encouraging greater debt financing of real estate could substantially exacerbate the swings in the normal business and real estate cycles, harming the economy over the long term.

In early 1998, the Clinton administration proposed legislation as part of its fiscal 1999 budget that would affect certain REITs. One of the proposals would specifically target those REITs whose ability to engage in certain non–real estate activities (such as hotel management) through a sister corporation has previously been "grandfathered" under prior legislation ("paired-share" REITs). This proposal, which would affect REITs such as Starwood Hotels & Resorts, Patriot American, MediTrust, and First Union, would restrict their competitive advantage by treating the REIT and its non-REIT corporation as one entity with respect to properties acquired after the date the congressional committee approves the legislation. This would effectively prevent these paired-share REITs from operating businesses that generate income that doesn't qualify under the existing REIT laws, but only with respect to new properties or businesses acquired.

Another proposal would tighten the restrictions on the ability of a REIT to own controlling interests in non-REIT corporations; the existing rules are designed to prevent a REIT from indirectly generating impermissible non–real estate income through controlled subsidiaries. The proposal would tighten existing rules by preventing REITs from owning stock representing more than 10 percent of the voting power or value of all outstanding shares of the non-REIT corporation.

These proposals, if enacted by Congress in their present or a related form, could negatively affect certain REITs whose present or future business activities go beyond the traditional business of owning and operating commercial real estate (for example, those REITs that—through non-REIT subsidiaries—operate, or intend to operate, such businesses as hotels, golf courses, and self-storage facilities management). However, it's quite possible that these new restrictions will be enacted in a form with which these REITs will be comfortable, and would actually be beneficial in some aspects by eliminating present uncertainties. While these issues had not been resolved by the time this book went to press, they are unlikely to have a substantial negative effect in the long run upon the great majority of REITs. In the near term, however, growth expectations for some of the more aggressive REITs could be pared back a bit, depending upon the final form of any such legislation.

So far, Congress has deemed it important to encourage a regular flow of funds into the real estate sector of the economy, and has enabled individuals to own real estate through the REIT vehicle. Over the years, thanks to the efforts of The National Association of Real Estate Investment Trusts (NAREIT), Congress has, if anything, liberalized the laws to expand the scope of REITs' authorized business activities. While the Clinton proposals appear to be moving in the other direction, they are designed to make sure that REITs remain essentially in the real estate business.

PROBLEMS AFFECTING INDIVIDUAL REITS

SOMETIMES ONE REIT in a sector has a problem and all the other REITs in its sector suffer from guilt by association. The following is a good illustration: In early 1995, two of the newly created factory outlet center REITs, McArthur/Glen and Factory Stores of America, got into trouble; the former by being unable to deliver the many additional developments it promised Wall Street, the latter by expanding too aggressively and taking on too much debt. The market, often prone to shooting first and asking questions later, assumed that the illness was sectorwide and destroyed the stock prices of such steady performers as Chelsea/GCA and Tanger, as well as the two problem-plagued outlet REITs. However, by the end of 1995, Chelsea/GCA's stock was back near its all-time high, and Tanger's stock was in the process of recovering as well. Investors who dumped their Chelsea/GCA stock in the low $20s because of their inability to distinguish between a major, sectorwide problem and problems with a couple of individual REITs had to swallow a bitter pill but learned a valuable lesson.

RECESSIONS

AN ECONOMIC RECESSION can hurt real estate owners, including REITs, even when supply and demand for space in a particular market are in equilibrium. A retail property, for example, located in a healthy property market may be 95 percent leased, but its tenants' sales might decline in response to a severe recession.

This will result in lower "overage" rentals (additional rental income based on sales exceeding a preset minimum), lower occupancy rates, and even tenant bankruptcies. Apartment units, especially newly built ones, may be slow to lease, perhaps because of declining job growth. Generally speaking, during recessionary conditions, both consumers and businesses will cut back on their spending patterns. In this situation, rents cannot be raised without jeopardizing occupancy rates.

We've mentioned that focusing on a specific geographical area is something that REIT owners like to see, but the downside is that local or regional recessions can be more damaging for a geographically focused REIT. In recent years, we've learned that economic conditions in the United States aren't always the same in every geographical area. We can have an oil-industry depression in the Southwest, while the rest of the country is doing fine. Or the Northeast can be in the dumps, while Florida's economy is humming along. Local or regional economic declines often result in slower FFO growth, shareholder nervousness, and declines in the affected REIT's stock price.

HEALTH CARE REITS

THE GOOD NEWS is that health care is one sector that has been quite recession resistant, because the need for health care services is continuous and government reimbursement is dependable.

The bad news is that some health care REITs are now moving into a new, economically sensitive area— assisted-living facilities. Since there is less likelihood of substantial government reimbursement in this area, REITs that own assisted-living facilities could become more sensitive to general economic conditions, including overbuilding.

CHANGING CONSUMER AND BUSINESS PREFERENCES

INVESTORS MUST ALSO watch for trends and changes in consumer and business preferences that can reduce renters' demands for a property type, causing supply to exceed demand and reduce owners' profits.

Today, for example, because of our increasingly mobile population, self-storage facilities are popular. Will they always be so? Will a large segment of the U.S. population continue to enjoy the flexibility provided by apartment living, or, as we move into the 21st century, will single-family houses become more affordable and attract an ever increasing percentage of the population? Will businesses continue to lease the industrial properties they've always found necessary, or will some new form of business practice render many of the current facilities obsolete? Will companies continue to absorb space in large office buildings as they have in the past, or will telecommuting make a major dent in the demand for traditional office space? What effect will Internet shopping have on traditional retailers? These are questions about basic trends in how we live and how we work. No one can answer them now with absolute certainty, but REIT investors will need to look for indications of changing trends, or they will suffer the consequences.

CREDIBILITY ISSUES

PROBABLY THE MOST common type of specific-REIT problem that can cause investor headaches is the error in judgment that raises significant management-credibility questions.

Here, for example, are just some of the situations that have occurred in prior years:

◆ Overpaying for properties and later having to write them down (*e.g.,* American Health Properties)
◆ Expanding too quickly and taking on too much debt in the process (*e.g.,* Factory Stores of America)
◆ Underestimating the difficulty of assimilating a major port-

folio acquisition (*e.g.,* Manufactured Home Communities)

◆ Providing investors with "bad" information by underestimating the expenses of operating a public company (*e.g.,* Holly Residential Properties)

◆ Overstating the number of new development properties expected to be completed in the year (*e.g.,* McArthur/Glen)

◆ Overestimating future FFO growth prospects *(e.g.,* Crown American Realty)

◆ Discovering that newly developed properties are falling short of promised operating income (*e.g.,* Horizon Group)

◆ Setting a dividend rate, upon going public, that exceeds anticipated FFO, thus raising concerns about the adequacy of dividend coverage (*e.g.,* Mills Corp.).

Yet another kind of credibility issue arises when there is a material conflict of interest between management and shareholders. REITs that are externally managed are always subject to such conflicts, but even those that are managed internally can sometimes exhibit conflicts. The most serious of these include a REIT's executive officer's selling his or her own properties to the REIT; allowing an executive officer to compete for available properties with the REIT; and allowing high-profile CEOs to spend too much of their time on other ventures or serve as officers of other companies with which the REIT does business. Excessive executive compensation for mediocre operating results, on the other hand, while annoying to shareholders, is not usually as damaging as the other types of conflicts mentioned.

Many investors are wary of the "UPREIT" format, which poses knotty conflict-of-interest issues. UPREITs, as you may recall from earlier chapters, are those whose assets are held by a limited partnership in which the REIT owns a controlling interest and in which REIT "insiders" may own a substantial interest. Since these insiders may own few shares in the REIT itself, their usually low tax basis in the partnership interest creates a conflict of interest should the REIT be subject to a takeover offer, or in the event it receives an attractive offer for some of its properties.

Most problems like these can be remedied by a REIT's management if it is forthright with investors, quickly recognizes any mistakes it has made, and promptly takes action to rectify the situation. In 1996, Highwoods Properties (HIW) agreed to acquire the assets of Crocker Realty, and advised investors that the acquisition would substantially increase FFO. However, it refrained from also advising investors that most of that increase would result from the substantial additional debt HIW would be taking on in order to pay for Crocker. Investor concern over the prospects of a highly leveraged balance sheet helped to depress HIW's shares shortly after the deal was announced. Management reacted promptly, however, and announced a major equity financing so that most of the debt could be repaid. With that financing completed, investor confidence was soon restored, and eventually HIW's stock hit new all-time highs.

The key issue here is management's loss of credibility with investors. When a REIT has some difficulty, unless prompt action is taken, it can be very hard to regain investors' confidence; in extreme cases, the only alternatives for such a REIT are to become acquired or to obtain new management.

Loss of management credibility can be crippling to a REIT.

There is obviously no way for REIT investors to avoid such problems altogether. The most conservative strategy is to invest only in those blue-chip REITs where management's reputation is beyond question. Of course, this policy of going only for pristine quality will often mean investors will have to pay a substantial price premium, and will miss out on lesser-known

REITs or those REITs that are primed for a rebound.

Another strategy is to avoid REITs that have been public companies for only a short time, since most of these management-credibility issues seem to have arisen in "unseasoned" REITs. This approach, unfortunately, could mean missing out on some very promising newcomers. The "right" strategy depends on market conditions, good research, and the individual investor's risk tolerance.

BALANCE-SHEET WOES

DEBT IS ALWAYS a problem, as well as an opportunity, for people, for nations, and, no less, for REITs. If management overburdens the REIT's balance sheet with debt, investors must be particularly careful. High debt levels often go hand in hand with impressive FFO growth and high dividend yields, but investors need to be wary of such attributes when they have been subsidized by excessive debt. Too much debt, particularly short-term debt, can virtually destroy a REIT. Earlier, we discussed the importance of a strong balance sheet in recognizing a blue-chip REIT. The importance of a strong balance sheet cannot be overstressed, because those REITs that are overloaded with debt will not only be looked upon with suspicion by investors, but may, if their property markets deteriorate, have to be sold to a stronger company at a fire-sale price or—worse—dismembered.

A weak balance sheet results from a number of different factors: high debt levels in relation to the REIT's market capitalization or net asset value (NAV), a low coverage of interest expense from property cash flows, or a large amount of short-term or variable-rate debt. A weak balance sheet can seriously restrict the REIT's ability to expand and increase FFO, and excessive debt leverage only serves to magnify the effects of declining net operating income (NOI). Further, a weak balance sheet can make equity financing expensive (new investors will have the greatest bargaining power); and it also creates the danger that lenders will not roll over existing debt at maturity, that covenants in credit agreements will not be complied with, and that should interest rates rise substantially, the REIT will be exposed to significantly higher operating costs and reduced FFO.

The market has usually factored potential problems like these into the price before the REIT actually feels their effects. A REIT, therefore, that is perceived to be overleveraged or to have too much short-term or variable-rate debt will see its shares trade at a low P/FFO ratio in relation to its peers and to other REITs.

SMALL MARKET VALUATIONS

REIT INVESTORS NEED to be aware that, despite REITs' 35-year history, very few are large companies compared to major U.S. corporations. Let's take Hewlett-Packard (HP) as an example. At the end of its 1997 fiscal year, HP had more than one billion shares outstanding; at its market price of $62 $3/8$ per share at the end of 1997, HP's total outstanding shares had a market value of $64.9 billion. General Motors, as of the end of 1997, had shares outstanding worth approximately $43 billion. Moving away from the real giants, let's look at Genuine Parts, a supplier of automotive parts and accessories. As of December 1997, their outstanding common stock had a market value of $6 billion.

Compare these market caps to some major REITs' market caps. Equity Office Properties, which had the largest equity market value in the REIT world in early 1998, could muster an equity market cap of only $8.9 billion. The next largest, Simon DeBartolo, had an equity market cap of $5.6 billion.

In January 1998, only nine REITs could boast of equity market caps in excess of $3 billion, with the average being $726 million.

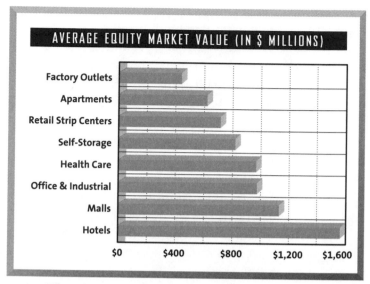

AVERAGE EQUITY MARKET VALUE (IN $ MILLIONS)

Factory Outlets
Apartments
Retail Strip Centers
Self-Storage
Health Care
Office & Industrial
Malls
Hotels

$0 $400 $800 $1,200 $1,600

The chart above shows average equity market caps for the larger market cap REITs, according to Green Street Advisors' Real Estate Stock Index, as of December 31, 1997.

The market cap of the entire REIT industry, as well as many of the individual REITs within it, has been growing rapidly during the last few years. According to NAREIT, by the end of 1997, the total equity market capitalization for just the equity REITs amounted to $128 billion. This compares with only $11 billion at the end of 1992, just five years earlier.

Nonetheless, while the "typical" REIT is by no means a tiny company, it is hardly a major U.S. corporation. As of the end of 1997, the equity market cap of the entire REIT industry was smaller than the equity market cap of even one such industry giant as General Electric, Coca-Cola, Microsoft, Exxon, or Merck.

There are several potential problems that can result from small size: A REIT with a small market cap may not be able to obtain the public awareness and sponsorship necessary to enable it to raise the equity capital necessary for its growth. Further, to the extent that pension and institutional ownership of REITs could be a new trend fostering the growth of the entire REIT industry or perhaps just a few REITs, a particularly small market cap is likely to discourage such entities from investing in a REIT due to its lack of market liquidity. Finally, a minor misjudgment on the part of management of a small REIT *(see "Credibility Issues," above)* could have a major impact on the REIT's future business prospects, FFO growth, and reputation with investors.

DEPTH OF MANAGEMENT AND MANAGEMENT- SUCCESSION ISSUES

PERHAPS A MORE serious potential problem related to the relatively small size of many REITs is the issue of management depth and succession. Smaller companies, whether REITs or other businesses, because of their limited financial resources, are often unable to develop the type of extensive organization found in a major corporation such as, for example, General Electric. We must ask ourselves whether the REIT might be at a competitive disadvantage if, perhaps, it cannot afford to hire a staff of employees of the highest caliber or obtain the very best market information available concerning supply and demand for properties in its market area. Other questions might relate to the depth and experience of the REIT's property acquisition or property management department, or perhaps the sophistication and strength of the REIT's financial reporting, budgeting, and forecasting systems. There are certain efficiencies that can be enjoyed by companies of substantial size, among them, greater bargaining power with suppliers and tenants. These are issues that must be addressed separately for each REIT, but small size can limit any company's ability to attract high-quality management, particularly at the middle-management level, and small size can limit a REIT's ability to remain a strong competitor in its markets.

Even if we, as investors, are comfortable with a

REIT's management capabilities, notwithstanding its modest size, still, modest size often means we must rely on the management of a few brilliant people to produce superior long-term results with the least risk. Let's face it, while we sometimes see "superstar" management in large corporations (*e.g.*, Warren Buffett at Berkshire Hathaway, Michael Eisner at Disney, Jack Welch at General Electric, or the late Roberto Goizueta at Coca-Cola), investors quite often see what they might consider "high-profile" management in smaller companies such as REITs.

Knowledgeable investors are attracted to such REITs as Crescent Real Estate Equities, Kimco Realty, Equity Office Properties, Simon DeBartolo Group, and Vornado Realty Trust, to name a few, because they are managed by such well-known real estate investors and managers as Richard Rainwater, Milton Cooper, Sam Zell, the Simons, and Steven Roth, respectively.

WHAT HIGH-PROFILE MANAGEMENT CAN MEAN

IN LATE 1996, Vornado Realty hired well-known real estate executive Mike Fascitelli away from a major investment banking firm. While his compensation package was the talk of the REIT world for a couple of weeks, investors gave Steven Roth a vote of confidence by boosting Vornado's shares substantially in the days immediately following the announcement.

The challenge for REIT investors, therefore, is to determine whether such superstar managers have developed a strong business organization, with highly capable individuals to succeed them when they no longer run the company. Earlier, we parenthetically referred to the much revered Roberto Goizueta of Coca-Cola, who made that company what it is today and who died, somewhat unexpectedly, in his 50s. Certainly not the least of Mr. Goizueta's talents was that he had created a strong and deep management team that made Coca-Cola's management transition practically seamless. There are always events: retirement, death, disability—expected and unexpected—that necessitate a backup plan in the event a company loses its superstar. It's never good for an organization to be dependent upon the efforts of one individual, no matter how talented.

Related to the superstar problem is determining how much the REIT's stock price reflects the "star" status of its top management. For example, if Richard Rainwater were to decide next week that he were tired of managing Crescent, what would happen to Crescent's share price? In other words, is the price of a REIT's stock based so much on the ability and reputation of just one individual that the sudden departure of that person would cause the price to collapse by 20 to 25 percent? A REIT's stock price is less likely to tumble if senior management has done a good job bringing along talented younger management, and has convinced investors that such is the case.

Larry Miller is another case in point. Mr. Miller was the extremely capable and respected CEO of Bradley Real Estate, a shopping-center REIT, for approximately ten years when he was struck down by a heart attack in his mid-50s. As with the case of Mr. Goizueta, Mr. Miller's foresight in developing additional high-quality managerial talent meant that Bradley's stock price moved very little immediately following his untimely death.

Management succession is a sensitive issue that is, for obvious reasons, difficult for both investors and REIT managements to discuss, but it is of vital concern to investors. Genius is tough to replace in any organization, no matter how large, but it's even tougher to replace in "mid-cap" companies like REITs. However, as important as the succession issue is today, it is only a part of the larger issue of how successful a particular REIT has been in building a strong, deep, and motivated management team.

SUMMARY

◆ All REITs are subject to two major hazards: an excess supply of available rental properties, and rising interest rates.

◆ While a recessionary economy sometimes results in a temporary decline in demand for space, the excess supply that is brought on by overbuilding can be a much larger and longer-lasting problem.

◆ Higher interest rates are generally not good for any company since they soak up purchasing power from consumers as well as businesses, and can cause recession.

◆ Overleveraged balance sheets and conflicts of interests by management can create problems for specific REITs—and their stock prices.

◆ Major disasters and gross misjudgments have been very rare among REITs; and even in such cases, major share price collapse has been infrequent.

◆ Encouraging greater debt financing of real estate could substantially exacerbate the swings in the normal business and real estate cycles, harming the economy over the long term.

◆ Since no investment is completely free from risk and since REIT investors are conservative by nature—seeking not only income but also preservation of capital—the greatest security comes from diversity among one's REIT investments.

12

Tea Leaves:
WHERE WILL REITs GO FROM HERE?

NE THING is for certain with REITs: their mention at cocktail parties will no longer draw blank stares. If the REIT world was unknown, then after the much publicized Hilton Hotels and Starwood Lodging bidding war for ITT, there was hardly an investor left who didn't learn what a REIT was. Does this mean the REIT industry will continue to distance itself from the murky backwaters of the investment world? Will the ongoing securitization of real estate continue to attract billions of investment dollars from institutions and individuals? Will the "graying" of America mean that more and more investors will need high current yields as well as growth, and look to REITs to fill that need? Here, we'll break out the crystal ball and look at some of the issues that could affect the size and landscape of the REIT industry over the next several years.

Before we start forecasting the future, though, let's look at the past and the present. The total equity market cap of equity REITs did not reach $1 billion until 1968, 5 years after the first REIT was organized. By the end of 1997, almost 30 years later, it was $128 billion—a compounded annual growth rate of 17.6 percent. However, most of this growth occurred only recently. At the end of 1992, the equity REITs' market cap was only $11 billion, but, by the end of 1993, it had increased to $26 billion and by the end of 1994, to $39 billion, primarily as a result of the IPO binge in those two years. The growth in 1995 and 1996 came primarily from secondary offerings and price appreciation, while in 1997 it came from virtually all sources. There were only 34 publicly traded equity REITs at the end of 1971. By the end of 1997, 26 years later, there were 176.

Despite this impressive growth, as we discussed briefly in the last chapter, the REIT industry remains small in comparison with both the stock market and the total value of commercial real estate in the United States. While REITs own a significant portion of the approximately $1.45 trillion of institutionally owned commercial real estate (as estimated by ERE Yarmouth), they own a much smaller percentage of the total value of all commercial real estate in the United States (which has been estimated at between $3 trillion and $4 trillion).

REITs' property ownership percentage is low, not only on an absolute basis, but also in relationship to that of other countries. The National Association of Real Estate Investment Trusts (NAREIT) has estimated that in the United Kingdom, for example, approximately 50 percent of the market value of that country's commercial real estate has been securitized and is publicly traded. Should securitization become as prevalent here as in the United Kingdom, the market cap of the U.S. REIT industry would expand almost fivefold, to over $600 billion. *Can* this happen? Will it happen? In order to hazard a guess, we will need to consider two key questions: (a) *Will* a signifi-

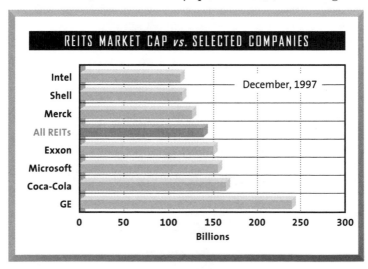

cant number of private real estate owners want either to become REITs or to sell their properties to REITs, and (b) *Will* investors want to own substantially more REITs in their portfolios?

SUPPLY SIDE: REAL ESTATE COMPANIES WILL WANT TO "REITIZE"

A SUCCESSFUL AND growing real estate organization could list several reasons why it might choose to go public as a REIT. In fact, as recent history illustrates, the trend of going public is becoming more and more prevalent.

Two outstanding real estate companies that have gone public in the past few years are Kimco Realty, which completed its initial public offering in November 1991, after having operated successfully as a private company for 25 years, and Spieker Properties, which went public in November 1993. These companies both have long track records of successful operations in their respective fields (neighborhood shopping centers and office/industrial), and they both have managements that have been innovative, that maintain significant ownership of the outstanding stock of each REIT, and that are devoted to strengthening their organizations and motivating their employees. These policies, in both cases, have resulted in well–above-average long-term growth for their shareholders.

TAX ADVANTAGES

PERHAPS ONE OF the most obvious reasons a corporation might choose to become a REIT is that, unlike most corporations, REITs pay no taxes at the corporate level, thus enabling them and their shareholders to avoid double taxation.

Although many property-owning companies can avoid taxation entirely by taking on a large amount of debt and writing off the interest expense, the REIT format allows the owner to do business with less risk. This is no small advantage in an increasingly uncertain and more competitive world economy.

Finally, it's possible that a significant number of publicly traded, non-REIT, real estate–owning corporations might elect to become REITs in order to take advantage of the lack of double taxation. For example, in 1997, The Rouse Company became a REIT—notwithstanding many years of successful operation as a regular "C-Corp." Others will likely follow.

That REITs pay no taxes at the corporate level is a factor that will, for a long time to come, motivate many real estate companies to join the trend to REITize.

ACCESS TO CAPITAL

A PRIMARY INDUCEMENT for going public is the greater access to capital and financing flexibility that publicly traded companies enjoy. Successful and growing real estate organizations constantly need additional capital for building and buying real estate, for improving and upgrading individual properties, and for continually strengthening management ranks. As we discussed earlier, successful REITs must constantly return to the capital markets if they want to continue to grow at above-average rates, but, as Kimco CEO Milton Cooper reminds us, lenders have been manic-depressive over the years when it comes to lending to real estate owners, developers, and operators. During some periods they seem almost to be throwing money at these enterprises, while at other times they are absolute skinflints. It's difficult to finance and manage a growing business under such stop-and-go conditions.

This is not to say that the traditional sources of financing will be discarded when a REIT is formed. Successful REITs normally obtain traditional short-term financing from banks, and longer-term, private-placement financing from other lenders—such as

insurance companies—in the same way that they did
earlier as private companies. They can also enter into
joint-venture deals with financial partners, whether the
company is public or private.

**Access to the public markets provides flexibility
and financial resources to REITs and allows managements
to have access to reasonably priced capital to plan for the
long term and to safeguard it from the whims of private
lenders.**

The issuance of common stock, while expensive,
provides the most permanent type of financing since
there is no obligation to repay it. Furthermore,
common-stock issuance allows the REIT to leverage
this additional capital by adding debt to it. Before a
borrower becomes eligible for certain types of loans,
most lenders insist on a substantial cushion of shareholders' equity, as well as a certain minimum "coverage" of interest-payment obligations. Thus, selling
common stock provides permanent capital and allows
the REIT to borrow more.

The sale of preferred stock is another avenue normally open only to publicly traded companies.
Although preferred stock adds financial leverage to
REITs' balance sheets and investors should therefore
treat it as debt in analyzing a REIT's financial strength,
it is not recorded as debt on the company's balance
sheet and is not treated as such by lenders. Furthermore, nonconvertible preferred stock does not dilute
shareholders' equity interest in the REIT.

Finally, a significant number of REITs have been
able to raise capital by the issuance and sale of notes,
bonds, and debentures, all of which enable the REIT
to access the public debt markets and diversify away
from a reliance on banks and other private lenders.
The broad mix of available financing options is of significant value to a real estate company. It is likely that

at various times the public markets will be closed to a
REIT as a result of depressed market conditions or for
some other reason; private financing may then be
readily available. Conversely, at other times private
lenders may be exceedingly tightfisted, while the public markets extend an open hand.

Finally, becoming an UPREIT or a DownREIT gives
the real estate organization a significant advantage in
the acquisition of properties from sellers who, by
accepting operating partnership (OP) units, can defer
capital gains taxes. This approach to financing real
estate acquisitions has become very popular over the
past few years, and gives REITs a competitive edge.

Expanded access to capital via common stock, preferred stock, and debt securities, as well as through the
issuance of OP units, is a key reason why many well-run
and growing real estate companies will become REITs
in the years ahead.

ABILITY TO STRENGTHEN AND MOTIVATE THE ORGANIZATION

TODAY, MORE THAN ever before, owning and operating commercial real estate successfully is a
business—no matter whether the real estate be apartments, office buildings, retail properties, or any other
type. For a business, a strong organization is essential
to success; competition is fierce everywhere, and
strong real estate organizations can often operate at
lower costs and are likely to have a significant competitive edge.

Although private companies, even large ones, can
build solid organizations and motivate employees and
management, it is clearly easier to accomplish these
objectives if the company is publicly held. Stock
options are a good motivational tool for employees—
from the most recently hired all the way to top management.

Today, stock option plans and stock purchase plans (allowing employees to buy their company stock at a discount) are strong employee incentives in companies, including REITs.

Discipline and control are becoming increasingly important to managements in their efforts to stay a step ahead of the competition. Many public companies find that the requirements imposed upon them, while often costly, strengthen the organization in the long run. These requirements include having a board of several outside directors with whom business plans and projects must be discussed and justified; having to answer to the shareholders with respect to expense control, compensation programs, and other shareholder concerns; and implementing strong financial systems and controls.

These factors, by strengthening the organization and its financial discipline, allow public REITs to become more efficient owners and managers of real estate. As such, they will be able to continue to take tenants and market share from the smaller, less-capitalized and less-disciplined real estate owner.

LIQUIDITY AND ESTATE PLANNING

ANOTHER FACTOR LIKELY to induce well-run real estate companies to go public is the ability of the public markets to provide liquidity for the ownership interests of management and employees. In all businesses—real estate, manufacturing, or service providing—management changes from time to time, and individuals who have devoted years to a successful operation may want to cash out for retirement or for some other reason. Even key personnel who stay with the company need to convert some of their capital to cash from time to time, perhaps to buy a house or to pay their children's college tuition. The public market provides the

liquidity necessary for selling their shares, since trans-
fers of privately held shares or partnership interests are
costly, time-consuming, or simply not available.

Estate-planning concerns may also induce successful
real estate companies to "REITize." Uncle Sam takes a
big bite out of substantial estates. This is not to say that
an entrepreneur who goes public will be able to avoid
estate taxes, but going public may keep heirs from
being forced to sell all or part of the business or promising real estate assets to pay estate taxes. Public shares,
however, can be sold in the public markets, which will
allow the business itself to remain undisturbed.

Admittedly, there are some reasons for a company not
to go public: Management will have to operate in a "fish-
bowl." Almost every major decision must be explained
to the investors, who will be constantly looking over
management's shoulder. Independent directors will
need to be consulted on all major projects. There will be
significant pressure to perform, often on a very short-
term basis. The costs of running a public company will
be large, including premiums for directors' and officers'
insurance, expensive audit fees, costs of maintaining an
investor-relations department, transfer agent fees, and
legal and other costs for SEC compliance.

These drawbacks notwithstanding, for a REIT the
benefits of being a public company greatly outweigh
the drawbacks for long-term success. In 1997 alone, 25
REITs went public, and a significant additional number will make their public debuts in 1998. If these
recent developments are any indication of what the
"best and the brightest" real estate entrepreneurs
intend to do over the next several years, then the
entire REIT industry has a very bright future ahead.

DEMAND SIDE: MORE INVESTORS
WILL WANT TO OWN REITS

IT OBVIOUSLY WON'T MATTER how many great real
estate companies want to become REITs if there is

insufficient investor demand for REIT shares. Following the end of the IPO boom of 1993–94, many well-run and experienced real estate organizations were told that investor enthusiasm for REITs had chilled and that the IPO window had slammed shut. That situation was reversed in 1996–97, when not only individual investors began buying REITs as they never had before, but institutional investors, money managers, and pension funds also started moving into REITs in a big way. How long will this enthusiasm last? Will investment interest in REITs continue to be great enough in the future to allow for continually increasing IPOs and the secondary offerings that will enable REITs to continue their portfolio expansions?

INDIVIDUAL INVESTORS

A PERCEPTIVE OBSERVER once noted that the baby-boomer generation is like a rather large rat that has just been swallowed by a snake—it greatly changes the form of the snake as it wends its way through the snake's long body. The baby boomers created over-crowded classes when they started school, and spiral-ing tuition rates as they pursued higher education; they stoked demand for houses, BMWs, and Brie as they got jobs and began climbing the corporate ladder. More recently, they inspired an awesome explosion in the growth of mutual funds as they began to contemplate future retirement. These boomers are now serious indeed about investing.

Although these new investors have channeled billions of dollars into mutual funds, they are also exploring other alternatives. Many are investing on their own, and both the full-service and discount brokerage firms have benefited from their business; other new investors are turning to financial planners and investment advisers.

The number of mutual funds devoted primarily to REITs and real estate investing has grown from 6 to 34 from 1992 to 1997, and their assets have increased from $342 million to $11 billion.

More than $4.8 billion poured into REITs and real estate mutual funds in 1997 alone. There are now even REIT-indexed mutual funds. But how much of the aggregate amount of the new investment funds that will be deployed through the end of the '90s and into the 21st century will REITs be able to capture?

All signs point to a significant amount. New investors start with small investments, and mutual funds are one obvious beneficiary; a mutual fund is a cost-effective way for new investors to get into a regular investment program. It is not necessary to become a financial analyst or keep detailed records of every transaction. Popular 401(k) plans also encourage employees to invest through mutual funds. Over time, however, these investments will grow larger and investors' needs will grow and become more complex. Many investors will want to get more personally involved. For tax reasons, they will want to time their financial transactions. They will use individual stock-brokers to help them review specific investments. They will seek the help of professional financial planners and investment advisers. They will want to diversify their investments among different asset classes to mini-mize the adverse effects of the occasional crash in a particular market. Therein lies a golden opportunity for REITs to attract new investors.

As the years go by, REITs will continue to be an attractive method of diversification for these serious, new investors. Even if they don't make up the lion's share of these investments dollars, a 10 to 15 percent asset allocation would result in huge additional demand for REIT shares. As investors' assets become

FROM AN INVESTOR'S STANDPOINT

THE JUSTIFICATION FOR banking on REITs is clear: REITs have, over many years, delivered total returns to their investors that approximate those of the S&P 500 Index; they have low betas, which means that the REIT sector of one's portfolio won't move in lockstep with the rest of the market; and they have shown themselves to be less volatile. They provide substantial dividend yields—well in excess of most other common stocks—and they respond to a different set of economic conditions and market developments from other common stocks.

larger and the investors themselves become more knowledgeable about the investment world, they will want to diversify into REIT investments.

In the November 19, 1997 edition of the *Wall Street Journal*, Bernard Winograd, CEO of Prudential Real Estate Investors, observed that "the kind and quality of the offerings and the players are beginning to improve, and the REIT business is shifting from being a cottage industry to a mainstream investment choice." He adds that as more large real estate companies go public, the growing liquidity will draw still more investors to the sector.

We are already seeing this; financial publications catering to individual investors are extolling the benefits of REIT investing. America Online's "Motley Fool," for example, has a very popular real estate–industry discussion group that focuses primarily on REITs and real estate investing. And more will come.

Brokerages firms, too, are expanding their coverage of REIT investments. At the end of 1992, 39 investment firms covered REITs; this number had expanded to 59 in 1996. The big brokerage firms now all have REIT analysts, something that would have been unheard of only a few short years ago. Additionally,

NAREIT has a program to educate financial planners about REIT investing as an excellent form of diversification for their clients' assets. Investment advisers, more than ever before, are looking at REITs as a strong alternative to utility stocks, and perhaps even bonds. And, once again, there are the ever-present baby boomers. As they get longer in the tooth and near retirement age, the high, steady, and growing dividend income provided by REITs will become more and more attractive to them.

INSTITUTIONAL INVESTORS

EARLIER, WE NOTED that institutions and pension funds were originally slow to embrace REITs, but, for many reasons, that is quickly changing. First of all, REIT stocks were, until very recently, limited in diversity of property sector. No more. It seems that with each passing month another whole sector is added. Who would have dreamed five years ago of prison REITs, fast-food–franchise REITs, or movie-theater REITs? The REIT industry was dismissed as insignificant, and many desirable types of properties, such as offices, malls, hotels, and self-storage facilities that dominate the whole REIT industry today weren't even represented or were available only in very small quantities.

Objections were raised with respect to the small market caps of REITs, which have made it difficult to buy and sell REIT shares in large blocks without affecting their market price. If an institution found a REIT it would like to own, it couldn't buy a significant position without finding itself owning practically a controlling position in the REIT. Liquidity is still an issue for some REITs, but this has not prevented institutional investors from significantly increasing their ownership of REIT shares in the aggregate, as the market caps of many have grown dramatically.

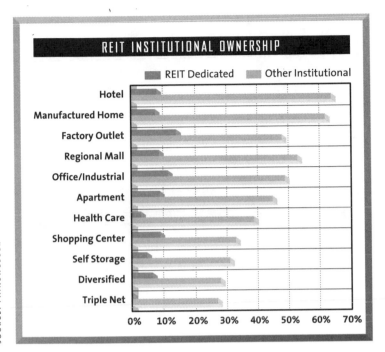

REIT INSTITUTIONAL OWNERSHIP

■ REIT Dedicated   ■ Other Institutional

Hotel
Manufactured Home
Factory Outlet
Regional Mall
Office/Industrial
Apartment
Health Care
Shopping Center
Self Storage
Diversified
Triple Net

0% 10% 20% 30% 40% 50% 60% 70%

SOURCE: PAINEWEBBER

REITS' QUALITY

BETWEEN THE TIME that the REIT industry was born
in the early 1960s and until just a few years ago, most
REITs were managed in a passive way by small real
estate staffs. Those days are gone and internal management is now the order of the day. To have called
these old-style REITs "organizations" would have been
a euphemism. Insider stock ownership was nil, conflicts of interest were numerous, and most REITs had
limited access to capital. Institutional investors would
have found investing in such REITs almost laughable.

Today, a large number of the sophisticated real
estate companies that had operated successfully for
many years as private companies have become REITs
and have earned excellent reputations—no less as
public REITs than as private companies. Some of these
include, among mall REITs, DeBartolo Realty, Simon
Property Group, and Taubman Centers; among neighborhood shopping centers, Developers Diversified,

Kimco, and Vornado; among apartments, Bay Apartment Communities, Irvine Apartment Communities, Post Properties, and Summit Properties; and, among office and industrial, Mack-Cali Realty, Reckson Associates, Spieker Properties, and Weeks Corp. Yes, there were some outstanding organizations operating under the REIT format prior to 1991, such as Federal, New Plan, United Dominion, Washington REIT, and Weingarten, but they were few in number.

INSTITUTIONAL OWNERSHIP OF REITS

SINCE INSTITUTIONAL INVESTORS historically have elected to own real estate as one asset class within their portfolios, it is easy to see why they would choose REITs instead of direct ownership of real estate:

1 REITs provide much greater liquidity.
2 Institutions can now choose from an increasing number of high-quality organizations with good management depth.
3 The number of REIT sectors has expanded geometrically.

The bottom line is that investing in REITs is a smart move for institutional investors.

EARNINGS GROWTH

ANOTHER FACTOR THAT has and will continue to increase the amount of institutional funds flowing into REIT investments is that investors are now recognizing the strength of many REITs' past and prospective growth rates. In the late 1980s and early 1990s, institutions learned to their great disadvantage that management can be as important as location as a determinant of success for a portfolio of properties. Most REITs today can boast outstanding property management skills. Furthermore, because of their managements' extensive tenant contacts, their strong financial resources, in-house research capabilities, and, in some cases, their ability to issue OP units allowing sellers to defer capital gains taxes, many REITs are often able to obtain some great properties at discount prices. These capabilities add up to steady and impressive earnings growth, which is not going unrecognized by institutions, since they are likely to generate better real estate–related investment returns by buying REITs than by buying and owning properties directly.

INCREASED MARKET CAPS AND SHARE LIQUIDITY

IF SMALL MARKET CAPS were a factor in keeping institutional fund mangers away from REIT shares in the past, these folks must have been relieved to see REIT market caps increasing, thus guaranteeing increased liquidity for REIT shares. Before the 1993–94 IPO boom, not a single REIT could boast an equity market cap of as much as $1 billion. By the end of 1997, according to NAREIT, a total of 47 REITs had passed that milestone. Rapidly growing REITs have continued to expand their property holdings; for reasons discussed earlier, they will continue to sell additional shares in order to finance growth. While these offerings have the effect of reducing the ownership interests of the existing shareholders, they also increase REITs' equity market cap and the public "float" of available shares. Furthermore, property acquisitions are often made through the issuance of stock and OP units convertible into shares. Finally, the tremendous merger activity among REITs and acquisitions of private companies result in a larger number of outstanding shares and in larger market caps.

The trading volume of many REITs today matches that of many midcap companies, and such volumes will increase with their increasing market caps. The institutions, if patient, should be able to establish sizable positions without overweighting in a single REIT, without significantly affecting the current market price. Further, as institutions become more comfortable with REITs, they might find it less important to be able to dump hundreds of thousands of shares within 20 minutes.

One experienced REIT observer, William Campbell, an analyst with Boston-based Equity Research Collaborative, has noted several other advantages for pension funds and other institutions that own REITs rather than specific real estate. Some of these include the use of leverage in real estate investing (which is often not legally permitted in direct investments by pension funds); the greater ability of REITs to assemble multiple properties in a single geographical area, which can increase operating efficiency and bargaining power with tenants and thus generate better real estate returns; the ability for most pensions and institutions to obtain greater diversification by way of management style, geography, and property sector; and the ease with which management can be replaced, should the investment prove disappointing.

In what form will institutions continue to invest in REITs? There are several. They can, of course, simply buy REIT shares in the open market. They can negotiate private placements directly with a REIT, either through common stock or through a special issue of convertible preferred stock, and they can buy shares in "spot offerings" that are completed within a single trading day. They can form joint ventures with a REIT, putting up the funds for the acquisition of significant property portfolios or for the development of one or more new properties. Or they can swap properties they already own for REIT shares. This institutional interest will continue to augment the credibility of REITs as investments, provide REITs with needed capital at reduced costs, and enable many more privately held, successful real estate companies to become REITs.

It is not important how institutions and pension funds choose to invest in REITs; it is important only that they are choosing REITs as a strong alternative to direct ownership of real estate and that they are investing in them at a greatly accelerating pace.

The move toward greater institutional ownership of REIT shares has already begun in earnest. A June 14, 1996, *Wall Street Journal* article, "Dutch Fund Makes Splash in U.S. REITs," highlighted the REIT investment activities of Stichting Pensioenfonds ABP (ABP), a pension fund for almost one million Netherlandic public employees. The article said that ABP, which manages $125 billion in assets, had already invested more than $1 billion in U.S. REITs and intended to "quadruple the size of its $1.2 billion U.S. real estate portfolio" by the year 2000. Further, the California State Teachers' Retirement System announced in mid-1996 that it wanted to exchange all or much of its $1.8 billion worth of properties for REIT shares. In the fall of 1996, Prudential Insurance Company of America announced that it would sell almost all of its remaining $5.6 billion worth of hotels, office buildings, and other properties and, in connection with such new strategy, swap some of its properties for shares of REITs. In the July 1996 issue of *Barron's,* well-known REIT observer Barry Vinocur observed that "it's estimated that tax-exempt pension funds own some $150 billion worth of properties," and noted that Douglas Abbey, a principal with real estate adviser AMB Investments, "expects the funds to shift gradually toward a mix of 80 percent publicly traded real estate stocks and 20 percent direct real estate investments."

CHANGES IN THE NATURE OF REITS

A CRUCIAL POINT concerning the nature of today's REITs is that, until the IPO boom of 1993–94, most

REITs were fairly small companies with limited capabilities. They acquired real estate, and most were able
to manage it quite well. Many were able to upgrade
their properties, and thus increase their value and FFO
at a faster pace than if they had employed a purely passive "buy-and-hold" strategy, but very few were able to
develop properties. In 1993 and 1994, however, this all
changed when a very large number of new REITs, with
well-established development capabilities, went public.
There *are* times in various real estate cycles when it is
simply not cost efficient to develop new properties,
such as when existing rental rates are insufficient to
justify the costs of land acquisition, property entitle-
ment, and construction. At other times, however, as in
the case of most real estate sectors today, new development is clearly warranted. REITs capable of new
development clearly have an advantage, since they will
be able to avail themselves of opportunities when conditions are appropriate, and thus gain an edge by their
ability to increase their FFO faster than those not so
well situated.

In the future, much of the available real estate capital will flow to those REITs that "can do it all." While
solid real estate companies without development capabilities will continue to attract capital on the basis of
their track records and managerial and acquisitions
skills, the lion's share of the new capital will be captured by those organizations that can create the most
additional value for their shareholders. These companies (most of which are likely to be REITs) will have
the acquisition skills to buy properties at bargain
prices, the research abilities to determine where
growth will be strongest, the staff necessary to manage
existing properties in the most creative and efficient
manner, the size necessary to become the low-cost
space provider and to negotiate the best deals with
suppliers and tenants in their markets, the capability
of developing the kinds of properties most in demand

and in the best locations, and the foresight to create highly incentivized managements and well-thought-out succession plans. Such real estate organizations, by their continual attraction of new capital, will become far larger than most of today's REITs, and will attract large institutional followings.

As the securitization of real estate in this country continues to grow, these companies will become increasingly powerful and national in scope. They will account for an ever-increasing percentage of new properties being owned, managed, and developed, and, if we assume they remain disciplined, will help to moderate the severity of the real estate cycles that have plagued real estate owners over the years.

We are already seeing this evolution, particularly in certain sectors—such as the office and apartment sectors—where CarrAmerica, Crescent, Equity Office, Prentiss, Apartment Investment and Management, Camden, Equity Residential, and United Dominion are becoming nationwide in scope. In early 1998, Bay Apartment and Security Capital Pacific, which focus on the West Coast and the western states, respectively, each announced proposed mergers. Bay will merge with Avalon, an East Coast REIT, while Security Capital Pacific will merge with Security Capital Atlantic, a Southeast REIT. The merged companies will become national REITs. Other REITs will follow, perhaps first by expanding regionally. Those REITs that do not follow suit will either have to become very savvy "local sharpshooters" or eventually be acquired by the larger REITs.

CONSOLIDATION WITHIN THE INDUSTRY: M&A ACTIVITY

DESPITE THE LIKELIHOOD that many well-run, privately held real estate companies will become REITs in the years ahead, a countertrend has begun to manifest itself. Starting in 1995, there has been almost fre-

netic merger activity among REITs. According to Barry
Vinocur, editor and publisher of *Realty Stock Review,*
"There's been more merger activity in REIT land . . .
[the 12 months from March 1995 to March 1996]
than in the prior five or ten years combined." That was
written in early 1996. The trend was highlighted by
Wellsford's acquisition of Holly Residential,
McArthur/Glen's acquisition by Horizon Group, the
merger of REIT of California with BRE Properties, the
buyout of Tucker Properties by Bradley Real Estate,
and Highwoods's purchase of Crocker Realty Trust.
The pace picked up in late 1996 and early 1997 when
South West Property Trust was merged into United
Dominion Realty, Camden Properties agreed to
acquire Paragon Group, and Equity Residential and
Wellsford Residential merged. The largest 1996 deal
was the merger between DeBartolo Realty and Simon
Property Group, which created the largest retail real
estate organization in the United States.

The pace of REIT merger activity continued at a
dizzying pace well into 1997 and 1998. Noteworthy
deals in the apartment sector included Equity Residential's acquisition of Evans Withycombe, Post's combination with Columbus, and Camden's purchase of
Paragon (and its subsequent agreement to buy Oasis).
In the retail area, Price agreed in early 1998 to merge
with Kimco, and Prime Retail made a deal to buy Horizon Group. Chateau and ROC Communities completed
their long-contested merger in the manufactured-
home-community sector, and MediTrust acquired the
Santa Anita Companies to become a paired-share
REIT. In early 1998, Bay Apartment Communities
agreed to join forces with Avalon Properties in a merger
of equals, with the purpose of becoming a nationwide
REIT specializing in upscale apartment communities
in high-barrier-to-entry areas across the United States.
Security Capital Pacific and Security Capital Atlantic
have likewise agreed to merge, which will create a sim-

ilar nationwide-oriented apartment REIT.

Two megamergers, however, dominated the head-
lines in the REIT world in late 1997: Equity Office
agreed to acquire Beacon Properties, a well-regarded
office REIT, in a $4 billion deal, creating the largest
REIT ever, with a total market cap of $11 billion. Not
to be outdone, Barry Sternlicht's Starwood Lodging
(since renamed Starwood Hotels & Resorts) won its
hotly contested bidding war against Hilton Hotels for
the right to acquire ITT/Sheraton. When the merger
closed in early 1998, Starwood became a mammoth
REIT with a total market cap of almost $20 billion.

**Mergers present shareholders with significant
advantages, both for the REIT being acquired and for the
REIT doing the acquiring.**

A premium to the previous market price is often
paid to the acquired company's shareholders, either
in cash or in stock of the acquiring company, reflecting expectations that FFO of the acquiring company
will be increased, and that the combined company will
become a stronger competitor. The acquiring company might have the financial resources and management expertise to improve the profitability of the
acquired company's properties by increasing revenues
and reducing costs. Legal, accounting, and other
expenses of operating a public company will be substantially reduced. Finally, as in the case of the
Simon/DeBartolo and Equity Office/Beacon mergers,
the new, larger company will often improve its bargaining position with tenants and be more likely to
attract low-priced investment capital.

Acquisitions of private real estate companies by
REITs, as well as mergers involving publicly traded
companies, *will* continue to occur regularly in the
REIT industry. Those that are well conceived and offer
many of the potential advantages discussed earlier will

be greeted with enthusiasm and will benefit the shareholders of both the acquiring and the acquired companies. However, it will be very difficult for REIT
investors to spot these deals ahead of time. It is noteworthy that the shares of other office REITs barely
budged in the wake of the Equity Office/Beacon
merger announcement, and the same shrugging of
shoulders occurred immediately following virtually all
of the apartment REIT merger announcements.
Investors do not seem to believe that one can predict
ahead of time where the wedding bells will chime next.

SO MUCH MORE TO COME

"WE'RE ONLY IN the top of the second inning in the
equitization of real estate in the United States," says
real estate investor Sam Zell, and, in the autumn 1996
issue of *REIT Report,* Mr. Peter Aldrich, founder and
cochair of the real estate advisory firm Aldrich East-
man Waltch, agreed, prophesying that "the industry's
right on track now for a 25 percent compounded
annual growth of market cap. Nothing should slow it
now unless there's bad public policy."

A combination of rising real estate prices (which
makes it more difficult for acquisitive REITs to make
highly attractive deals) and investor uncertainties arising out of the Clinton administration proposals discussed in Chapter 11, coupled with an ever-rising stock
market, caused REITs' stock performance to turn lackluster in early 1998. The ebbs and flows of investor sentiment will always influence price movements of individual stocks and entire sectors in the short term, but,
over longer time periods, investors will base their buying and selling decisions on business prospects and
investment merits. REIT organizations, led by some of
the most innovative and creative management teams
that have ever been assembled in the world of real
estate, are truly capable of delivering outstanding
returns for their investors. This fact—more than any

other—will insure a home for REITs in virtually all investors' portfolios.

SUMMARY

◆ The rapid growth of the REIT industry is creating abundant opportunities, for both real estate companies and their shareholders, as publicly traded REITs have greater access to capital and investors have many more choices.

◆ The REIT vehicle allows successful real estate organizations that have vision tremendous access to needed capital and heretofore unfound flexibility in financing, enabling them more easily to grow their businesses and attract and motivate quality management.

◆ The availability of ever-larger and more capable REITs enables individual investors and large institutions alike to diversify their investment portfolios, while offering the prospects of outstanding total returns.

◆ If, as seems quite likely, ten years from now, REITs own at least $500 billion of commercial real estate, that would still be well under half of the nation's institutionally owned real estate, and would still not exceed the percentage of securitized ownership that prevails in many other major world economies, such as the United Kingdom.

◆ The argument for the individual investor to invest in REITs is a compelling one: REITs provide high, stable, and growing dividend yields along with significant opportunities for capital appreciation, with only a modest amount of risk.

◆ REIT investors have a wide choice, both in sector and REIT management strategy and objectives, and the choices are growing ever greater with the growth of the entire industry. For yield-oriented investors, REIT investing has provided outstanding rewards, but, based on the abundance of new opportunities, "the best is yet to be."

RESOURCES

APPENDIX A

DEATH AND TAXES

WHEN THEY'RE NOT held in individual retirement accounts (IRAs) or other tax-advantaged accounts, REITs have one major disadvantage with respect to their common-stock counterparts. The greatest portion of the total returns expected by holders of most common stocks consists of capital appreciation; today's dividend yields are pretty skimpy, averaging less than 2 percent. If a stock is held for 18 months (under the 1997 changes to the tax laws), the capital appreciation is taxed at a maximum tax rate of only 20 percent (or even at 18 percent if held long enough). With REITs, however, nearly half of the expected total return will come from dividend income, which can be subject to a marginal tax rate that's substantially higher.

Nevertheless, ownership of REIT shares does frequently provide the shareholder with some definite tax advantages—certainly *vis-à-vis* most electric utility stocks and virtually all preferred shares and bonds. Very often a significant portion of the dividends received each year from a REIT is not fully taxable as ordinary income, and may be treated as a "return of capital," which is not currently taxable. This portion of the dividend reduces the shareholder's cost basis in the shares, and defers the tax until the shares are ultimately sold (assuming the sale is made at a price that exceeds the cost basis). However, if held for at least 18 months, the gain is then taxed at long-term capital gain rates and the shareholder has, in effect, converted dividend income into a deferred, long-term capital gain.

How can this be? As we've seen in earlier chapters, REITs base their dividend payments on "funds from operations" (FFO), not net income; FFO, simply stated, is a REIT's net income but with real estate depreciation added back. As a result, many REITs pay dividends to their shareholders in excess of "net income" as defined in the Internal Revenue Code (IRC), and a significant part or all of such excess is usually treated as a "return of capital" to the shareholder and not taxable as ordinary income. It has been estimated that the "return-of-capital" component of a REIT's dividend is typically 25 to 30 percent,[1] although that percentage is lower today as a result of REITs' reducing their payout ratios.

For income tax purposes, dividend distributions paid to shareholders can consist of ordinary income, return of capital, and long-term capital gains. Therefore, if a REIT realizes long-term capital gain from a sale of some of its real estate, it may designate a portion of the dividend paid during the year of the sale as a "long-term capital gain distribution," upon which the shareholder will pay taxes, but at the lower capital gain rates.

A good example of the type of dividend allocation that REIT investors might see between ordinary income, capital gain distributions, and return of capital in a typical year is provided by the dividend distributions made by United Dominion Realty in 1995:

	DIVIDEND PER SHARE	PERCENT OF TOTAL
Ordinary Income	$0.715	82.2%
Capital Gains	$0.003	0.3%
Return of Capital	$0.152	17.5%
Total	$0.870	100.0%

Shareholders cannot predict the amount of the dividend that will be tax deferred merely by looking at financially reported net income, as the tax-deferred portion is based on distributions in excess of the REIT's taxable income pursuant to the U.S. IRC. The differences between net income available to common shareholders for financial reporting purposes, and *taxable* income for income tax purposes relate primarily to:

◆ differences between taxable depreciation (usually accelerated) and "book" (usually straight-line) depreciation;

◆ accruals on preferred stock dividends; and

◆ deferral for tax purposes of certain capital gains on property sales (*e.g.*, tax-deferred exchanges); realized gains or losses on sales of investments are normally distributed to shareholders if and when they are recognized for income tax purposes.

There is generally no publicly available information to determine, ahead of time, the portion of the dividend distribution from a REIT that will be taxed as ordi-

EXAMPLE

LET'S ASSUME AN INVESTOR purchased 100 shares of United Dominion Realty (UDR) at $15.00 in 1997 for a total cost of $1,500. For simplicity, we'll ignore commissions and assume a dividend rate for 1997 of $1.00 per share. By year-end, he or she will have received $100 in dividends. Let's further assume that the ratios of ordinary income, capital gains, and return of capital in effect for 1995 (as stated in the chart on the previous page) still apply. Therefore, $82.20 will be taxed as ordinary income, $0.30 will be taxed as long-term capital gain, and $17.50 will be tax deferred as a return of capital. The investor must then reduce his or her cost basis by the equivalent amount of the return-of-capital component ($17.50) so that the "new" cost basis of the 100 shares of UDR is now $1,482.50. Let's finally assume that the 100 shares are sold 18 months later for $16.00 per share, or a total of $1,600 (again ignoring commissions). The investor will then report a total long-term capital gain of $117.50 on Schedule D.

nary income. The primary problem is that, as noted above, for tax purposes certain income and expense items are calculated differently from what appears in the financial statements. Without extensive tax disclosure by the company, this number must be generated by the company itself, and the shareholder will have to wait until year-end to obtain the final figures.

Of course, all of the foregoing discussion is irrelevant if a REIT's shares are held in an IRA, Keogh, 401(k) plan, or other tax-advantaged account. The dividends won't be taxable while held in such an account, but the distributions (when eventually taken out of the account) will normally be taxable as ordinary income.

What happens upon death of the shareholder? The heirs get a "step-up in basis," and no income tax is *ever* payable with respect to that portion of the dividends that was classified as a return of capital. In this scenario, it's therefore possible to escape income taxation of a significant portion of a REIT's dividends entirely—though this is not a recommended tax-planning technique!

We should keep in mind that state tax laws may differ from federal law. Investors should confirm the status of their dividends under federal *and* state tax laws with their accountant or financial adviser.

None of the foregoing tax advantages will induce a nonbeliever to run out and buy REITs; furthermore, the lower tax rates on capital gains would tend to give other common stocks an edge over REITs if tax savings were one's only investment criterion. Nevertheless, being able to defer a portion of the tax on REITs' dividends can have significant advantages over time, and should not be overlooked.

---

[1] Robert A. Frank, in a December 18, 1995, *Barron's* interview, stated that the figure was close to 30 percent. David Kostin, at Goldman Sachs, calculated the figure for his group of REITs at between 23 and 28 percent between 1993 and 1995.

APPENDIX B

	REITS BY SECTOR		
STOCK SYMBOL	**REIT**	**MARKET**	**APPROXIMATE MARKET CAP (S MILLIONS)**
APARTMENT REITS			
EQR	Equity Residential Properties Trust	NYSE	4613.83
PTR	Security Capital Pacific Trust	NYSE	2087.12
PPS	Post Properties	NYSE	1550.61
AIV	Apartment Investment & Management Co.	NYSE	1245.82
UDR	United Dominion Realty Trust	NYSE	1223.24
AVN	Avalon Properties	NYSE	1185.75
SCA	Security Capital Atlantic	NYSE	1002.58
BYA	Bay Apartment Communities	NYSE	971.29
CPT	Camden Property Trust	NYSE	911.81
MRY	Merry Land & Investment Company	NYSE	906.18
CMM	CRIIMI MAE	NYSE	671.87
IAC	Irvine Apartment Communities	NYSE	607.54
GBP	Gables Residential Trust	NYSE	591.62
ESS	Essex Property Trust	NYSE	558.49
SMT	Summit Properties	NYSE	474.98
MAA	Mid-America Apartment Communities	NYSE	473.31
TCR	Cornerstone Realty Income	NYSE	450.63
SRW	Charles E. Smith Residential Realty	NYSE	450.59
WDN	Walden Residential Properties	NYSE	448.50
BRI	Berkshire Realty Company	NYSE	425.29
AML	Amli Residential Properties Trust	NYSE	373.86
AEC	Associated Estates Realty Corp.	NYSE	347.85
OAS	Oasis Residential	NYSE	346.09
PEI	Pennsylvania REIT	AMEX	325.58
TCT	Town & Country Trust	NYSE	263.00
HME	Home Properties of NY	NYSE	237.34
AAH	Ambassador Apartments	NYSE	215.66
GVE	Grove Property Trust	ASE	91.93

STOCK SYMBOL	REIT	MARKET	APPROXIMATE MARKET CAP (S MILLIONS)
NIRTS	National Income Realty Trust	OTC	67.67
RPI	Roberts Realty Investors	ASE	41.30
SHOPPING-CENTER REITS			
NPR	New Plan Realty Trust	NYSE	1490.14
KIM	Kimco Realty Corp.	NYSE	1441.54
WRI	Weingarten Realty Investors	NYSE	1177.99
DDR	Developers Diversified Realty Corp.	NYSE	1101.09
FRT	Federal Realty Investment Trust	NYSE	972.13
XEL	Excel Realty Trust	NYSE	674.18
JDN	JDN Realty Corp.	NYSE	657.39
REG	Regency Realty Corp.	NYSE	603.20
RET	Price REIT (Series B)	NYSE	522.52
PREN	Price Enterprises	OTC	470.66
BTR	Bradley Real Estate Trust	NYSE	460.88
IRT	IRT Property Company	NYSE	371.18
BPP	Burnham Pacific Properties	NYSE	345.78
ACH	Alexander Haagen Properties	AMEX	257.26
WIR	Western Investment Real Estate Trust	AMEX	254.98
BFS	Saul Centers	NYSE	221.46
KRT	Kranzco Realty Trust	NYSE	197.89
FRW	First Washington Realty Trust	NYSE	189.53
MRR	Mid-Atlantic Realty Trust	AMEX	181.14
PNP	Pan Pacific Retail Props	NYSE	155.75
RPT	Ramco-Gershenson Properties Trust	NYSE	140.68
FAC	FAC Realty Trust	NYSE	112.29
AER	Aegis Realty	ASE	95.60
HRE	HRE Properties	NYSE	95.59
ADC	Agree Realty Corp.	NYSE	93.69
MDI	Mid-America Realty Investments	NYSE	90.62
MCT	Mark Centers Trust	NYSE	78.06
MAL	Malan Realty Investors	NYSE	66.28
MALL REITS			
SPG	Simon DeBartolo Group	NYSE	3332.50
WEA	Westfield America	NYSE	1310.76
GGP	General Growth Properties	NYSE	1301.81

STOCK SYMBOL	REIT	MARKET	APPROXIMATE MARKET CAP (S MILLIONS)
MAC	Macerich Company	NYSE	749.66
TCO	Taubman Centers	NYSE	647.16
CBL	CBL & Associates	NYSE	599.73
MLS	Mills Corp.	NYSE	592.05
URB	Urban Shopping Centers	NYSE	589.59
GRT	Glimcher Realty Trust	NYSE	526.60
JPR	JP Realty	NYSE	436.45
CWN	Crown American Realty Trust	NYSE	239.93
EKR	EQK Realty Investors	NYSE	13.90
OUTLET-CENTER REITs			
CCG	Chelsea/GCA Realty	NYSE	572.11
PRT	Prime Retail	NYSE	397.50
HGI	Horizon Group	NYSE	285.80
SKT	Tanger Factory Outlet Centers	NYSE	234.73
OFFICE REITS			
EOP	Equity Office Properties	NYSE	7342.22
BXP	Boston Properties	NYSE	1995.60
CLI	Mack-Cali Realty Trust	NYSE	1970.20
CRE	CarrAmerica Realty Corp.	NYSE	1753.71
CPP	Cornerstone Properties	NYSE	1749.51
ARI	Arden Realty Group	NYSE	1748.33
HIW	Highwoods Properties	NYSE	1628.15
PP	Prentiss Properties	NYSE	995.61
BDN	Brandywine Realty Trust	AMEX	866.40
KRY	Kilroy Realty	NYSE	689.40
KE	Koger Equities	AMEX	522.17
TOW	Tower Realty	NYSE	397.63
ARE	Alexandria Real Estate	NYSE	389.18
PKY	Parkway Properties	NYSE	333.47
SLG	SL Green Realty	NYSE	326.52
GL	Great Lakes REIT	NYSE	300.00
GLR	G&L Realty	NYSE	78.03
NRTI	Nooney Realty Trust	OTC	8.16
RRF	Realty ReFund Trust	NYSE	4.27

STOCK SYMBOL	REIT	MARKET	APPROXIMATE MARKET CAP ($ MILLIONS)
INDUSTRIAL-PROPERTY REITS			
SCN	Security Capital Industrial Trust	NYSE	2971.29
AMB	AMB Property	NYSE	2018.05
FR	First Industrial Realty Trust	NYSE	1291.06
TRI	TriNet Corp. Realty	NYSE	900.98
MDN	Meridian Industrial Trust	NYSE	756.08
CNT	CenterPoint Properties	NYSE	675.65
WKS	Weeks Corp.	NYSE	612.95
EGP	EastGroup Properties	NYSE	329.89
PGE	Prime Group Realty	NYSE	253.79
CTR	Cabot Industrial Trust	NYSE	184.89
IND	American Industrial Properties REIT	NYSE	147.75
MPH	Meridian Point Realty Trust VIII Company	AMEX	13.48
MPTBS	Meridian Point Realty Trust, '83	OTC	4.36
HEALTH CARE REITS			
MT	MediTrust	NYSE	2715.44
HRP	Health & Retirement Properties Trust	NYSE	1939.70
HCP	Health Care Properties	NYSE	1101.01
NHP	Nationwide Health Properties	NYSE	1099.76
NHI	National Health Investors	NYSE	1019.34
OHI	Omega Healthcare Investors	NYSE	757.92
HCN	Health Care REIT	NYSE	657.40
AHE	American Health Properties	NYSE	630.69
HR	Health Realty Trust	NYSE	581.74
CCT	Capstone Capital Corp.	NYSE	537.83
LTC	LTC Properties	NYSE	511.94
UHT	Universal Health Realty Income Trust	NYSE	195.89
ETT	ElderTrust	NYSE	126.10
SELF-STORAGE REITS			
PSA	Public Storage	NYSE	3259.75
SUS	Storage USA	NYSE	1069.46
SHU	Shurgard Storage Centers	NYSE	794.87
SEA	Storage Trust Realty	NYSE	377.88
SSS	Sovran Self-Storage	NYSE	355.17
HOTEL REITS			
HOT	Starwood Hotels & Resorts	NYSE	9671.56

STOCK SYMBOL	REIT	MARKET	APPROXIMATE MARKET CAP (S MILLIONS)
PAH	Patriot American Hospitality	NYSE	1700.17
HPT	Hospitality Properties Trust	NYSE	1416.34
FCH	FelCor Suite Hotels	NYSE	1283.10
SSI	Sunstone Hotel Advisors	NYSE	609.55
ENN	Equity Inns	NYSE	559.24
AGT	American General Hospitality Corp.	NYSE	524.88
KPA	Innkeepers USA Trust	NYSE	488.62
RFS	RFS Hotel Investors	NYSE	439.00
BOY	Boykin Lodging	NYSE	335.26
WXH	Winston Hotels	NYSE	213.57
JAMS	Jameson Inns	OTC	112.42
HUMP	Humphrey Hospitality	OTC	42.65
HFD	Host Funding	AMEX	9.73

MANUFACTURED-HOME REITS

STOCK SYMBOL	REIT	MARKET	APPROXIMATE MARKET CAP (S MILLIONS)
CPJ	Chateau Communities	NYSE	745.06
MHC	Manufactured Home Communities	NYSE	639.62
SUI	Sun Communities	NYSE	579.49
UMH	United Mobile Homes	AMEX	77.72

DIVERSIFIED PROPERTY REITS

STOCK SYMBOL	REIT	MARKET	APPROXIMATE MARKET CAP (S MILLIONS)
CEI	Crescent Real Estate Equities	NYSE	3939.44
VNO	Vornado Realty Trust	NYSE	2845.37
RSE	Rouse Company	NYSE	2223.16
CUZ	Cousins Properties	NYSE	919.14
GLB	Glenborough Realty Trust	NYSE	845.89
CLP	Colonial Properties Trust	NYSE	642.93
WRE	Washington Real Estate Investment Trust	AMEX	600.38
ALCC	Allied Capital Commercial Corp.	OTC	491.16
PEI	Pennsylvania REIT	AMEX	305.78
PAG	Pacific Gulf Properties	NYSE	423.48
FUR	First Union Real Estate Investments	NYSE	337.65
MGI	MGI Properties	NYSE	326.73
LXP	Lexington Corp. Properties	NYSE	241.45
PCC	PMC Commercial Trust	AMEX	168.85
CVI	CV REIT	NYSE	117.51
ICH	Impac Commercial	ASE	111.48

STOCK SYMBOL	REIT	MARKET	APPROXIMATE MARKET CAP (S MILLIONS)
SIZ	Sizeler Property Investors	NYSE	93.21
BNP	Boddie-Noell Properties	AMEX	85.28
BSRTS	Banyan Strategic Realty Trust	OTC	82.75
FSN	Franklin Select Realty Trust	AMEX	80.39
CMETS	Continental Mortgage and Equity Trust	OTC	64.92
BRT	BRT Realty Trust	NYSE	64.12
TCI	Trancontinental Realty Investors	NYSE	60.44
ANM	Angeles Mortgage Investment Trust	AMEX	50.05
BMCC	Bando McGlocklin Capital	OTC	35.52
IOT	Income Opportunity Realty Investors	AMEX	17.67
AZL	Arizona Land Income Corp.	AMEX	12.98
PCT	Property Capital Trust	AMEX	6.59
HMG	HMG/Courtland Properties	AMEX	5.25

OFFICE/INDUSTRIAL MIXED

SPK	Spieker Properties	NYSE	2241.72
DRE	Duke Realty	NYSE	1764.53
LRY	Liberty Property	NYSE	1508.64
RA	Reckson Associates	NYSE	956.88
BED	Bedford Property Investors	NYSE	443.21
REA	American Real Estate Investment Corp.	AMEX	96.74

SPECIALTY

PZN	Prison Realty Trust	NYSE	827.24
CARS	Capital Automotive	OTC	378.64
TEE	National Golf Properties	NYSE	378.12
EPR	Entertainment Properties Trust	NYSE	272.00
GTA	Golf Trust of America	NYSE	219.76
PW	Pittsburgh and West Virginia Railroad	ASE	11.13

FREE STANDING RETAIL

FFA	Franchise Finance of America	NYSE	1151.50
O	Realty Income Corp.	NYSE	682.74
NNN	Commercial Net Lease Realty	NYSE	503.44
ALX	Alexander's	NYSE	471.33
USV	U.S. Restaurant Properties	NYSE	218.14
CRRR	Captec Net Lease Realty	OTC	168.77
OLP	One Liberty Properties	ASE	22.84

APPENDIX C

REIT MUTUAL FUNDS		
FUND	ASSETS (IN $ MILLIONS)	1997 RETURN
Cohen & Steers Realty Shares	$3,433	21.2%
Fidelity Real Estate	2,478	21.4
Vanguard REIT Index *	1,278	18.8
Longleaf Partners Realty	737	29.7
Franklin Real Estate	429	19.9
Alliance Real Estate	420	23.0
CGM Realty	477	26.7
Morgan Stanley U.S. Real Estate	382	24.5
Davis Real Estate	291	25.1
Heitman Real Estate	218	21.2

•INCEPTION DATE 5/13/96

	THREE-YEAR RETURN	FIVE-YEAR RETURN	PHONE NUMBER
	23.1%	19.1%	800-437-9912
	22.4	16.1	800-544-8888
			800-662-7447
			800-445-9469
	23.3		800-342-5236
			800-221-5672
	29.8		800-345-4048
			800-548-7786
	26.4		800-279-0279
	22.9	18.0	800-435-1405

SOURCE: REALTY STOCK REVIEW, DECEMBER 1997

APPENDIX D

Example of income statement derivation of adjusted funds from operations (AFFO), and funds or cash available for distribution (FAD or CAD)

POST PROPERTIES (PPS): THIRD QUARTER, 1996

(In thousands of dollars, except for per share.)

Revenue

Rental—owned property	$40,583,000
Property management	722,000
Landscape services	1,199,000
Interest	50,000
Other	1,661,000
Total Revenue	$44,215,000

Property Expenses

Property operating & maintenance	$15,115,000
Depreciation—real estate assets	5,877,000
Total Property Expenses	$20,992,000

Corporate and Other Expenses

Property management—third party	$558,000
Landscape management	1,013,000
Interest	5,970,000
Amortization of financing costs	293,000
Depreciation—non–real estate assets	197,000
General and administration	1,769,000
Minority interest	0
Total Corporate & other expenses	$9,800,000
Total Expenses	$30,792,000
Income before minority interests and extraordinary items	$13,423,000
Gain on sale of assets	$693,000
Minority interest in operating partnership	(2,535,000)
Net Income	$11,581,000

Plus

Depreciation and amortization—real estate assets	$5,877
Minority interest	2,696

Less

Net gain on sale	$(854)
Amortization of financing costs	(55)
Funds from Operations (FFO)	$19,245
FFO per share	$0.71

Less

Recurring Capital Expenditures	$(692)
Adjusted funds from operations	$18,553
AFFO per share	$0.69

Less

Nonrecurring capital expenditures	(687)
Funds or cash available for distribution	$17,866
FAD or CAD per share	$0.66
Weighted average number of shares/operating units	26,929,000

NOTES

1. Depreciation of "hard assets" such as apartment buildings and other structures can be deceptive. The property (including the underlying land) could actually appreciate in value, particularly if well maintained; however, for accounting purposes, depreciation must be deducted in order to derive net income. Funds from operations (FFO) is calculated by adding back real estate depreciation and amortization to net income. However, property owners incur recurring expenditures that are certainly real and that need to be taken into account to provide a true picture of the owner's cash flow from the property. Examples include the necessary replacement, from time to time, of carpets and roofs. In some cases, property owners may make tenant improvements (and/or provide tenant allowances) that are necessary to retain the property's competitive position with existing and potential tenants, and may pay leasing commissions. Since many of these expenditures are capitalized, they must be deducted from FFO in order to determine "adjusted funds from operations," or AFFO, which is the "truest" picture of economic cash flow.

"Funds (or Cash) Available for Distribution" (FAD or CAD) is sometimes calculated in a slightly different manner. Unlike AFFO, which deducts the amortization of real estate–related expenditures from FFO, FAD or CAD is often derived by deducting nonrecurring (as well as normal and recurring) expenditures. Unfortunately, there is no widely accepted standard for making these adjustments.

2. Another major consideration is the use of variable-rate debt. If the balance sheet reflects a significant portion of variable-rate debt or short-term maturities, there is a significant risk of increasing interest costs in the future should interest rates rise. An assessment of this risk can be made by adjusting the cost of the variable-rate-debt coupon to fixed-rate levels in order to make an "apples-to-apples" comparison with other REITs and operating companies. This adjustment can also be made for operating entities with substantial levels of tax-exempt financing.

3. When reviewing a REIT's revenues, it is a good idea to analyze lease expirations and existing rents and compare them to market rates. This approach may help in determining whether rental revenues may decrease when leases are renewed at market rates.

4. Always distinguish revenues from services as opposed to revenues from rents. Rental revenue tends to be of higher quality and more stable, as service clients can easily terminate the relationship.

5. Always analyze the type of debt and debt maturities. REIT investors would obviously prefer long-term debt to short term, and fixed-rate debt to variable rate.

6. Look for recurring "capital expenditures" that do not improve or prolong the life of the property, as well as financing traps (*e.g.*, "buydowns" of loan-interest coupons).

APPENDIX E

COST OF EQUITY CAPITAL

THERE IS NO GENERAL agreement on how to calculate a REIT's "cost of equity capital." There are, however, several ways to approach this issue. One quick way to determine a REIT's "nominal" equity capital cost is to estimate the REIT's per-share FFO in the most recent quarter, or—perhaps what is more appropriate—the expected per-share FFO for the next 12 months and annualize it. This per-share FFO should then be adjusted for any additional shares to be issued, and the expected incremental FFO to be earned from the investment of the proceeds from such new share issuance. Finally, we would then divide such "pro forma" FFO per share by the price the REIT receives for each new share sold (after deducting underwriting commissions).[1]

Let's assume, for example, that "Apartment REIT USA" has 10 million shares outstanding and is expected to earn $10 million in FFO over the next 12 months. It intends to issue an additional 1 million shares and receive net proceeds of $9 per share (after underwriting commissions), which will be used to buy additional apartments providing an initial yield of 9 percent; this investment of $9 million will thus provide $810,000 of additional FFO (9 percent of $9 million). Therefore, on a pro forma basis, this REIT will have $10.81 million in FFO which, when divided by 11 million shares outstanding, will produce FFO of $.98 per share. Dividing this by the $9 net offering price results in a nominal cost of equity capital of 10.88 percent. Note that this is higher than the entry yield (9 percent) available on the new apartment investments, as a result of which this stock offering would be dilutive to FFO. However, if we were to hypothesize that Apartment REIT USA were able to sell its new shares at a net price of $12, its nominal cost of equity capital would be 8.4 percent. Thus, the higher the price at which a REIT can sell new shares, the cheaper its nominal cost of capital will be, making it more likely that the offering and the investment of the offering proceeds will be accretive to FFO.

The above approach measures only a REIT's *nominal* cost of equity capital; its *true* cost of equity capital should be measured in a very different way. In the first approach, we divided pro forma expected FFO per share by the net sale proceeds per share, using expected FFO only for the next 12 months. But what about the *additional* FFO that will be generated by the REIT for many years into the future? This additional FFO will be forever diluted by the new shares being issued, and, for this reason, it may not be appropriate to use expected FFO for just the next 12 months (*e.g.*, why not 24 months? 36 months?) How can longer time periods be taken into account?

A REIT's true cost of equity capital may be best measured by the total return expected by investors on their investment in the REIT. For example, if investors price a REIT's shares in the trading market so that 12 percent total annual returns are demanded—and expected—well into the future (on the basis of existing and projected dividend yields, anticipated FFO or AFFO, and expected growth rates), why isn't the REIT's true cost of equity capital the same 12 percent? A few REITs may be so conservative and their FFO and dividend growth so predictable that mere 10 percent annual returns might satisfy investors; in such a case, the REIT's true cost of equity capital might very well be 10 percent. A difficulty with this approach is determining the total returns that are demanded by investors; this isn't as easy as it might appear. All of this gets us into capital-asset-pricing models, "modern portfolio theory," and the like, which are topics beyond the scope of this appendix. Nevertheless, REIT investors who want to delve into this issue might want to try to determine the total returns expected by investors in particular REITs, and use those figures to determine the REIT's true cost of equity capital. (See, for example, "The True Cost of Capital," *Institutional Real Estate Securities,* January 1998.) Keep in mind, however, that in view of REITs' historical total returns of close to the mid-teens, very few REITs would have expected total returns of less than 12 percent.

REITs' legal requirement to pay out 95 percent of net income to their shareholders each year in the form of dividends makes it very difficult to grow externally (*e.g.,* through acquisitions or new development) without frequently coming back to the markets for more equity capital. Keeping payout ratios low certainly helps reduce the overall cost of equity capital, as does periodically selling off properties with less than exciting long-term potential. However, innovative REIT managements who continue to find attractive opportunities will undoubtedly need to raise additional equity capital from time to time. It is, therefore, important for REIT investors to understand how to analyze a REIT's nominal cost of equity capital, and its true longer-term cost of equity capital as well.

---

[1] Some investors have simply looked at a REIT's dividend yield, which is quite misleading; FFO and AFFO are far more important than dividend payments in the context of determining most REITs' valuations, and thus the dilution from issuing additional shares.

GLOSSARY

AFFO (Adjusted Funds from Operations). FFO (Funds from Operations), less normalized recurring expenditures that are capitalized by the REIT and amortized, but which are necessary for property leasing and maintainance (*e.g.*, new carpeting and draperies in apartment units, leasing expenses, and tenant improvement allowances); the effects of straight-lining of rents are also adjusted for.

Base Year. In a commercial lease, the year used as a reference against which revenues or expenses in subsequent years are measured to determine additional rent charges or the tenant's share of additional operating expenses of the building.

Basis Point. One one-hundredth of one percent (.01 percent). Thus, a one-basis-point increase in the yield of a ten-year bond would result in a yield increase from, for instance, 6.81 percent to 6.82 percent.

Beta. The extent to which a stock's price moves with an index of stocks, such as the S&P 500.

Bond Proxies. The shares of a REIT that provide a high dividend yield to its shareholders but where FFO/AFFO and dividend growth are expected to be quite low, *e.g.*, 3 to 4 percent annually.

Book Value. The net value of a company's assets less its liabilities, as reflected on its balance sheet pursuant to GAAP *(see GAAP)*. Book value will reflect depreciation and amortization, which are expensed for accounting purposes, and may have little relationship to a company's "net asset value" if evaluated at market prices. *See also Net Asset Value.*

C-Corporation. A "C-Corp." is a typical corporation

organized under the provisions of "Subchapter C" of the Internal Revenue Code, and may be publicly or privately held. It must pay taxes on its net taxable income, at the prescribed corporate tax rates in effect from time to time, and its shareholders must also pay income taxes on any dividends that they receive from such corporation.

Cap Rate. The unleveraged return expected by the buyer of a property, expressed as a percentage of an all-cash purchase price. It is determined by dividing the property's expected net operating income (before depreciation) by the purchase price. Generally, high cap rates indicate greater perceived risk by the buyer. A "nominal" cap rate excludes, in determining the expected net operating income from a property, such normal but often capitalized expenses as new carpeting or draperies (*e.g.* in apartment units), tenant improvements, or leasing commissions; an "effective" or "economic" cap rate includes the effects of such expenditures.

Cash Flow. With reference to a property (or group of properties), the owner's rental revenues from the property minus all property operating expenses. The term ignores depreciation and amortization expenses, as well as interest on loans incurred to finance the property. Sometimes referred to as "EBITDA."

Cash-on-Cash Return. The yield an investor would receive as a result of buying a specific property for a specific purchase price, assuming a given level of rental income and operating expenses, but without taking into account the additional leverage provided by debt. For example, if an investor buys an office building for $2 million and expects the building's first-year rental income to be $500,000 and operating expenses to be $300,000, the net operating income would be $200,000 and the investor's "cash-on-cash return" would be $200,000 divided by $2 million, or 10 percent.

Collateralized Mortgage Obligations (CMOs). Real estate

mortgages which are packaged together and sold in the form of participating interests.

Cost of Capital. The cost to a company, such as a REIT, of raising capital in the form of equity (common or preferred stock) or debt. The cost of equity capital takes the form of diluting the interests of the existing equity holders in the company. The cost of *debt* capital is merely the interest expense on the debt incurred.

Debt Capital. The amount of nonequity debt that a REIT carries on its balance sheet. This could be long-term mortgage debt, secured or unsecured debentures issued to public or private investors, borrowings under a bank credit line, or any other type of indebtedness. It does *not* include equity capital, such as common or preferred stock.

Discounting. In financial markets, the process by which expected future developments and events that will affect an investment are anticipated and taken into account by the price at which the investment currently trades.

DownREIT. A DownREIT is structured much like an UPREIT *(see UPREIT)*, but is formed *after* the REIT has become a public company and generally does not include members of management among the partners in the controlled partnership.

EBITDA. *See Cash Flow.*

Equity Capital. Permanent capital that has been raised through the sale and issuance of securities that have no right to repayment by the issuing company. This normally takes the form of common stock. Preferred stock is also sometimes regarded as equity capital, although often the company has an obligation to redeem such shares at certain times or under certain conditions.

Equity Market Cap. The total equity value of a public company, such as a REIT, which is determined by multiplying the company's total common shares outstanding by the market price of the shares as of a particular date *(see also Market Cap)*. The term "implied market cap" is sometimes used to refer to the market cap of an UPREIT or a DownREIT that has operating partnership units outstanding that are convertible into common shares. The "implied market cap" takes the value of these units into account.

Equity REIT. A REIT that owns, or has an equity interest in, real estate (rather than one making loans secured by real estate collateral).

FFO (Funds From Operations). Net income (determined in accordance with GAAP), excluding gains or losses from debt restructuring and sales of property, plus depreciation of real property, and after adjustments for unconsolidated entities, such as partnerships and joint ventures, in which the REIT holds an interest.

GAAP. Generally accepted accounting principles, to which financial statements of public companies must conform.

GLA. Acronym for "gross leasable area," a measurement of the total amount of leasable space in a commercial property.

Hurdle Rate. The required rate of return in a discounted cash flow analysis, at or above which an investment makes sense and below which it does not.

Hybrid REIT. A REIT that both owns real estate and holds mortgages secured by real estate.

Interest-Coverage Ratio. The ratio of a company's operating income (before amortization, depreciation, and interest expense) to total interest expense. This ratio measures the extent to which interest expense on existing debt is covered by existing cash flow.

Leverage. The process by which the owner of a property may expand both the economic benefits and the risks of property ownership by adding borrowed funds to his or her own funds that have been committed to the venture.

Market Cap. The total market value of a REIT's (or other company's) outstanding securities and indebtedness. For example, if 20 million shares of a REIT are trading at $20 each, 2 million shares of the REIT's preferred stock are trading at $10 each, and the REIT has on its books $100 million of debt, its "market cap" would be $520 million ($400 million in common stock, $20 million in preferred stock, and $100 million in indebtedness). *See also Equity Market Cap.*

Mortgage REIT. A REIT that holds mortgages secured by real estate collateral.

NAREIT. The National Association of Real Estate Investment Trusts.

Net Asset Value, or NAV. The net market value of all a REIT's assets, including but not limited to its properties, after subtracting all its liabilities and obligations. Such net asset value, which is usually expressed on a per-share basis, must be estimated by analysts and investors since REITs generally don't obtain periodic property appraisals.

Net Income. An accounting term used to measure the profits earned by a business enterprise after all expenses are deducted from revenues. Under GAAP *(see GAAP),* depreciation of real estate owned is treated as an expense of the business.

Overage. A provision in a retail lease that requires the payment of rent in addition to the base rental prescribed in the lease if the store's sales exceed certain specified levels during the measurement period.

Overbuilding. A situation in which so much new real estate has been recently completed and offered to tenants in a particular area that the supply of available space significantly exceeds the demand by renters and users.

Payout Ratio. The ratio of a REIT's annual dividend rate to its FFO or AFFO, on a per share basis. For example, if FFO is $1.00 per share and the current dividend rate is $.80 per share, the payout ratio would be 80 percent.

Positive Spread Investing (PSI). The ability to raise funds (both equity and debt) at a nominal cost significantly less than the initial returns that can be obtained from real estate acquisitions.

Price/Earning (P/E) Ratios. The relationship between a company's security price and its per share earnings. It is calculated by dividing the stock price by the company's earnings per share.

Profitless Prosperity. Describes a situation whereby, because of a strong economy, either the owner enjoys higher rentals or the tenant enjoys higher sales, but where higher costs offset most or all of the benefits of the higher rentals or sales.

Real Estate Investment Trust Act of 1960. Legislation passed by Congress and signed into law authorizing the REIT format, for the purpose of allowing individuals to "pool their investments" in real estate to receive the same benefits they would receive from direct ownership.

REIT or Real Estate Investment Trust. Either a corporation or a business trust that has certain tax attributes prescribed by federal legislation, the most important of which is that the entity does not pay federal taxes on its income if certain requirements are satisfied (such as the requirement to pay out at least 95 percent of net annual income to shareholders).

Resolution Trust Corporation or RTC. A public corporation organized by Congress in response to the banking and savings and loan crisis of the early '90s, to acquire and resell real estate and real estate loans from bankrupt and near-bankrupt lenders.

Retail REITs. Retail REITs include those specializing in neighborhood (or "strip") shopping centers, malls, and factory outlet centers.

Same-Store Sales. The term used originally to analyze retail companies, meaning sales from stores open for at least one year but excluding sales from stores that have been closed and from new stores, which often have unusually high sales growth. The "same-store" concept is applied to REITs' rental income, operating expenses, and net operating income from those of its properties that have been owned and operated in the same fiscal period of the prior year.

Securitization or Equitization. The process by which the economic benefits of ownership of a tangible asset, such as real estate, are divided among numerous investors and represented in the form of publicly traded securities.

Total Return. A stock's dividend income plus capital appreciation, before taxes and commissions. For example, if a stock rises 6 percent in price and provides a 7 percent yield during the measurement period, the investor's total return would be 13 percent.

Triple Net. A type of lease that requires the tenant to pay its pro rata share of all recurring maintenance and operating costs of the property, such as utilities, property taxes, and insurance.

UPREIT. A REIT that does not own its properties directly, but owns a controlling interest in a limited partnership that owns the REIT's real estate. Other partners (besides the REIT itself) might include management and other private investors. *See also Down-REIT.*

Volatility. The extent to which the market price of a stock tends to fluctuate from day to day, or even hour to hour.

INDEX

ABOUT BLOOMBERG

Bloomberg L.P., founded in 1981, is a global information services, news, and media company. Headquartered in New York, the company has nine sales offices, two data centers, and 80 news bureaus worldwide.

Bloomberg Financial Markets, serving customers in 100 countries around the world, holds a unique position within the financial services industry by providing an unparalleled combination of news, information, and analytic tools in a single package known as the BLOOMBERG® service. Corporations, banks, money management firms, financial exchanges, insurance companies, and many other entities and organizations rely on Bloomberg as their primary source of information.

BLOOMBERG NEWS℠, founded in 1990, offers worldwide coverage of economies, companies, industries, governments, financial markets, politics, and sports. The news service is the main content provider for Bloomberg's broadcast media, which include BLOOMBERG TELEVISION®—the 24-hour cable television network available in ten languages worldwide— and BLOOMBERG NEWS RADIO™—an international radio network anchored by flagship station BLOOMBERG NEWS RADIO AM 1130℠ in New York.

In addition to the BLOOMBERG PRESS® line of books, Bloomberg publishes BLOOMBERG® MAGAZINE and BLOOMBERG PERSONAL FINANCE™.

To learn more about Bloomberg, call a sales representative at:

Frankfurt:	49-69-920-410	San Francisco:	1-415-912-2960
Hong Kong:	852-977-6000	São Paulo:	5511-3048-4500
London:	44-171-330-7500	Singapore:	65-438-8585
New York:	1-212-318-2000	Sydney:	61-29-777-8686
Princeton:	1-609-279-3000	Tokyo:	81-3-3201-8900

ABOUT THE AUTHOR

Ralph L. Block has been a REIT aficionado for over 20 years. He is Executive Vice-President, Chief REIT Analyst, and a Senior Portfolio Manager at Bay Isle Financial Corporation, a San Francisco–based investment advisory firm which manages over $370 million for institutions and individuals. Prior to joining Bay Isle, Mr. Block had a 30-year career as a corporate attorney and has been a Board member and general counsel to a number of public and private corporations.

Mr. Block graduated with a B.A. degree with honors in Political Science from U.C.L.A. and with a J.D. degree from the U.C.L.A. School of Law, where he was an Associate Editor of the *UCLA Law Review* and Member of the Order of the COIF. He lives with his wife, her mother, and their dog, Beauregard, in Westlake Village, California.